T0259995

SAP MII

Functional and Technical Concepts
in Manufacturing Industries

Suman Mukherjee

Saptaparna Mukherjee (Das)

Apress®

SAP MII: Functional and Technical Concepts in Manufacturing Industries

Suman Mukherjee
Kolkata, West Bengal, India

Saptaparna Mukherjee (Das)
Kolkata, West Bengal, India

ISBN-13 (pbk): 978-1-4842-2813-5
DOI 10.1007/978-1-4842-2814-2

ISBN-13 (electronic): 978-1-4842-2814-2

Library of Congress Control Number: 2017948407

Cover image designed by Freepik

Managing Director: Welmoed Spahr
Editorial Director: Todd Green
Acquisitions Editor: Nikhil Karkal
Development Editor: Poonam Jain
Technical Reviewer: Antonio A. B. da Silva
Coordinating Editor: Prachi Mehta
Copy Editor: Kezia Endsley
Compositor: SPi Global
Indexer: SPi Global
Artist: SPi Global

Distributed to the book trade worldwide by Springer Science+Business Media New York, 233 Spring Street, 6th Floor, New York, NY 10013. Phone 1-800-SPRINGER, fax (201) 348-4505, e-mail orders-ny@springer-sbm.com, or visit www.springeronline.com. Apress Media, LLC is a California LLC and the sole member (owner) is Springer Science + Business Media Finance Inc (SSBM Finance Inc). SSBM Finance Inc is a **Delaware** corporation.

For information on translations, please e-mail rights@apress.com, or visit http://www.apress.com/rights-permissions.

Apress titles may be purchased in bulk for academic, corporate, or promotional use. eBook versions and licenses are also available for most titles. For more information, reference our Print and eBook Bulk Sales web page at http://www.apress.com/bulk-sales.

Any source code or other supplementary material referenced by the author in this book is available to readers on GitHub via the book's product page, located at www.apress.com/978-1-4842-2813-5. For more detailed information, please visit http://www.apress.com/source-code.

Printed on acid-free paper

In January 2016, I got a call from Apress, whereby they asked me to author a book on SAP MII. It was kind of unbelievable to me and is a dream come true. On that day, I felt that all my effort the past six and a half years was rewarded by God with this offer. The first gratitude I feel is toward my father, Sasthi Charan Mukherjee, and mother, Mina Mukherjee, as without them I would never be part of this human society. I thus dedicate this book to them. It is only by their love, care, and education that I became an IT professional. Thank you mom and dad.

Secondly, I want to dedicate the book to one of the most supportive people I know—my beloved wife Saptaparna. She is a great lady who handles all our family chores exceptionally while I was concentrating fully on writing the book and also worked with me as the coauthor of this book. Without her support, it would have been impossible to complete the book in the tight schedule. I salute her for her unbelievable support and inspiration, and for always coping with my moods.

If I didn't mention a few other people, this dedication would be incomplete. One of my inspirations is my brother-in-law, the Late Sudipta Bhattacherjee, who always supported, enlightened, and encouraged me to be a man who was unique in the crowd. May his soul rest in peace. I must also mention my mentors—Dipankar Saha, Abesh Bhattacherjee, and Sudipta Mukherjee. Because of their guidance, I am working in the manufacturing domain. They selflessly helped me build my base in this domain. I also dedicate this to my friends—Lopamudra Mukherjee and Swapna Mukherjee—who selflessly shared their technical experience to enrich the book. From my heart to all of them.

This book is also dedicated to all of my friends who inspired me to write this book. It's dedicated to the SCN, which gave me the chance to write many technical blogs to share my knowledge and to the manufacturing community, which may find this book useful.

—Suman Mukherjee

First, I would like to dedicate this book to my father, Mr. Sudhendu Das, who is an amazingly hard working and self-made person. I have always admired him for his great career achievements. To my sweet and humble mother, Mrs. Nibedita Das, who nurtured me to become what I am today as a human being. Due to their blessings, I have accelerated to this position in my career. Thanks to them for being my parents.

Secondly, I would like to dedicate this book to my very talented, supportive, and beloved husband, Suman, who inspired me to sit and gather my thoughts on SAP MII and convinced me to write a book on SAP MII. I thank him from the bottom of my heart for giving me the confidence and courage to put my knowledge into a book so I can help others.

I also thank my mentors—Mr. Sanjay Bhide, Mr. Soham Shah, Mrs. Vinayprabha Gautam, and Mr. Sanjeev Nadhkarni—who provided strong support to me during my IT career. I also dedicate this book to my friends—Swapna Mukherjee and Lopamudra Mukherjee—for being a great support while writing the book and would further like to dedicate the book to the SCN community and the manufacturing industry professionals.

—Saptaparna Mukherjee (Das)

Contents at a Glance

Contents

About the Authors

Suman Mukherjee has nearly seven years of IT experience, specializing in the SAP manufacturing domain. He is currently working at Cognizant Technology Solutions as a technical lead in the SAP manufacturing business unit. He worked on many high-quality global manufacturing solutions by defining the architecture design. He also managed deliverables by leading the team for custom SAP MII, MEINT, and OEE applications. He worked as a technical reviewer for a SAP OEE book. He is actively involved in SCN SAP MII/OEE articles and discussions and has authored several technical blogs. He has been recognized as SCN Topic Leader for SAP MII. Previously he worked with IBM India Pvt. Ltd and Infosys India Limited. He has a Bachelor's Degree of Technology in electronics & instrumentation engineering.

Saptaparna Mukherjee (Das) is associated with Cognizant Technology Solutions as a SAP MII subject matter expert and business analyst in the engineering manufacturing business unit. She has nearly seven years of IT experience with specializations in several SAP domains. She worked on several manufacturing implementation projects and proposals involving SAP MII, SAP OEE, SAP MEINT, and SAP ECC. She managed the deliverables by leading the team in an onsite-offshore role. She contributed to several SCN technical discussions, forums, and blogs. Previously, she worked with L&T Infotech Solutions. She has a Bachelor's Degree of Engineering in computer technology from Nagpur University.

About the Technical Reviewer

Antonio Alexandre Barbosa da Silva is a mechanical engineer with solid experience in several different manufacturing industries. He has been involved in the IT environment for 17 years in several different continents (the Americas, Asia, and Europe). Currently located in Switzerland, where he was introduced to MII in 2008, he has been implementing this tool in different sectors, including the automotive, agricultural, chemical, and pharmaceutical industries. He is currently working as project manager for a major consulting company from the US/India. Together with a very strong team of developers and technical leaders (including the authors of this book), Antonio has been increasing his scope of work with the tool by dealing with tasks related to project management and business analysis in MII implementations.

Acknowledgments

It had always been a vision only for us to do something distinguishing in our career together, as we share this common technology. When this book proposal happened, we thought, "This is it!" We are so happy to have started and completed this project successfully considering we have recently gone through some very tough situations in our personal lives.

We could not have written this book without the help and support of many important people in our day-to-day lives.

To Nikhil Karkal, Prachi Mehta, Welmoed Spahr, and Todd Green, for proposing this book, which helped us express our knowledge and experience gained throughout our SAP MII careers, and for their mentoring and providing valuable suggestions on authoring a book.

To others on the Apress team, without whose continuous sincere effort and hard work the idea of writing a book would never have materialized. We thank the whole Apress team from the bottom of our hearts for making this possible. Thanks to all of you.

To our parents and relatives, our friends Swapna Mukherjee and Lopamudra Mukherjee, and others who in one way or another shared their selfless support and dedication. Thank you.

To Amol Akre, Amol Kurdukar, Balu Durai, Praveen Odughat, and Shylaja Veerakyathaiah from the Cognizant leadership and management team, as well as our valuable colleagues Abhijeet Nevaskar and Vipin Verma for their support and motivation and for arranging the logistics that helped in the completion of the book. Thanks to all of you.

To all our clients and vendors, who have gifted us with their knowledge and trust as we traveled and ventured many new and old roads together. We have all continued to sharpen each other with patience, perception, and perseverance. Thank you all.

To our dearest friend and technical reviewer of the book—Antonio A.B. da Silva—for providing his support in reviewing the content of the book during different points of time, despite being on a busy professional and personal schedule. He constructively criticized the content when required and also provided facts and shared his experience. Thank you.

To the SAP community network, without which we would not have been able to collaborate, enhance our learning, and always find help from the community of developers, users, and experts.

Above all, to the Great Almighty, the most powerful force, who gave us the courage to complete this book even in difficult and most challenging personal times, and for blessing us with his kindness to finish it.

—Suman Mukherjee
—Saptaparna Mukherjee (Das)
Pune, India. February, 2017

Introduction

Manufacturing is a vast and complex industry and it uses automation to handle processes quickly and efficiently and to integrate with other intelligent systems accurately. Most of the time, there is a gap between the management stakeholders and production units, which makes the management people unaware of the real-time situations happening on the shop floor. This causes a huge deviation in the industry KPIs. Furthermore, shop floor operators struggle with manual data maintenance during different machine readings. SAP MII fills these gaps and provides the intelligence and seamless integration of multiple systems in the manufacturing industry.

This book explains what SAP MII is and how it is becoming a necessary platform in the manufacturing industries. It also explains the usability and flexibility of SAP MII to business owners across various functional domains. Along with that, it will help technical and functional practitioners of SAP MII understand the various hidden features of the product and its best practices. It will help beginners quickly get a better grasp of MII by using the FAQs provided for quick reference.

The Target Audience

This book is suitable for all levels of SAP manufacturing professionals, starting with business process owners, production engineers, and architects who manage and design infrastructure, to functional and technical consultants and practitioners.

The Structure of this Book

This book is organized into eight chapters:

Chapter 1 explains the concept of manufacturing and the revolution that took place in manufacturing industries. It also explains the different processes involved during manufacturing and how to fill the gap between the manufacturing stakeholders and the production units during any manufacturing processes. It explains what SAP MII is and what it is capable of doing with its product architecture, installation concepts, and the system configuration features.

Chapter 2 explains the key challenges of the manufacturing industries and why you should use SAP MII from the functional, technical, and business perspectives. It also explains when MII is preferred over SAP BI/BW and vice versa. In addition to this, PI is explained, including its advantages and disadvantages, and when it's best to use MII or PI or both.

Chapter 3 explains the basics of SAP MII, the steps related to its various configurations and its development components and other basic features required for initial knowledge to start working on SAP MII.

Chapter 4 explains the basic functionalities of different manufacturing sectors involved in discrete manufacturing processes like automobiles, aviation and airspace defense, power generation, and mining. It discusses the possible scenarios in which automation is preferred and explains how SAP MII can be used to fulfill the requirements and need for automation.

Chapter 5 explains the basic functionalities of different manufacturing sectors involved in process manufacturing processes, such as pharmaceutical, consumer packaged goods, and oil and gas manufacturing industries, and the possible scenarios where automation is preferred for these industries. It explains how SAP MII is capable of providing the exact solution to all these problems.

Chapter 6 explains the different integrations possible through SAP MII and their respective configuration steps. It also explains the basics of SAP MII query templates, transactions, and different action blocks that new developers need to know in SAP MII. It further explains the concept of SAP MII integrations with other SAP manufacturing product integration module, i.e., MEINT and OEEINT.

Chapter 7 explains the new features of SAP MII, such as the general concepts associated with MDO, visualization services, UI5 and SSCE, KPI and Alerts, PIC, PCo, session handling for queries and JRA, and the new action blocks introduced in SAP MII.

Chapter 8 explains the best practices, recommendations, and frequently asked questions in SAP MII.

Foreword

Management thinker Peter Drucker is often quoted as saying, "If you can't measure it, you can't improve it." While the meaning of this statement is widely understood, measuring brings some inherent difficulties on the manufacturing shopfloor. The first among them is the different maturity levels of the factories and a heterogeneous system landscape that needs to be connected. Finding a single tool to connect these systems seamlessly and provide visualizations is a difficult and costly affair. This is exactly where SAP Manufacturing Integration & Intelligence (SAP MII) has created the highest impact in manufacturing, by not only providing seamless connectivity, integration, and visualizations, but also by bringing actionable intelligence right to the end user. SAP MII is a great enabler of measurement and visualizations, which forms the backbone of continuous improvement on the manufacturing shop floor. SAP MII, being a toolset, has extensive coverage of implementation scenarios across the manufacturing industries. The recent releases of SAP MII also bring pre-delivered content like SAP OEE (Overall Equipment Effectiveness) and EMA (Energy Monitoring and Analysis), which reduce the TCO of the MII implementation.

It has been more than a decade since SAP acquired Lighthammer Software Development, which is today SAP MII (Manufacturing Integration and Intelligence). I have been fortunate enough to be associated with SAP MII nearly since its inception in SAP. Since then, SAP MII has seen massive customer adoption and many success stories on the manufacturing shopfloor.

Although SAP MII has come a long way, when I talk to customers across the globe, I still see that there is a need for more MII consultants to execute their projects. While on one hand, this shows there is more demand than supply of consultants, it depicts the need for more training and resources to be easily accessible. Though there are a few books and trainings available on MII, having more books written by consultants from their real-life implementation experiences always adds value to the topic and goes way beyond in explaining concepts during training. This is where I see the value this book is bringing to the SAP manufacturing community.

Last but not the least, we all know that writing a book needs that extra enthusiasm and hard work, and I highly appreciate the time Suman and Saptaparna have taken after their busy consulting hours to pen their customer experiences on MII implementations. I'm sure that this book will enrich the SAP manufacturing community with additional dimensions of using MII on the shopfloor. I also thank Suman and Saptaparna for their passion for SAP manufacturing and their dedication to write this book for the community of SAP consultants. I wish them all the success going forward.

—Sumanta Chakraborty
Global Product Owner (SAP MII OEE Management), SAP Labs India, Bangalore
March, 2017

CHAPTER 1

SAP MII Overview

This chapter explains the manufacturing industry. It also discusses SAP MII and how it fills the gap of information flow between management and production. Along with that, it explains the history and features of SAP MII introduced in the manufacturing sector and how to work with it.

Concept of Manufacturing

Manufacturing basically involves the steps that convert the different raw materials into a finished product. It starts by collecting the material or creating the semi-finished material. It also involves designing the final product. These materials are modified and processed further to get the desired result. In industrial production, raw materials are converted into finished goods. Such finished goods are produced on a very large scale and can be further sold to other manufacturers depending on demand and needs. These finished goods may also be sold to wholesale buyers who in turn prefer to sell them to retailers, who then sell them to end users or customers. Thus, this selling and buying is a long chain, where different buyers and sellers are involved and use the manufactured product.

Revolution in Manufacturing

In earlier days, manufacturing was limited to a few experts and was carried out on a very small scale. After the industrial revolution, this changed and manufacturing became large scale but the processes were still completely or partially manual and very time consuming.

Later, with the modernization of manufacturing, the processes became very complex and multiple sub-components were added to the process. Shopfloor machines were connected to PLCs and sensors and the sensor data was stored in DCS, LIMS, SCADA, and Historian devices. Along with that, enterprise modules like production planning, master data governance, and others, came into the picture so that management could also get an understanding of production and its related business statistics. This created a pyramidal structure of layers in the industry where at the ground level are the shopfloor machines and the highest level includes ERP (Enterprise Resource Planning).

© Suman Mukherjee and Saptaparna Mukherjee (Das) 2017
S. Mukherjee and S. Mukherjee (Das), *SAP MII*, DOI 10.1007/978-1-4842-2814-2_1

There was a gap between the production shopfloor and the enterprise module, as there was no scope to connect them. Higher management never received real-time or near real-time information from their production plants. Other challenges, such as getting wrong information from the production plants, was also observed as data collection and production information gathering were manual processes (and therefore included human error).

Manufacturing Processes

The manufacturing industry follows certain process steps to complete production. This process is different for each type of industry domain. There can be some set of processes for automobile industries, but they will not be the same for the pharmaceutical industry. In the upcoming chapters of this book, we explain the domains and their expected processes, including explaining where SAP MII is best fitted and where the capability of SAP MII can be fully utilized.

Types of Manufacturing

In the manufacturing industry, there are multiple types of manufacturing depending on industry standards, region, and even continent. Although the processes and sub-processes are different for each domain, at a very broader level, there are two types of manufacturing:

- Discrete manufacturing
- Process manufacturing or batch manufacturing

Discrete Manufacturing

Discrete manufacturing is the production of distinct items where part of the final production can be further manufactured separately and can be used as input to the next manufacturing module in the whole process. In short, discrete manufacturing consists of all the produced components that are easily identifiable and can be de-assembled to get the main input component at which the process started.

The processes involved in discrete manufacturing are not continuous in nature. Sometimes, each process can be individually started or stopped and can run with different production rates. The final product can be produced with single or multiple raw or semi-finished inputs.

Discrete manufacturing runs with two concepts—one is low volume and high complexity and another is high volume and low complexity. Low volume with high complexity can change as market need changes, and high volume with low complexity needs a very good inventory capacity and proper control over the inventory. Controlled, high quality inventory stock reduces production cost as well as waste.

Good examples of discrete industries are automobile, electronics, aviation, etc., where the main concept is to assemble multiple raw or semi-finished products and create a new finished material which might not be the same as the base material.

Process Manufacturing

Process manufacturing, commonly known as continuous manufacturing, refers to the production of any finished material, which is the same base component ingredient but in a different form. In process manufacturing, products can be manufactured in lots or batches. Bulk production is possible in this case. The raw material consists of several ingredients that were mixed, churned, transformed, and converted to manufacture the final end product. This means the end product of process manufacturing cannot be de-assembled back to the raw materials.

In process manufacturing, processes are continuous in nature. Final products are manufactured only after a good market survey and a good understanding of the customer demand.

Quality control is a major factor during process manufacturing. A strong and very good quality control process involves quality inspection to pass any batch or lot. A batch can be recalled for retesting and verification at a later stage for quality reasons. Due to the huge scale of produced components, the quality check always happens in batches, which provides for more efficiency and speed. When any issue is found in the quality samples of any batch, the complete batch may be scrapped. In-process quality control is also possible. Based on a quality report, the raw material ratio can be changed to make the final product better.

Process manufacturing requires a good warehouse management to store stock, and this might require backup warehouses sometimes. Process manufacturing also monitors the product expiry date and distributes product across the market as per the requirement.

Good examples of process industries are chocolate, food, oil, natural gas, lens, medicines, etc.

Filling the Gap in Manufacturing

The biggest challenge in the manufacturing industry is to reduce the manual work and the human intervention during work so that the processes can be automatic. Another challenge is to fill the gap between management and the shopfloor, which closes the gap between business and production. Manufacturing industries have been looking for a solution that can provide real-time integration so that management can get real-time visibility of production happenings. This allows management to plan production accordingly.

There were a few local solutions available in the market to fix this gap, but these homegrown solutions were only fit for certain manufacturing environments. It was a revolution in the manufacturing industry, when in 2005, SAP AG launched the product SAP xMII. It was not only capable of providing near real-time integration, but could also provide a rich visualization to the user interface solution. This allowed management as well as the shopfloor to use reports to make key decisions. SAP xMII got an overwhelming acceptance in the manufacturing industry and so is SAP MII currently.

History of SAP MII (Manufacturing Integration and Intelligence)

SAP MII is derived from Lighthammer CMS (Collaborative Manufacturing Suite), developed by Lighthammer software. Development of Lighthammer Software was initiated in 1998 with a product code named as "Morning Coffee." Its intention was to enable manufacturing personnel to have access across operational information every morning, which would help them prepare for their daily production meetings.

SAP AG acquired Lighthammer in 2005 and rebranded the product as SAP xMII, where "x" stands for xApp. Later it was renamed SAP MII (SAP Manufacturing Integration and Intelligence). The initial version of SAP xMII was 11.5 and it ran on Microsoft Internet Information Server. Later on, they migrated it to SAP NetWeaver 7. SAP MII is nothing but the evolution of the original vision (SAP xMII), expanded to include not only visualization and analytics, but also the integration of multiple manufacturing systems on the shopfloor with each other and with the rest of the enterprise systems.

SAP MII is expanding continuously and many new features have been added to enhance the previous versions of SAP MII.

Figure 1-1 displays the evolution of features from 2005 through 2009.

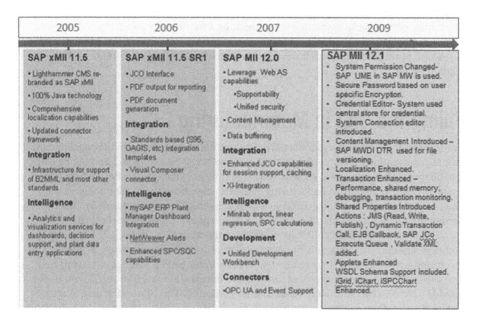

Figure 1-1. *SAP MII 11.5 through 12.1*

Figure 1-2 displays advancements from 2010 until 2015.

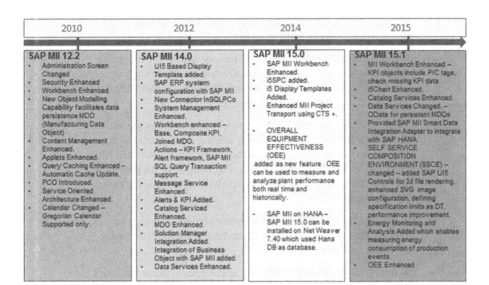

2010	2012	2014	2015
SAP MII 12.2	**SAP MII 14.0**	**SAP MII 15.0**	**SAP MII 15.1**
• Administration Screen Changed	• UI5 Based Display Template added.	• SAP MII Workbench Enhanced.	• MII Workbench Enhanced – KPI objects include PIC tags, check missing KPI data
• Security Enhanced	• SAP ERP system configuration with SAP MII	• i5SPC added.	• i5Chart Enhanced.
• Workbench Enhanced	• New Connector InSQLPCo	• i5 Display Templates Added.	• Catalog Services Enhanced.
• New Object Modelling Capability facilitates data persistence MDO (Manufacturing Data Object)	• System Management Enhanced.	• Enhanced MII Project Transport using CTS +.	• Data Services Changed. – OData for persistent MDOs
• Content Management Enhanced.	• Workbench enhanced – Base, Composite KPI, Joined MDO.	• OVERALL EQUIPMENT EFFECTIVENESS (OEE)	• Provided SAP MII Smart Data Integration Adapter to integrate with SAP HANA.
• Applets Enhanced.	• Actions – KPI Framework, Alert framework, SAP MII	added as new feature . OEE can be used to measure and analyze plant performance both real time and historically.	• SELF SERVICE COMPOSITION ENVIRONMENT (SSCE) – changed – added SAP UI5 Controls for 3d file rendering.
• Query Caching Enhanced – Automatic Cache Update.	SQL Query Transaction support.		enhanced SVG image configuration, defining specification limits as DT, performance improvement.
• PCO Introduced.	• Message Service Enhanced.	• SAP MII on HANA – SAP MII 15.0 can be installed on Net Weaver 7.40 which used Hana DB as database.	• Energy Monitoring and Analysis Added which enables measuring energy consumption of production events.
• Service Oriented Architecture Enhanced.	• Alerts & KPI Added.		
• Calendar Changed – Gregorian Calendar Supported only.	• Catalog Serviced Enhanced.		• OEE Enhanced
	• MDO Enhanced.		
	• Solution Manager Integration Added.		
	• Integration of Business Object with SAP MII added.		
	• Data Services Enhanced.		

Figure 1-2. *SAP MII 12.2 through 15.1*

A Glimpse of SAP MII

SAP MII is a flexible platform where the basic design can be customized to fit the customer's needs. It provides robust integration and high-quality intelligence. SAP MII can provide near-to real-time data integration between the shopfloor and enterprise systems. SAP MII also provides a development environment that's model driven, which means it doesn't follow any traditional line-by-line coding style. It is a drag-and-drop kind of hierarchical design development.

SAP MII can develop many kinds of logic using Business Logic services. Also, with the help of the visualization engine, it can provide excellent intelligence with the user interface. SAP MII has built-in connectivity and content to connect to the SAP business suite, like ERP, SAP SCM, and SAP PLM. SAP MII can persist data within MDO so that customers do not need to set up additional databases for data storage, which reduces cost and maintenance. Currently, SAP MII has standard alerts and KPI-generation mechanisms.

SAP MII uses web standards such as XML and Java adapters as integration components to connect to ERP and other related business components. SAP MII can integrate with multiple sources and with different data connectors at a time and can provide a web-based analytical dashboard. Currently, SAP MII can connect to HANA and can also leverage the HANA in-memory database for its design.

In short, SAP MII can be explained based on the following points:

- SAP MII can integrate all the available manufacturing systems as well as the information systems to provide the enterprise users with a common interactive platform.

- SAP MII has successfully helped in the revolution of wireless applications by supporting manufacturing employees in monitoring critical applications through PDAs (Personal Digital Assistants), smartphones, and other digital devices.

- XML is the backbone for SAP MII as a structural language and it can handle different integrity issues among the manufacturing systems on the shopfloor with the business applications like ERP, CRM, etc. It also helps integrate the shopfloor with supply chain optimization using standards like SOAP (Simple Object Access Protocol) and others.

- SAP MII helps get real-time monitoring of manufacturing so that the planning in the supply chain will be smooth and better decisions can be made.

- SAP MII can reuse the already available legacy systems to unlock the data for the end users within the enterprise. It provides a user-friendly environment to the users to establish link between different forms of data coming from multiple systems in a single browser interface.

- The SAP MII software does not need to be managed at the client site and there is no requirement for complex data warehouses or data models to be maintained in an SAP MII implementation.

- SAP MII allows the designing of smart solutions for computer integrated manufacturing, IIoT, machine-to-machine capabilities, and real-time intelligence.

- SAP MII can boost employee productivity by delivering information like real-time notifications and acknowledgement for any activity in the shopfloor. This helps the employees take immediate action on the received information.

- SAP MII can also provide enterprise-wide insights from Big Data manufacturing analytics.

- It is possible to define manufacturing metrics and KPIs and deploy the same standardized calculations across the sites globally using SAP MII.

SAP MII Architecture

In SAP MII, integration and intelligence are the key factors to consider when designing an automated manufacturing solution. So, if you consider the construction of SAP MII at a more detailed level, it splits into a few layers. From the integration side, SAP MII can connect to any of the shopfloor systems using SAP PCo or OPC connector and from the management side, SAP MII can connect to ERP through the Java connector. From the intelligence side, it is possible to develop all kinds of dashboards, reports, analytics, and other indicators using SAP MII rich visualization services to get real-time visibility. See Figure 1-3.

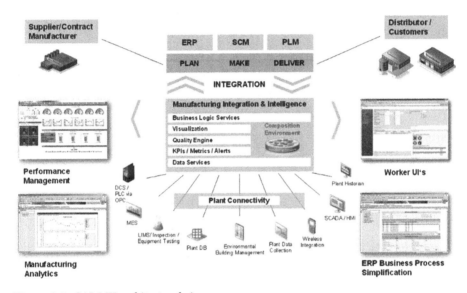

Figure 1-3. *SAP MII architectural view*

The following points explain these SAP MII architectural concepts:

- SAP MII is an open platform which integrates different systems used for manufacturing operations, regardless of purpose.

- SAP MII uses advanced web server technologies to extract data from multiple data sources and aggregates at the server. It transforms these sources into business contexts, personalizes them, and then delivers the results to the end users.

- SAP MII seamlessly connects to the ERP system using standard protocols like SAP Java connector and web service.

- SAP MII provides various data connectors specific to various standard manufacturing shopfloor systems.

- SAP MII provides bi-directional data access in both synchronous and asynchronous modes to ERP and shopfloor systems.

- SAP MII is browser independent, scalable, and extensible.

- Data functionality can be accessed using standard transports like HTTP, SMTP, and FTP.

When you begin to install SAP MII, one important question can arise. How do you place the solution? Based on the customer's requirements and budgets, SAP MII can be installed in three ways: locally, regionally, or globally.

- *Local installation*: SAP MII is installed at the manufacturing plant site. For each plant site, there is one SAP MII system. All those systems are connected to the Global ERP. See Figure 1-4.

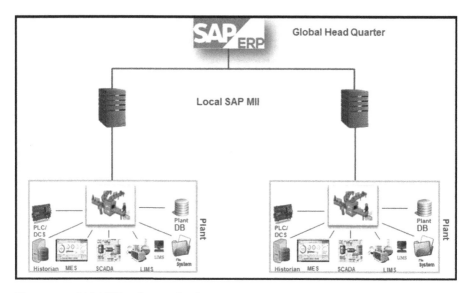

Figure 1-4. *SAP MII local server landscape*

- *Regional installation*: There is one SAP MII server for each region, and one region can consist of multiple manufacturing plants. A regional SAP MII can connect to the global ERP. This architecture is the one most commonly used. See Figure 1-5.

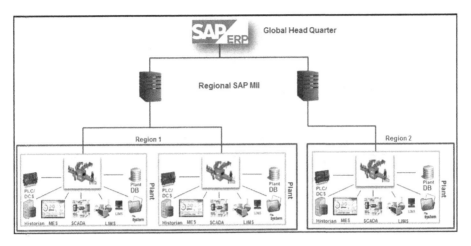

Figure 1-5. SAP MII regional server landscape

- *Global installation*: There is only one SAP MII globally and it's located at headquarters or a datacenter. It is shared by all the manufacturing plants. See Figure 1-6.

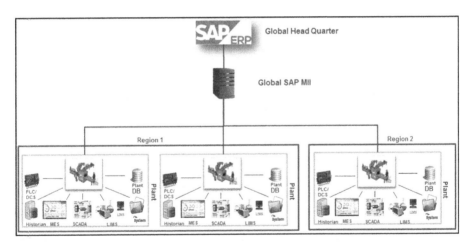

Figure 1-6. SAP MII global server landscape

SAP MII System Overview

In order to explain the SAP MII platform overview and its related configuration, the area of developments are detailed in the following sections.

SAP MII Installation

SAP MII is generally installed on the SAP NetWeaver platform on the application server, but the latest version (from SAP MII 15.0) can be installed on a SAP HANA platform. Prerequisites for SAP MII installation include the NetWeaver version and the corresponding Java J2EE engine version. From SAP MII version 12.0, all versions have a fixed NetWeaver version. Here we explain the settings for SAP MII version 15.1, which is the latest version.

SAP MII 15.1 can be installed on SAP NetWeaver 7.4 or SAP NetWeaver 7.5 Java Application Server.

In order to run SAP MII 15.1, JRE 1.6 or higher is required in the client machine. SAP MII doesn't support JRE 1.7.8 and above properly. Sometimes it crashes.

To install SAP MII 15.1, log in to SAP Service Marketplace (http://service.sap.com). Choose the SAP MII option from the software download support package and select the 15.1. Then download the version specific SAP MII sca component file and the SAP MII admin sca component file. Follow the SAP installation guide to complete the installation (https://help.sap.com/viewer/p/SAP_MANUFACTURING_INTEGRATION_AND_INTELLIGENCE).

To explain the server hardware sizing, SAP provides an insta-tool in the SAP Marketplace called Quick Sizer (service.sap.com/sizing).

System Configuration of SAP MII

SAP MII has different basic configurations depending on your needs. This is further explained next.

Security

As with any other tool, security is a major and important part of SAP MII. As SAP MII is a platform and it is possible to develop customer-specific solutions, SAP MII must provide security within the solution.

User Management

SAP MII has multiple security procedures. One of the most important parts of the procedure is the user management or user admin.

User management is handled by SAP NetWeaver J2EE Web.AS User Management Engine (UME). Here are the basic roles for SAP MII system access.

- *xMII Read Only*: Role for users who will have read-only access to the SAP MII system and to the workbench.

- *xMII Users*: Role for users with basic access to the SAP MII system and the solution developed with SAP MII. With this access, users cannot carry out any kind of configuration.

- *xMII Developers*: Role for developers working to develop composite applications using SAP MII Workbench. Developers can carry out certain configurations required for development, such as schedule a job configuration.

- *xMII Administrators*: Role for system administrators. All SAP MII system and NetWeaver configuration capabilities are available to this role.

- *xMII Super Administrators*: Role with full access in SAP MII and its related configurations in NetWeaver and in the user administrator.

Architecture of the UME

As shown in Figure 1-7, there are three main layers in a UME architecture. The lowermost level includes the data sources with individual persistence adapters. The user data is stored in the multiple data sources and so the lowermost layer is dedicated to user data storage purposes only. The second layer is the persistence manager. It helps the persistence adapters create, read, write, and search data related to user management. The topmost level is called the application programming interface (API). All configurations related to data write or read from the data source are done through the persistence manager so as to keep the information secure and ensure that there is no leakage to the applications using the API. These applications can determine details as to where exactly the user management data is stored.

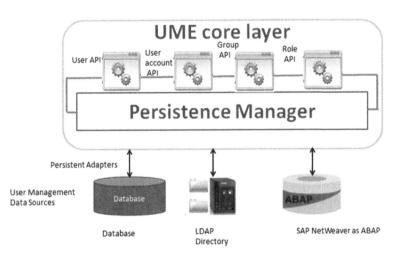

Figure 1-7. *Architecture of UME*

In SAP MII, it is possible to create project-specific multilayer roles. By using this functionality, it is possible to restrict the solution from all users so that the admin user can do certain configurations as permitted. Apart from that, project- or application-specific roles can also be created in UME to assign security permissions to develop objects on the workbench.

In addition to role creation, it is necessary to create users in NetWeaver in order to access SAP MII. If a customer already maintains users in NetWeaver for some other application, these same users can be reused in SAP MII, as SAP MII is also NetWeaver based.

There are two ways to access User Management or user admin:

1. Type the following URL in the browser:
    `https://<server>:<port>/useradmin`

2. From the MII Menu, go to the Security Services ➤ User Management. See Figure 1-8.

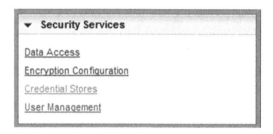

Figure 1-8. *Menu option for User Management*

From User Management, it is possible to create a new user, copy or modify an existing user profile, and delete existing users.

The same actions for user creation are also possible for role and group creation from the User Management screen. See Figure 1-9.

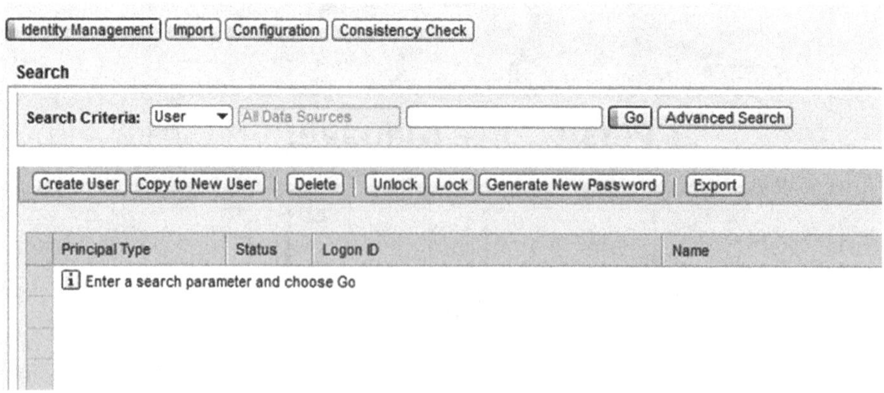

Figure 1-9. *User management in NetWeaver*

The following are the standard suffixes that SAP MII uses to identify authorized actions:

- _R: Permits read access

- _RW: Permits read and write access

- _RWD: Permits read, write, and delete access

- _deploy: Forces an immediate deploy

- _transport: Permits transport access

- _all: Permits read, write, delete, and transport access

Data Access

SAP MII Data Access is used to assign the SAP MII roles to SAP MII data servers. Admin and Data Access Security Editor are two system security services that are required to be assigned in order to perform specific functions on data access.

To configure data access, select a server from the Available Servers list and click on Edit. From the Available Roles list, select a role and use the Add All, Add, Remove, and Remove All buttons to add it to or remove it from the roles assigned to the server list. To select multiple roles, press and hold Ctrl and then click the appropriate roles. Then click on Save. See Figure 1-10.

Figure 1-10. Data Access screen

Encryption Configuration

Encryption configuration uses the encryption algorithm for encoding data servers, schedules, and credentials that are saved in SAP Manufacturing Integration and Intelligence. See Figure 1-11.

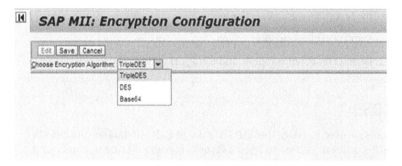

Figure 1-11. *SAP MII Encryption Configuration screen*

The available encryption algorithms are determined by the SAP NetWeaver instance and may include the following:

- TripleDES, which provides the strongest data encryption. It's the default setting. It is based on the Data Encryption Standard (DES), where the data is encrypted three times.

- DES provides the second strongest data encryption.

- Base64 provides the least amount of data encryption. When no other encryption method is available, the system uses Base64 encoding.

Credential Stores

You use the Credential Stores screen to add an alias for a username and password, which can be changed or deleted (see Figure 1-12). These aliases are used in SAP Manufacturing Integration and Intelligence workbench actions, instead of entering the username and password in the action configurations. Credential storage with password encryption is available with all objects that require a username and password for configuration. The aliased credentials can then be used to configure:

- SAP servers

- BLS actions

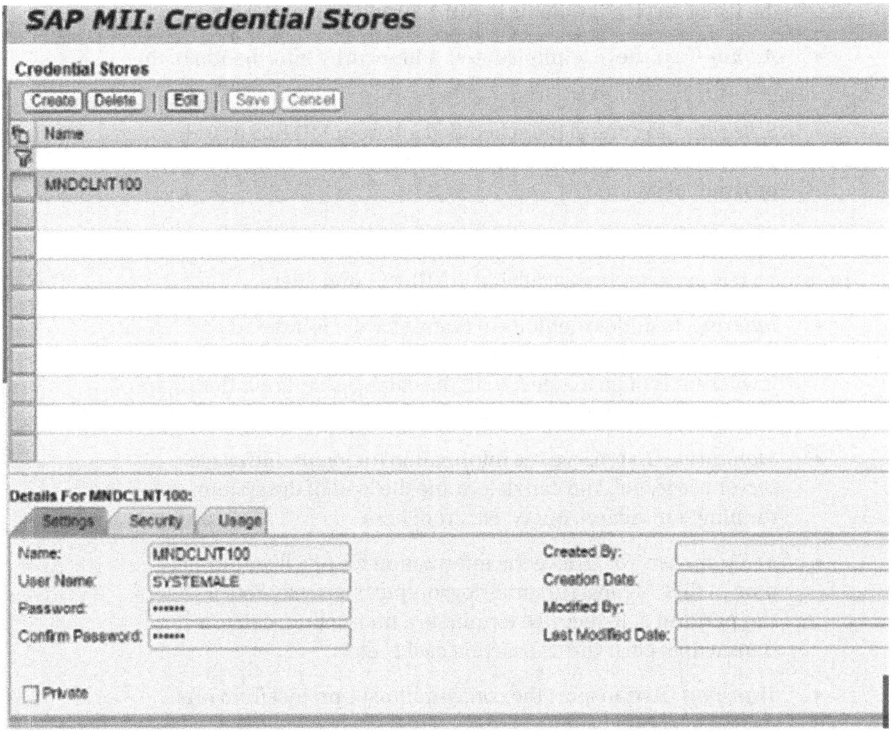

Figure 1-12. *SAP MII Credential Alias Configuration*

Illuminator Services

Illuminator services are the backbone of data service in SAP MII. SAP MII illuminator services are basically a set of HTTP services that provide some core functionality of SAP MII. You can call these services externally by XML message exchange.

Each illuminator service has a service name and one or more modes, which are service operations. At the time of execution, you must specify both the service name and mode with the input parameter if any. The services can be called independently or from the web pages by using AJAX or BLS. Here are the three main uses of these services:

- As the only way to fetch data from MII internal Table

- Performance-wise, one of the best ways to use this in the code

- Easy to use directly from IRPT or JS

Here is the syntax for the illuminator services:

```
http://<server>:<port>/XMII/Illuminator?service=<service name>&mode=<mode
name>&content-type=text/xml
```

Here is the list of services available in MII 12.0 and later:

- *Admin*: To retrieve administrative and security information of the SAP MII server.

- *Scheduler*: To control the scheduled job from MII BLS or web pages automatically without any user intervention based on the program logic.

- *SystemInfo*: To get system-related information of SAP MII.

Here are a few more services available in MII 12.1 and later:

- *Indexing*: Includes methods to examine what is indexed and monitor an indexer. The indexer rebuilds the index information. It will run through all the files in the database and re-index them. This should be used only if the indexes get out of sync somehow.

- *Monitoring*: To retrieve the information for logins, file usage, server usage, etc. You can determine the load of the system, running transaction, query, etc. from here.

- *BLSManager*: To retrieve the information for BLS like running time of BLS, highest run time, log, output, stats, etc. You can perform activities like terminate a transaction, delete a transaction, clear the transaction cache. etc.

- *Transport*: To transport the configuration or project from one system to another.

- *DataServer*: To carry out the basic functionalities of the data server, like enabling, disabling, deleting, exporting, and importing it.

In the latest version of SAP MII, several new services are included:

- *Alert*: Provides the basic features like list, view, delete, etc.

- *oData*: Newly added in SAP MII and now supports SAP HANA integrations. SAP MII can be hosted on SAP HANA.

Refer to the SCN blog written by the author: `https://blogs.sap.com/2013/01/02/illuminator-services-of-sap-mii/`.

SAP MII Admin Configuration

To develop a SAP MII solution, the developer with the administrator role needs to do certain configurations to proceed. There are multiple sections in the SAP MII Admin menu page that need to be configured. The most important sections are explained in this section. They are mandatory and must require proper knowledge before starting a SAP MII project.

To access the SAP MII menu page, access the following URL through the browser.

```
https://<host>:<port>/XMII/Menu.jsp
```

System Management Menu Options

The SAP MII menu includes system management options. This menu allows you to configure the system-wide settings. These system administration activities need admin and other administrative security service permissions. They need to be assigned to the user role to access and manage the administrative tasks available in the System Management menu. This menu consists of the configurations shown in Figure 1-13.

Figure 1-13. SAP MII System Configuration menu options

The System Properties Screen

The System Properties screen is used to configure the general administrative configurations of SAP MII, as shown in Figure 1-14.

Figure 1-14. SAP MII System Properties configuration screen

17

The System Jobs Screen

System jobs are the tasks that run in the background at regular intervals and perform internal maintenance of SAP MII server and content. See Figure 1-15.

SAP MII: System Jobs

Name	Description	Frequency (Min)	Next Run Time
Activation Request Cleaner	Clean activation request IDs that are older than 7 days	1440.0	Dec 1, 2016 12:40:27 PM IST
Alert Expiration Job	Job for checking expired alerts	60.0	Nov 30, 2016 5:40:28 PM IST
Cache Cleanup	Triggers cleanup for multiple MII caches	1.0	Nov 30, 2016 5:00:38 PM IST
Catalog Delete Old Logs	Delete old tag catalog logs	1440.0	Dec 1, 2016 12:40:27 PM IST
Catalog Scan Inactive Tags	Check for deleted tags in plant historians	1440.0	Dec 1, 2016 12:40:27 PM IST
Data Buffer Job Scanner	Process items in the data buffer queue	1.0	Nov 30, 2016 5:00:39 PM IST
Indexing Cleaner	Clean bad file references from indexing	1440.0	Dec 1, 2016 12:40:27 PM IST
JCO Connection Monitor	Clean JCo connections where hops timeout has been reached	5.0	Nov 30, 2016 5:00:30 PM IST
Job History Cleaner	Clean job history table	30.0	Nov 30, 2016 5:10:28 PM IST
MDO Data Source Watcher	MDO Data Source Watcher	360.0	Nov 30, 2016 7:22:41 AM IST
MDO Log Cleanup	MDO Log Cleanup	720.0	Dec 1, 2016 12:40:34 AM IST
Message Sequence Cleaner	Remove message sequences that have no messages under them	1440.0	Dec 1, 2016 12:40:27 PM IST
Monitor Data Cleaner	Remove monitoring data older than the specified number of days	1440.0	Dec 1, 2016 12:40:27 PM IST
Query Cache Scanner	Clear expired query content from the systemcache	1440.0	Dec 1, 2016 12:40:27 PM IST
SQL Connection Timeout Monitor	Clean SQL connections for connections that exceeded timeout	0.2	Nov 30, 2016 5:00:09 PM IST
Scheduler Checker	Checks that the MII scheduler is working correctly	1.0	Nov 30, 2016 5:00:39 PM IST
Security Object Reference Cleaner	Clean obsolete references to users and roles	10080.0	Dec 6, 2016 12:40:26 PM IST
Session Logger	Log session information	30.0	Nov 30, 2016 5:00:39 PM IST
Shared Property Cleanup	Remove expired properties	1.0	Nov 30, 2016 5:00:40 PM IST
Temp File Cleaner	Clean Temp file table	60.0	Nov 30, 2016 5:40:28 PM IST

Figure 1-15. SAP MII internal system job details

The default system jobs running on a SAP MII server as highlighted in Figure 1-16 are as follows:

- *Session Logger*: Runs every 30 minutes to log system usage by the number of active unique users.

- *Security Object Reference Cleaner*: Runs once every seven days to delete invalid system and performance roles, custom attribute roles, and users in the respective database tables.

- *Temp File Cleaner*: Runs every hour to clean the temporary files table.

SAP MII: System Jobs

Name	Description	Frequency (Min)	Next Run Time
SQL Connection Timeout Monitor	Clean SQL connections for connections that exceeded timeout	0.2	Nov 30, 2016 5:00:09 PM IST
Scheduler Checker	Checks that the MII scheduler is working correctly	1.0	Nov 30, 2016 5:00:39 PM IST
Security Object Reference Cleaner	Clean obsolete references to users and roles	10080.0	Dec 6, 2016 12:40:26 PM IST
Session Logger	Log session information	30.0	Nov 30, 2016 5:10:28 PM IST
Shared Property Cleanup	Remove expired properties	1.0	Nov 30, 2016 5:00:40 PM IST
Temp File Cleaner	Clean Temp file table	60.0	Nov 30, 2016 5:40:28 PM IST

Figure 1-16. Important system jobs in SAP MII

The Transaction Manager Screen

The Transaction Manager screen monitors the BLS transactions that are being executed in the system (see Figure 1-17).

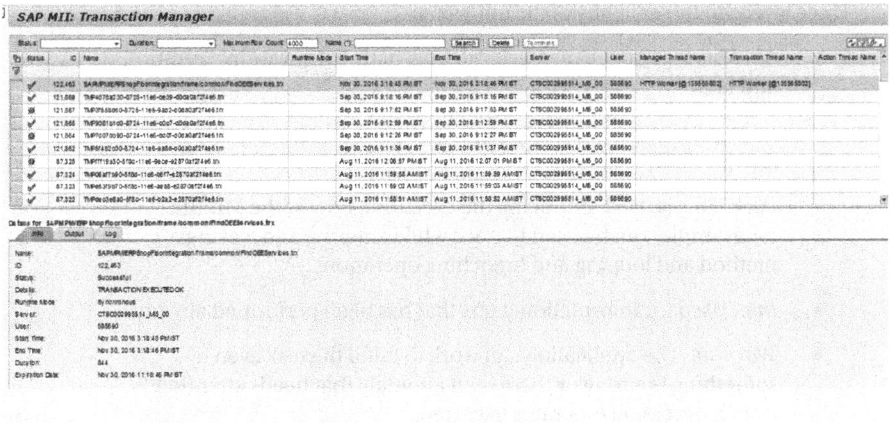

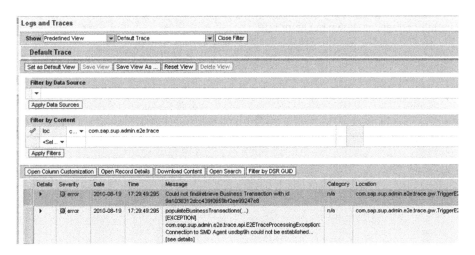

Figure 1-17. *SAP MII Transaction Manager screen*

The Log Viewer Screen

The Log Viewer screen (see Figure 1-18) displays the SAP NetWeaver log viewer. System logs can be viewed from SAP NetWeaver Administrator (NWA). It can be viewed with the NWA_READONLY role through the https://<host>:<port>/nwa link. Further, NWA_SUPERADMIN allows the user to have full view access and control over the NetWeaver interface and the configurations required for MII, as well as permissions to access the data in the managed system. The read-only role (NWA_READONLY) does not allow users to make changes to the managed system. The other role (NWA_SUPERADMIN) allows full control. You can view logs from the last 24 hours. The tracing level defaults to error and can be modified by navigating to SAP NetWeaver Administrator ➤ System Management ➤ Configuration ➤ Log Configuration.

Figure 1-18. *The SAP MII Log Viewer*

Trace level can be set to any of the following:

- *All*: This logs all the messages: debug, path, info, warning, error, and fatal.

- *Debug*: This is used for debugging purposes, with extensive and low-level information.

- *Path*: This is used for tracing the execution flow of the MII BLS, for example, can be used to trace while entering and leaving a method and looping and branching operations.

- *Info*: Used for informational text that has been performed already.

- *Warning*: The application can work to fulfill the task even if something is wrong or there is an anomaly that needs attention from a developer/operator to correct.

- *Error*: The application can recover from an error, but it cannot fulfill the required task because of the error and needs to be corrected.

- *Fatal*: The application cannot recover from an error, and this severe situation causes fatal termination of the application.

- *None*: Logs no messages.

The Scheduler Menu

The Scheduler menu provides information about all the jobs that are scheduled by the user. Any Business Logic (BLS) transactions, queries, and MDOs can be executed periodically using Scheduler. It is also possible to view a status of the jobs that are running, pending, or stopped.

You need to assign the Scheduler Security service to a user to enable access to the Scheduler screen, as shown in Figure 1-19.

Figure 1-19. *SAP MII Scheduler configuration*

The scheduler has three tabs:

- Transaction Scheduler

- History

- Execution Schedule

Transaction Scheduler

The elements on this tab are described here:

- *Name*: The scheduled job's name.

- *Description*: The job details and what it is supposed to do.

- *Enabled*: A checkbox option that, when checked, enables the job to run periodically according to the cron pattern. The job is not scheduled if this checkbox is not checked.

- *Transaction, Query, or MDO (Manufacturing Data Object)*: Indicates the BLS transaction, data query, or MDO query that will be scheduled to run.

- *Run As Username*: Indicates the user, whose credentials are used to run the job.

- *Run As Password*: Signifies the password of the user mentioned above.

21

- *Parameters*: Indicates the input parameters, if any, of the transaction selected above. The user should ideally enter the values of the input parameters to be used while running the transaction as a scheduled job.

- *Pattern*: Indicates a cron pattern, which determines the schedule of the job to be run. You can create the cron pattern, which is used to determine the job schedule, either manually or by using the Build Pattern screen. The Build Pattern screen is invoked by clicking the Build Pattern button. It enables you to create cron patterns with ease.

The Scheduler Service checks every 500 milliseconds for jobs that are ready to be run and then executes them. Using the Scheduler, any business logic transaction, query, or MDO can be executed periodically to do various activities, such as pull data from manufacturing plant floor systems by data queries, execute a web service or RFC, and calculate and update a KPI.

The Scheduler screen also displays the following information regarding the scheduled jobs.

Status signifies the status of the job. The values can be Stopped, Pending, and Running.

- *Stopped*: Indicates the job is currently stopped. Tasks that are not enabled have this status.

- *Pending*: Indicates the job is scheduled and pending its next run.

- *Running*: Indicates the scheduled job is running at the current moment.

- *Name*: Signifies the name of the job as set in the Scheduler.

- *Next Run Time*: Indicates the time when this scheduled job will run next.

- *File*: Signifies the full path of the business logic transaction, query, or MDO that has been scheduled to run.

- *Description*: Illustrates the job as set in the Scheduler.

History

The Scheduler also lets the administrator or any user with sufficient authorization privileges view the Job Execution History screen, as shown in Figure 1-20.

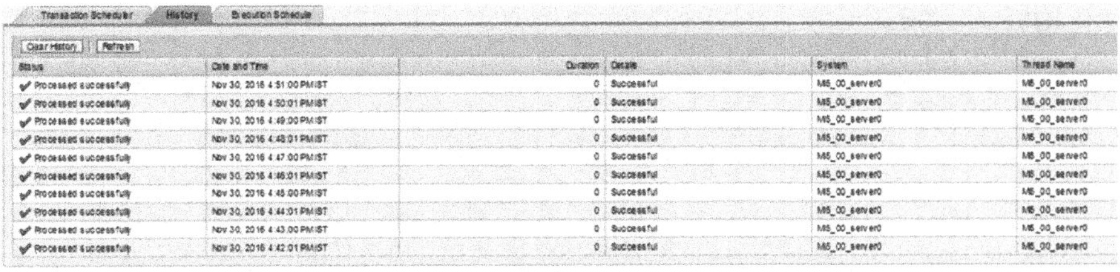

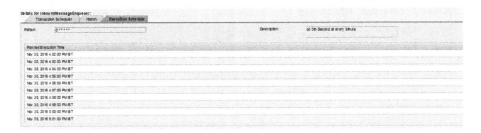

Figure 1-20. *Scheduler Execution History screen*

This screen displays details of the previous execution attempts of the scheduled job with the status, duration, and details.

Execution Schedule

Lastly, the Execution Schedule functionality displays a schedule for the next 20 scheduled times the job will run, as shown in Figure 1-21.

Figure 1-21. *Scheduler Execution schedule*

The Active Sessions Screen

If the user is assigned the administrative role, it is possible to view the list of users who are logged in to the SAP MII server through the Active Sessions screen. In addition to the user login name, this screen also provides the full names of the users, their e-mail addresses, the date and time of initial login, the date and time when the system was last accessed, and when the session expires. See Figure 1-22.

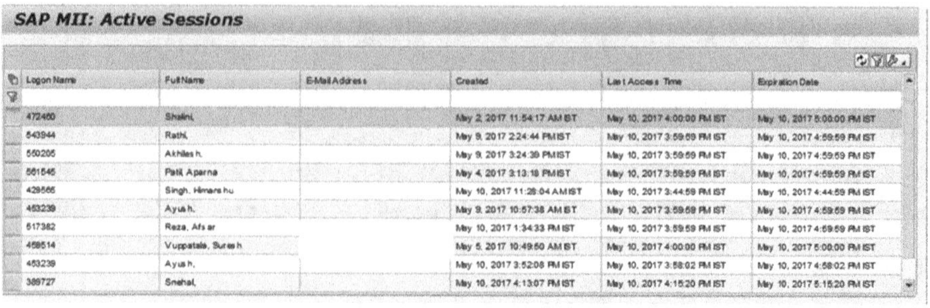

SAP MII: Active Sessions

Logon Name	Full Name	E-Mail Address	Created	Last Access Time	Expiration Date
472460	Shalini,		May 2, 2017 11:54:17 AM IST	May 10, 2017 4:00:00 PM IST	May 10, 2017 5:00:00 PM IST
543944	Rathi,		May 9, 2017 2:24:44 PM IST	May 10, 2017 3:59:59 PM IST	May 10, 2017 4:59:59 PM IST
550205	Akhiles h,		May 9, 2017 3:24:39 PM IST	May 10, 2017 3:59:59 PM IST	May 10, 2017 4:59:59 PM IST
561546	Patil, Aparna		May 4, 2017 3:13:18 PM IST	May 10, 2017 3:59:59 PM IST	May 10, 2017 4:59:59 PM IST
429566	Singh, Himans hu		May 10, 2017 11:26:04 AM IST	May 10, 2017 3:44:59 PM IST	May 10, 2017 4:44:59 PM IST
453239	Ayus h,		May 9, 2017 10:57:38 AM IST	May 10, 2017 3:59:59 PM IST	May 10, 2017 4:59:59 PM IST
517382	Reza, Afs ar		May 10, 2017 1:34:33 PM IST	May 10, 2017 3:59:59 PM IST	May 10, 2017 4:59:59 PM IST
458514	Vuppatala, Sures h		May 5, 2017 10:49:50 AM IST	May 10, 2017 4:00:00 PM IST	May 10, 2017 5:00:00 PM IST
453239	Ayus h,		May 10, 2017 3:52:06 PM IST	May 10, 2017 3:58:02 PM IST	May 10, 2017 4:58:02 PM IST
389727	Snehal,		May 10, 2017 4:13:07 PM IST	May 10, 2017 4:15:20 PM IST	May 10, 2017 5:15:20 PM IST

Figure 1-22. *SAP MII Active Sessions screen*

The Custom Attributes Screen

The Custom Attributes screen is used to manage custom attributes to store configuration or business data used by the application. See Figure 1-23.

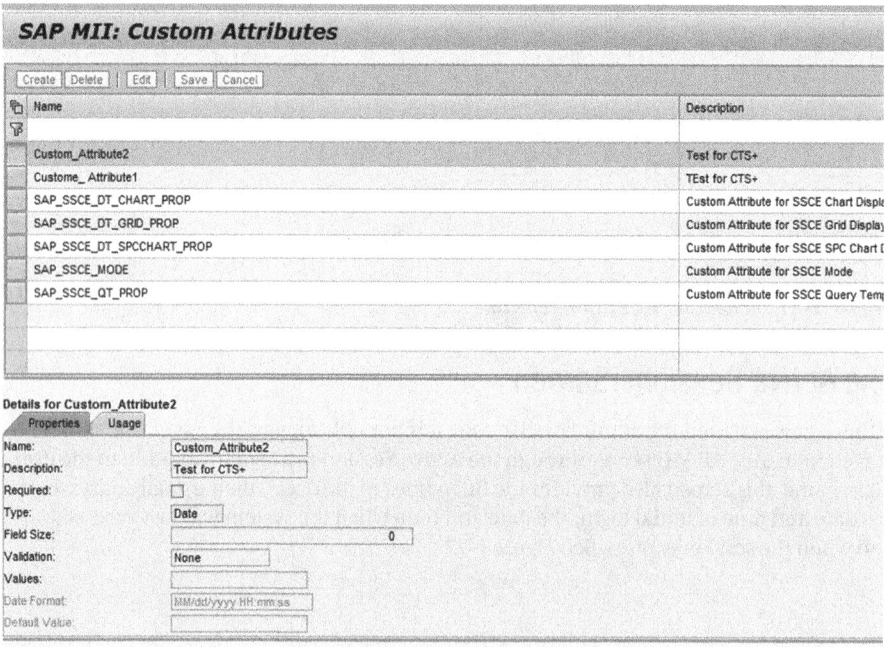

SAP MII: Custom Attributes

Create | Delete | Edit | Save | Cancel

Name	Description
Custom_Attribute2	Test for CTS+
Custome_ Attribute1	TEst for CTS+
SAP_SSCE_DT_CHART_PROP	Custom Attribute for SSCE Chart Displa
SAP_SSCE_DT_GRID_PROP	Custom Attribute for SSCE Grid Display
SAP_SSCE_DT_SPCCHART_PROP	Custom Attribute for SSCE SPC Chart D
SAP_SSCE_MODE	Custom Attribute for SSCE Mode
SAP_SSCE_QT_PROP	Custom Attribute for SSCE Query Tem

Details for Custom_Attribute2

Properties | Usage

Name:	Custom_Attribute2
Description:	Test for CTS+
Required:	☐
Type:	Date
Field Size:	0
Validation:	None
Values:	
Date Format:	MM/dd/yyyy HH:mm:ss
Default Value:	

Figure 1-23. *SAP MII Custom Attributes configuration*

The Custom Attribute Mapping Screen

The Custom Attribute Mapping screen is used to assign the custom attributes to existing users or user roles to be used as session variables. See Figure 1-24.

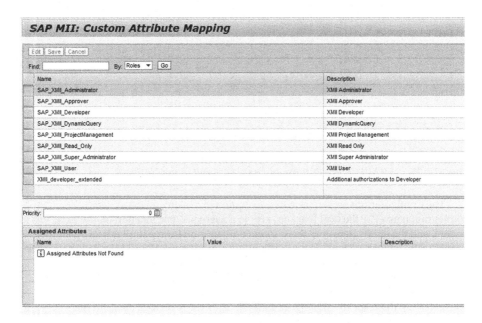

Figure 1-24. SAP MII Custom Attribute Mapping configuration

The Configurations Screen

The Configurations screen is used to import or export configuration backup as a ZIP archive to and from the system. The configurations shown in Figure 1-25 can be exported and imported.

25

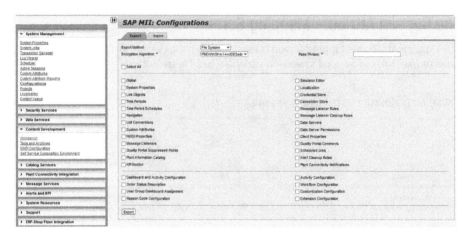

Figure 1-25. *SAP MII Configurations and its export and import features*

The Configurations screen provides the option of backing up the system configuration as a ZIP file (xmiibackup.zip) to a user-specified location on the local system, and the ability to restore the system configuration from a similar backup archive. This is useful while transporting the configurations from one SAP MII installation to other (for example, from development to production).

You need to assign the configuration management security service to a user to enable access to the Configurations screen. According to the options that are checked on the screen, the respective configurations are exported to an XML file, and the corresponding file is included in the xmiibackup.zip archive when the Export button is clicked. In the case of an import, you need to browse the backup archive file containing a previous export of the configuration from the local file system and click on Import to import the configuration archive file into SAP MII.

The configuration types explained here are available for export or import in SAP MII:

- *System Properties*: The system properties are backed up in the SystemProperties.xml file.

- *Simulator Instances*: Each instance is backed up as a separate XML file as <SimulatorServerName>.xml in a folder called Simulator_files in the archive. The default simulator instance is backed up as DefaultSimulator.xml.

- *Scheduled Jobs*: Each scheduled job is backed up as a separate XML file as <ScheduleName>.xml in a folder called Scheduler_Jobs in the archive.

- *Message Listeners*: The message listeners configuration created in message services are backed up in the MessageServers.xml file.

- *Message Listener Rules*: The processing rules for message listeners created in message services are backed up in the MessageProcessRules.xml file.

- *Data Server Permissions*: The security permissions for the data servers configured in security services are backed up in the ServerPermissions.xml file.

- *Message Listener Cleanup Rules*: The cleanup rules created in message services are backed up in the MessageCleanupRules.xml file.

- *Data Servers*: The data servers configured in data services are backed up in the Servers.xml file.

- *Localization*: Localization settings are backed up as a separate XML file, <Language>.xml, in a folder called Localization in the archive.

- *Link Objects*: The navigation link objects configured in the visualization services are backed up in the ContentMap.xml file.

- *Time Periods*: The time periods configured in data services are backed up in the TimePeriods.xml file.

- *Navigation*: Each role or profile that has navigation profiles associated with it is stored as the corresponding XML files named <Role>.xml or <User>.xml in the corresponding ROLE or USER folder under the common Profiles folder.

- *Time Period Schedules*: The time period schedules configured in data services are backed up in the Schedules.xml file.

- *Global*: The global properties defined in the SAP MII installation are backed up in the Globals.xml file.

- *Unit Conversions*: The unit conversion configurations are backed up in the UnitConversions.xml file.

- *Custom Attributes*: The custom attributes configured in system administration are backed up in the CustomAttributes.xml file.

The Projects Menu

The Projects menu in SAP MII allows the SAP MII administrator (and any users with the Project Management security service) to back up and restore SAP MII projects. This is useful while transporting development content from one SAP MII installation to other, such as from development to production. See Figure 1-26.

27

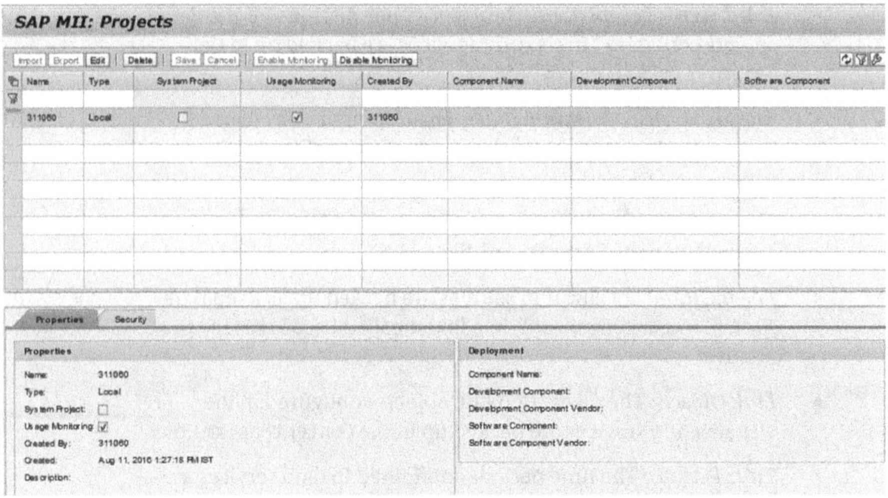

Figure 1-26. *SAP MII Projects configurations and its export & import feature*

The Projects screen lists the various projects and their details such as name, description, whether it is system project, when and by whom it was created, and options to delete and export it as a compressed ZIP file.

A project exported from SAP MII contains the project files in the same folder structure defined in the SAP MII Workbench, along with an ExportManifest.xml file, which contains necessary metadata regarding the exported project. It is not necessary to have an ExportManifest.xml to import a project into SAP MII. It is possible to externally create the project structure and import it into SAP MII. However, note that if a project with the same project name as an existing project is imported into SAP MII, the existing project will be overwritten, regardless of whether it is a system or a hidden project.

System projects in SAP MII are delivered by SAP and required internally by the SAP MII system. Those projects cannot be deleted, for example, Default and QualityPortal.

Localization

The Localization function provides different language support to the SAP MII platform (see Figure 1-27).

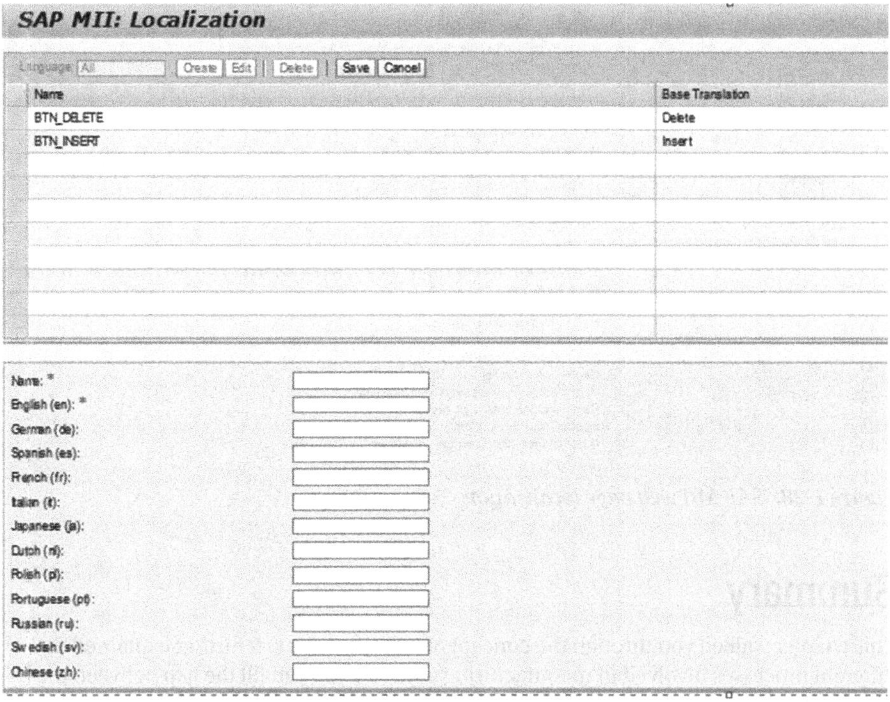

Figure 1-27. *SAP MII Localization configuration*

Localization can be set using two methods (see Figure 1-28):

- *Web Page Localization*: Any HTML page can be localized based on the regional language. The HTML page needs to be saved as an .irpt file. This file extension identifies the files as web pages that need to be processed by the system before being returned as HTML to the browser at runtime. During this process, the system replaces the localization keys with their translations based on the user's language. For this, the developer needs to define a localization key and its value as per specific language within the # tag, like {##KeyName}. During runtime the value determines the language that's displayed.

- *Project Localization*: This function can be used to fully localize the project. The localized strings are used in transactions and .irpt pages. The preference order for localizing the project is the user language, then the system language, then English (EN). If the localization value is not found, the key is returned by default. Further, from the meta-inf tab of SAP MII Workbench, you can create (under the Bundles folder) new .properties files for customer-specific local languages. Using this file, you can add name=value pairs for the specified language.

29

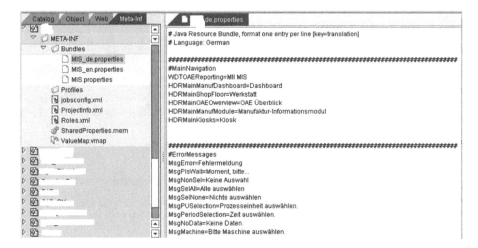

Figure 1-28. *SAP MII web page localization*

Summary

This chapter walked you through the concept of manufacturing. It further explained the different processes involved in manufacturing and how you can fill the gap between the shopfloor and management during the manufacturing processes. You also learned the history behind SAP MII evolution, what SAP MII is, and what it can do with its product architecture, installation concept, and system configuration features. In the next chapter, you will get to know what are the key challenges in manufacturing industries and why you should use SAP MII from it's functional, technical and business perspectives.

CHAPTER 2

Why Use SAP MII in Manufacturing Industries

This chapter explains why you should use SAP MII in the manufacturing industry. It explains the challenges that are being faced in manufacturing and the role SAP MII plays in overcoming these challenges.

Why Use SAP MII?

The previous chapter explained what SAP MII is. One of the biggest questions these days in the manufacturing world is why use SAP MII? The benefits of using SAP MII need to be considered from multiple perspectives, such as its functional aspects, technical advantages, and business benefits, to justify its usage. SAP MII is a powerful integration platform, which means that SAP MII can work as middleware among different third-party or legacy systems. It's not only for integration. SAP MII has intelligence capabilities also, as it is used to develop various smart real-time analytical and monitoring reports with high-end visualization using 3D graphics. Recently, SAP MII has been introduced with another "I" factored in it, which refers to "innovation". This silent feature of SAP MII helps you leverage innovation by connecting with IIoT (Industrial Internet of Things) smart mobile devices.

■ **Note** The term *innovation* refers to introducing a new idea to an existing method or modifying the existing method with a more enhanced solution. The new solution might be more user friendly or use new devices or technologies to achieve better results. For example, the smartphone was an innovation over the traditional cell phone and it was inspired by the market demand for more flexible communication.

IIoT refers to the Internet of Things technologies. The different technologies that are part of the IIoT include big data technology, machine learning mechanisms, methods controlling, and monitoring sensor data. How one machine communicates with another machine is also called M2M (machine-to-machine) communication. Another factor behind the use of IIoT is that it can integrate with mobile devices so users can stay connected to near-to real-time data even when they aren't on-site.

Key Challenges and Solutions in Manufacturing

The manufacturing sector has been facing various challenges, including increased cost of production, lower quality of the products, finding qualified manpower, competitive markets, and more. All these challenges are interconnected. For example, inefficient manpower tends to increase the cost of manufacturing and adversely affect the quality of the products. The organization is left behind in the long run. To overcome these issues more easily, quickly, and efficiently, the company needs a robust solution. The following sections explain in detail the challenges and the solutions applied to the manufacturing industry.

Competitive Markets and Lower Manufacturing Costs

Manufacturing is a complex sector but is an essential part of any country's economy. There is stiff competition in the manufacturing industries these days. The competitiveness of a manufacturing firm can be determined based on various interdependent factors like quality, innovation, efficiency, customer satisfaction, employee satisfaction, etc. Further, how fast these functions communicate with each other adds to the competitiveness factor of a firm. Multiple factors are involved to determine the competitiveness in manufacturing. To handle this challenge more efficiently, you must identify the core competencies to manage with minimal cost and high quality. These days, innovation is also considered a factor that provides better performance, which in turn helps reduce the cost of manufacturing.

SAP MII provides all these functions in one place to the manufacturing firm with minimal costs. From the server perspective, as it has the following:

- Internal database and low maintenance cost

- Capability to integrate with ERP systems using connectors to get near-to real-time data from the shopfloor

- No manual costs involved in various processes

- Automation of the processes so to avoid human error

■ **Note** ERP stands for *Enterprise Resource Planning*. This is the planning and management suite for the business, which helps manage the activities of planning for the production and product. This includes manufacturing costs, delivery, bill of lading, material management, shipping management, payment management, inventory management, sales management, etc. It helps you get an integrated view of the business from warehouse to production management and from planning to production management by providing control over various business processes in real-time using a strong RDBMS (relational database management system).

The *shopfloor* is the area of a factory or workshop where the operatives work; this term is used to distinguish the productive part of a factory from the administrative part.

Preference of Lean Supply Chain Strategy

Now a days, manufacturing industries prefer a lean supply chain strategy. This method promotes delivery of products quickly to the end customers with minimum waste. A lean supply chain helps deliver the customers a better solution while quickly predicting the customer's needs and easily delivering the product with great efficiency. This ultimately helps in superior financial performance. As SAP MII is a flexible platform, it is possible to develop customer-specific solutions as required. Further, SAP MII can connect to the shopfloor systems and ERP solutions and can automate the processes, so it is possible to design the solution in SAP MII in such a way that the production timeline will be reduced. SAP MII can further integrate with quality modules and monitor the production in real-time. It can put a check on production wastes more efficiently, which results in decision-making being reduced.

■ **Note** The *supply chain* is one of the components of enterprise resource planning that provides a clear view of the inventory's movement from supplier to end customer. This provides a transparent view and better control over the raw material to the finished product, and finally delivered to the end customer.

Lean supply chain encourages producing only the amount required and considering when and where products are required. This helps reduce unnecessary production, which can cause waste and drive up cost. Fewer resources are used to produce more or more resources are used to produce the exact amount, as per the end consumer need. This can be successful only if each product is attended to individually to remove the unnecessary methods involved in the processes, which are considered waste. Thus, the Lean approach focuses not only on removing waste from processes but also considers the enhancement of the value stream.

Disparate Manufacturing Plant Systems

Manufacturing plants involve multiple automation systems, machines, factories, headquarters, and securities of different manufacturing-related departments. In a larger manufacturing system it is very common for production plants to be scattered in multiple locations, regions, or geographies. These various units are disconnected and don't communicate with each other very well. Generally, ERP is implemented centrally at the headquarters or regional office and not at each plant. As there is no direct connection of the ERP systems with these units, it can be more time-consuming to fetch information from various sites and units. Also, as this information is handled manually, there is a very good chance of human error. If ERP is connected to MII locally, regionally, or globally, management will always be able to get near-to real-time data. As the process becomes automated with SAP MII, the data will always be accurate. Along with that, MII has guaranteed delivery of data and thus, if any plant or unit gets disconnected, MII can push queued data to ERP immediately on reconnection, without any data loss.

Business and Financial Impact of Production Issues

The business and financial impact of production issues or discrepancies is very difficult to monitor or control manually in manufacturing units. As an example, if the scenario arises where there is demand for 100 parts to be produced as the final product but, due to a fault in the line, 20 are scrapped and only 80 are produced, this is considered good production. If 80 were scrapped and 20 were good, the line or machine needs to be replaced or corrected, as number of scraps is higher than the good product. SAP MII can connect to ERP to monitor and raise plant maintenance notifications from both MII and ERP. These notifications tell the maintenance supervisors about such business losses in time so they can replace or rectify the machines or lines quickly.

Financial loss can also be curbed by having good performance line or machines that produce good products with minimal waste. MII can also connect to the quality module of ERP so whatever good quantity is being produced as a final product, MII can connect to ERP quality modules. SAP MII also has a plant maintenance schedule monitoring feature. This feature can be utilized by management and supervising teams. These teams can use the score card reports developed in MII to see why and when the lines went through states like scheduled downtime, unscheduled downtime, scheduled stop, malfunctions, and so on. These issues could happen because of labor error, material unavailability, deviation from planned production, utility of equipment in excess, improper logistics, and unavoidable incidents.

Lack of Control and Monitoring Mechanism for Production

Many times, manufacturing industries face problems because they cannot control and monitor the line running in production. Suppose there is a situation where they need to keep track of the temperature controllers used in large ovens in production, when it crosses a particular threshold and then manually track the exact time of this incident. This information may be erroneous if it's left to human intervention.

Another situation that could occur is that the boiler or tank valve needs to be closed, as it is exceeding its capacity. But again, due to the lack of a proper mechanism, the boiler/tank overflows and bursts. Human lives could even be lost due to such plant incidents. SAP MII provides a foolproof solution to avoid such incidents. It constantly checks for the threshold and sets alarms to automatically track such problems in production occurring in real-time. SAP MII can also trigger emails to the supervisors to let them know about such incidents. If the shopfloor machine is connected to SAP MII, then MII can stop the machine whenever it detects a malfunction or an abnormality in the machine.

■ **Note**   The temperature controller controls the temperature without needing human intervention. This intelligent tool gets input from thermal sensors like RTD (resistance temperature detectors) or thermocouples and continuously compares that information with the set-point, which is the safe desired temperature. It provides output to the control element, such as valves that control the temperature.

Lack in Decision-Making Process to Meet Production-Level Targets

Often, there is lack in the decision support information by the production personnel to meet production target goals. These goals are defined and measured by various KPIs (key performance indicators) differing from plant to plant. As there is no direct connection of the shopfloor to ERP, production operators and even sometimes supervisors can take advantage of this disconnection and can stop the machine or manipulate the data manually to meet the production targets, thus ignoring actual readings.

These human discrepancies can be avoided by completely automating the machines involved on the shopfloor using SAP MII and connecting to ERP. Once SAP MII is connected directly to both the shopfloor machines and ERP, it can use the real-time data available from the shopfloor and ERP to display valuable OEE (Overall Equipment Efficiency) reports and custom reports, such as machine reports, downtime analysis reports, yield overview reports, etc. SAP MII is capable of fully automating such situations very efficiently.

■ **Note**   *OEE* stands for Overall Equipment Effectiveness. It is one of the metrics for ISO and considered in the best solution practices to identify the percentage of planned production time, which is truly productive. GMP (Good Manufacturing Practices) suggests having practically no downtime in the plants while manufacturing only good parts. So, if the OEE comes out to 100%, that is considered perfect production. If over time, a very good result of OEE is reached, then it is used as a benchmark for other assets in the same setup or as an industry standard for other production assets. Similarly, it can be also used as a baseline to detect overtime, the progress of eliminating waste from a particular production asset.

Copies of Master Data Leading to Quality and Compliance Issues

If ERP is not connected to the shopfloor directly, the only way to transfer the master data to the shopfloor is by downloading and exporting it from ERP into Excel. In this case, there is sufficient time loss during the transfer of data, as it is human dependent and open to error. There is also a good chance of data manipulation. To fill this gap, MII can connect directly to ERP systems and load the master data automatically when it is pushed from ERP.

Functional Aspects of SAP MII

SAP MII is the one-stop solution for not only integration but also for intelligence. It establishes a direct connection to the shopfloor and business processes and operations. It ensures that the integration between the enterprise systems and plants is near-to real-time data and displays the integrated data to the users.

When you're considering SAP MII as a solution for integration and intelligence, consider the following functional aspects.

Availability of the SAP MII Product

Currently, it is easily available and one of the most trusted solutions from SAP labs and it now comes with manufacturing suites along with some other manufacturing products. Licensing is required for SAP MII, but if the manufacturing suite licensing is already incurred by the plant then it automatically includes SAP MII in it.

Integration Benefits

SAP MII has many default connectors, which makes it very easy for SAP MII to connect to any Level 4, Level 3, Level 2, or Level 1 systems. SAP MII can fill the gap between Level 3 and Level 4 and if any plant has no MES, then MII can be placed in Level 3 too. Further, MII using a SAP PCo or OPC connector can connect to Level 2 and Level 1 as well. See Figure 2-1.

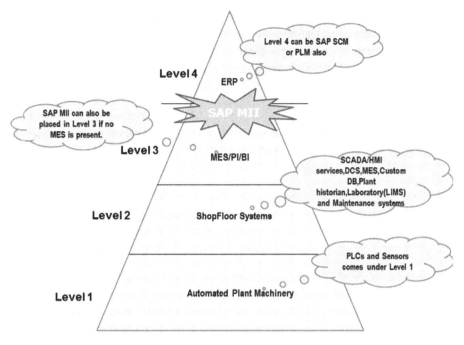

Figure 2-1. Placement of SAP MII in industrial leveling

■ **Note** *Product Lifecycle Management (PLM)* is the concept of managing the products involved in any process or system by integrating the business data in a people-oriented extended enterprise environment.

Manufacturing Execution System (MES) is a computerized system that is used in the manufacturing industries to monitor and capture the transformation of raw materials to finished products. It shows real-time happenings from the shopfloor to the authorized personals involved in decision-making. It captures the input, the output, any critical failure or error of machines, the operator's activity, and other support services.

Supervisory Control and Data Acquisition (SCADA) is software integrated with an application program to control the manufacturing process. In modern manufacturing, the automated systems mainly work with SCADA. It collects data from sensors and PLC devices and provides a sophisticated control to all those devices based on the real-time data acquired.

Historian can pull data from complex systems across multiple variables to paint a complete picture of the manufacturing environment. *Wonderware historians* can store large volumes of plant historical data by processing and storing high-speed data using a traditional RDBMS. It provides a secure, high-performance database to consolidate disparate data sources and provides rapid retrieval techniques to make sense of the increasing amount of industrial data.

A *Distributed Control System (DCS)* refers to the control system of the industrial processes of the production plant where the controllers are distributed across the plant's process control points. A centralized control is also in place in the central control room. DCS mainly follows the distributed hierarchical control philosophy to control processes in plant automation.

A *Programmable Logic Controller (PLC)* is a solid-state industrial computer control system that can continuously monitor the input state of the device and make a logical decision for the automated process or machines. PLC is a good replacement of industrial relay and provides more functionalities than relay. As PLC is modular, it can be placed in any setup to define the logic and can resist any kind of tough manufacturing environment like high heat, dust, extreme cold, or high moisture. Relay, on the other hand, can't correctly operate under these environments. PLC consists of a 16-bit or 32-bit microprocessor, which can be connected to a CPU. Any kind of executable control logic can be designed in the CPU and can be transferred to the PLC by a routine run.

Laboratory Information Management System (LIMS) or Laboratory Information System (LIS) takes into account all the laboratory apparatus and equipment involved in a laboratory operation. This system enables the laboratory to be completely automated with workflows defined by integrating the instruments or apparatus and managing the associated information of the sample readings automatically. This automation enhances performance and reduces the time needed to meet the customer's needs.

SAP MII has multiple standard connectors for smooth integration, as explained here:

- *Aggregate connector*: Can be used when you create an *aggregate query*. It combines multiple datasets into a single one. It's a default connector provided by SAP.

- *ECC connector*: SAP Java Connector (SAP JCo) and SAP Java Resource Adapter (SAP JRA) can be used to connect to SAP ECC.

- *Database connector (IDBC)*: This can be used with any JDBC (Java Database Connectivity)-(Oracle, SQL or any database), or ODBC (Open Database Connectivity) data source that is defined in SAP NetWeaver.

- *PCO connector*: This can be used to support the query capabilities of SAP PCo. It's a default connector provided by SAP.

- *Xml connector*: This connector allows connecting to and querying any XML returnable data source and is included in the system by default.

- *Alarm suite connector*: This connector is basically for alarm mechanism data source and enables you to connect to the Wonderware Alarm advisor software.

- *MDO connector*: This connector is specifically used with MDO queries and can have only one active MDO connector. It's a default connector provided by SAP.

- *Open connector*: The Open connector browses historical data in a relational database. One can create tag queries by browsing tag names and descriptions and using time periods instead of writing SQL queries.

- *Universal data connector (OLEDB)*: The UDC allows remote data access when the data source does not. The UDC communicates with remote universal data servers (UDS) using TCP/IP sockets. The OLEDB connector is a UDC that allows access to OLE DB data sources.

- *Xacute connector*: This connector is used to connect to a transaction through Xacute Query. It's a default connector provided by SAP.

- *KPI connector*: This connector is used with KPI queries. By default, only one active KPI connector is allowed. It's a default connector provided by SAP.

- *OLAP connector*: This connector allows connecting and querying multi-dimensional data sources that support the XML for Analysis (XMLA) specification. It is generally used to integrate BI queries.

- *Virtual connector*: This connector helps to query and connect virtually to other SAP MII instances without directly connecting to the data source server. It's a default connector provided by SAP.

- *IP21 and IP21OLEDB connectors*: The IP21 connectors connect SAP Manufacturing Integration and Intelligence (SAP MII) to AspenTech InfoPlus.21 (IP21) data sources.

- *HANA SDA connector*: This connector allows SAP MII to connect to HANA studio.

■ **Note**   *SAP Java Connector* is known as SAP JCo in short. It can leverage the development of the components and applications in Java, which are SAP compatible. SAP JCo communication is bidirectional with SAP ECC (i.e., it supports inbound and outbound calls). For an inbound call, Java calls ABAP and vice versa for the outbound call.

SAP JRA is the SAP Java Resource Adapter. It is the Java Enterprise edition connector that's used for connection with SAP systems. It allows you to integrate AS ABAP with remote Java application servers like AS JAVA and thus simplifies the communication among different distributable SAP JAVA applications along with AS ABAP (Application Server for ABAP).

Java Database Connectivity, known as *JDBC,* acts as an API for Java and defines the accessibility protocol for a client with database. It is a part of the Java Edition platform and is property of Oracle Corporation. It is based on relational database rules and provides functions and methods to query and update the data in the database.

ODBC stands for Open Database Connectivity and is another API for querying the database, but is an open source standard application. By using ODBC, you can access different databases like Access DB, Excel, DB2, Dbase, and Text. Other than the ODBC software, a Microsoft ODBC connector is needed for each database to connect and access the data using the ODBC software.

PCo is the freely distributable component with SAP MII. It is a .Net based application that can integrate with shopfloor and SPC systems. PCo can also host custom designed web services. SAP MII has a default connector to connect with SAP PCo. SAP Plant connectivity is called SAP PCo.

Manufacturing data object (MDO) is available to define object models and data structures and to persist data.

Aspen InfoPlus.21 is a kind of process historian that's highly flexible and can be involved with single processes to enterprise wide global deployments across multiple locations. This flexibility ultimately reduces the consumption of tags that generally happens and thus provides a better management of the metadata involved.

The *Plant Information Catalog (PIC)* contains the hierarchy of tags and groups created from the working version after approval. The hierarchical structure is created in order to provide business context to the tags and their data by interfacing to the tag data servers in a generic way.

SAP HANA has a built-in database memory, whereby all the data is stored in the RAM. As data is always in-memory, the data processing is faster. This is the recommended best approach to process real-time analytics and applications. It uses row based and column based technologies. It can process massive real-time data in a short time.

Infrastructure Benefits

MII can be installed on top of SAP NetWeaver and it is easily deployable. The solutions developed on SAP MII are more flexible than other middleware tools. MII can be integrated with NWDI, CTS+, and SAP Solution Manager and can be easily tracked for all changes. As SAP MII deployment is not time-consuming due to its simplicity, very little downtime is required to deploy a SAP MII solution.

Intelligence Benefits

SAP MII can provide performance management on the shopfloors through dashboards, scorecards, and rich analytics. SAP MII is also a powerful reporting platform that can provide enterprise reporting, ad hoc query/reporting, and advanced analysis in enterprise data warehousing and BI. It can execute reports from executive to plant to line levels on the shopfloor. SPC/SQC (Six Sigma) analyses are also possible using SAP MII.

Innovation Benefits

SAP MII can provide compatibility with IIOT, including mobile and tablet devices such as iPhone, iPad, etc. These kinds of innovations make SAP MII solutions user friendly and efficient. SAP MII can integrate with Google Maps and can communicate via platforms like SMS and e-mail.

Flexibility Across Plant-Level Machineries

As SAP MII is equipped with Open, UDC, and PCo connectors, it provides more flexibility to connect to systems like SCADA, DCS, PLCs (IFIX), Wonderware systems, etc., as most of the shopfloor system use standard OPC connectors. SAP PCo, which is a freely distributable component of SAP MII, has a built-in OPC connector so that it can connect directly.

■ **Note** SAP Manufacturing Execution is called SAP ME. *SAP ME* is one of the MES products of SAP used for discrete manufacturing. This solution helps manufacturers manage manufacturing on the shopfloor in an automated and granular way at each operations level. It can also connect to the ERP as well as to the shopfloor using SAP MII. SAP ME uses the integration component called SAPMEINT to connect to other systems.

Easy to Use with Other SAP Manufacturing Products

As SAP ECC is an enterprise solution of SAP and similarly SAP OEE and SAP ME are developed and maintained by SAP as a MES solution, connecting SAP MII to these three is very efficient, easily configurable, and reliable from the connection and integration perspectives. Manufacturing products like SAP OEE and SAP ME are also developed on top of the SAP MII platform.

Integration Per Industry Standards

ISA-95 is the international standard for integrating enterprise and control systems. B2MML is the Business to Manufacturing Markup Language. It is actually used to implement the data models of the ISA-95 standards and is a superset of XML schemas written using the World Wide Web Consortium's XML Schema language (XSD). SAP MII can integrate with the ISA-95 standard following B2MML.

Statistical and Other Mathematical Analyses

SAP MII can do mathematical and customer-specific statistical calculations. Standard functions for max, mean, average, standard deviation, and so on, are available by default in the SAP MII package. SAP MII can provide SPC/SQC analytics through logic as well as visualization.

Predictive Analyses Capability

It is possible to develop solutions of SAP MII, which are capable of providing predictive alerting as to when a machine should stop working based on certain parameters. SAP MII can analyze and create a predictive alert from all the historic values to determine when the machine will have downtime.

Technical Advantages of SAP MII

Due to the flexibility across the shopfloor execution, ERP systems and other legacy systems, easy development methodology and standardized coding techniques in SAP MII, it becomes a robust manufacturing solution development platform. The following are the technical advantages that you can leverage from SAP MII.

Easy Coding Standard

Unlike other technologies, where most of the coding needs to be done manually by writing and remembering the functions and keywords to be used to write the code, SAP MII provides very easy and standard coding standards in the form of a drag-and-drop tool. It is an easy-to-use software application platform for manipulating, transforming, and distributing the plant and production information via XMLs. Using SAP MII, you can just drag and drop the required action block and you don't have to worry about remembering the coding functions, expressions, and operators as they are built into the action blocks by default. The only thing the developer needs to think about is the logic behind handling the business cases using the built-in features of SAP MII.

Flexibility with the XML Language

SAP MII lets the developers store and use XML (Extensible Markup Language) robustly and efficiently in a structured way. As MII is a web based application, XML is used to transport and provide the data across the Internet and applications. Developers can use the XML data files to generate the dynamic content by applying different style sheets. XML provides easy parsing through data contents. In fact, it can represent any kind of data structure, including databases and other business information. XML is very easy to handle and transform as it is always a structured dataset. XSLT is one of the XML technologies that converts XML and is further compatible with SAP MII. Thus, using XML gives you flexibility in moving and translating data based on the customer's needs.

High-End Advanced Business Logic Services

SAP MII enables developers to encode the real-world business rules that can determine how data can be created, displayed, stored, manipulated, and changed as per the need of the business. In simple terms, SAP MII can handle any kind of customer-specific logic with its standard logic services. Business logic define the flow of logic from one business object to another and so on in the business landscape to interact with one another. The routes and methods by which the business object communicates should be defined in the Business Logic Services, commonly termed as BLS.

BLS basically defines the process or procedure by which data should be transformed or calculated, as well as the method by which it will be routed to other system. SAP MII provides many action blocks that can be used in the BLS to define the business process actions ranging from data input and output, web input and output, transformations, data calculations, e-mail communications, and process flow control.

Compliant with International Standards for Integration

The manufacturing industry follows certain standards for manufacturing. As per the current industrial automation, ISA-95 is one of the most acceptable standards used in manufacturing industries. ISA-95 generally follows the B2MML structure in order to interact with other systems. SAP MII can integrate with the ISA-95 standard and can handle B2MML restructuring with minimal (simple) coding and accept B2MML and generate B2MML as per ISA-95 standard.

UI5 Integrated SSCE

Self Service Composition Environment (SSCE) is extended to integrate UI elements and allow end users to create their own frontend views in the dashboard. The dashboard can be created by adding suitable UI controls from the selection panel, called UI elements. To integrate the UI elements with the backend data, query templates of the same MII instance can be selected from the MII content pane. Similarly, display templates can be selected and added by configuring visualization parameters. For UI controls, different events can be selected, including select, press, etc., just by the drop-down selection in the Properties tab. Suitable layouts can also be selected as per the dashboard design requirement.

SSCE creates the code in the backend, which can be seen and modified from the Source Code tab. Modification can be done in a specific area. The code that gets generated does not follow the MVC pattern but rather generates an HTML file at the backend. This is an additional functionality that can help to create a dashboard within minutes by just dragging and dropping with minimum effort.

An Easy-to-Configure and Flexible Solution

SAP MII comes with a very friendly frontend for developers. SAP MII is flexible enough to customize any of the customer-specific solution and can also be extended, if required. SAP MII has very strong illuminator services; i.e., it is possible to create a full plug-and-play kind of solution using it. SAP MII provides features like scheduler, connector, and message services to configure jobs as BLS or queries, and to connect and configure easily with other systems like SCADA, ERP, etc.

Flexibility to Communicate with Legacy Systems

SAP MII can easily connect via UDS or PCo connectors to legacy systems like SCADA/HMI, DCS, MES, plant historians, custom database, laboratory and maintenance systems, and SPC/SQC systems. It can fetch data accurately near-to real-time.

■ **Note** Statistical Process Control is known as *SPC* and Statistical Quality Control is known as *SQC*. Both of these controls use statistical tools. While SQC is more focused on the analysis of the variations occurring in the processes involved in manufacturing industries, SPC focuses on minimizing waste during production by predicting the problems in production processes and controlling them. Thus, SPC is kind of a SQC where it checks the flaws leading to low-quality production, whereas SQC is completely dedicated to checking the quality of the product by checking each sample. The samples undergo inspection and acceptability testing to finally introduce the product into the market.

Flexibility to Communicate with Plant-Level Devices

Even if the legacy systems are not present in the plant landscape, if machines like PLCs are compatible with the UDC/PCo connector then via tag recognition, data can be fetched to the SAP MII platform.

Compatibility of Connection to Files in Shared Network

PCo can easily be configured to connect to any files linked with SharePoint, which is stored in the shared drive via the Microsoft OLEDB connector to get data in the SAP MII platform. Using the OLEDB connector, SAP MII can fetch the data from any of the file systems.

■ **Note** *OLE DB* (Object Linking and Embedding, Database, sometimes written as OLEDB or OLE-DB), an API designed by Microsoft, allows you to access data from a variety of sources in a uniform manner.

Service Exposure to NetWeaver Stack

MII services are by default exposed to all elements of the enterprise as services via NetWeaver. All these services can be utilized by other NetWeaver components like PI, Portal, etc., for data exchange, advance reporting, and visualization.

High-End Visualization Capability

SAP MII supports integration with crystal reports so that these reports can be accessed by multiple reporting tools. MII can integrate with an enterprise portal for better visualization and integrate with the ERP users directly to access those reports. SAP MII has a lightweight portal to host the specialized visualization service developed by SAP MI. SAP recently introduced SSCE to create and host special visualization using SAP UI5.

Capability to Support Web Service

Web services can connect businesses to one another by using XML, SOAP, WSDL, and UDDI. Web services allow applications to communicate with one another without worrying about hardware, OSs, and programming languages. Web services can also be customized to meet user requirements. SAP MII can connect to other web services directly to access the data from other systems in a very secure way, because MII supports multiple encryption methodologies. Similarly, if any third-party systems do not have standard web services to invoke their data, MII can expose its BLS transactions as web services so that the third-party systems can use that to pass the data to MII in a more secure manner. MII also supports most of the REST and SOAP services to receive and pass data.

■ **Note** *Simple Object Access Protocol (SOAP)* is a universal messaging protocol that's operating system independent. It can run in all OSs, such as Windows, Linux, etc. SOAP communicates through HTTP and its base language is XML.

Web Services Description Language's (WSDL) interface is based on an XML defined language. The XML is used to define the methods with various functionalities that the web service is supposed to provide. Business users can easily call these services.

Universal Description, Discovery, and Integration (UDDI) is a registry based on XML. It helps developers publish the business services on the Internet. WSDL is the language behind this.

Provision of Flexibility for Language Support

SAP MII removes the language barrier for an application to be used by end users with simple configuration and minimal coding. It provides language support flexibility through web page localization and project localization features. For any business requirement that demands various cross-locational designs with different respective languages, it is possible to maintain the web page frontend application with the user's defined language through HTML or SAP UI5. This provides an end application that's globally standardized but is specific to local regions while adapting their regional language.

Support for Analytics with Graphical Representation

SAP MII features the graphics generation using iSPCC chart applets that can be used to create static image references. SAP MII is the only available middleware that can support SPC/SQC charts. SPC charts can enable label alarming points and custom levels and comments for different alarms. MII can show animated objects or vector images for the reporting designed in MII.

Easy Debugging Techniques

In terms of debugging, SAP MII provides breakpoints, watchpoints, color-coding of action success/failure/not executed items, ability to modify values at breakpoint, and the flexibility to copy and paste to analyze the output from various actions in another editor.

■ **Note**   A *breakpoint* is forcefully putting a stop or pause in the program during code debugging. It helps the developers check if the coding is done correctly while inspecting each step of the code used in the program.

A *watchpoint* is a kind of breakpoint that can be placed on a particular expression to be debugged. Whenever the value of a variable in that expression changes, it stops the execution flow of the program at the applied watchpoint. Moreover, the value change can be more than one variable. It can use operators such as a * b where a and b are variables with certain values and * is the operator between the two variables. This is sometimes also referred as a *data breakpoint.*

Alert and KPI Framework

SAP MII comes with standard alert and KPI mechanisms. This feature helps developers as well as customers in many ways. It reduces the effort needed to create an alert mechanism for every solution hosted on SAP MII server and is easily configurable. It is now possible to create the alert threshold and handle certain alerts. Apart from that, it is also possible to set acknowledgements for any alert recognized. It is possible to query these alerts too. In the latest version, it is possible to expose the KPI and Alert queries in HANA using OData services. It can also use the analytics engine of HANA to provide rich analytics and predictive analytics.

Internal Data Storage Capability

SAP MII has NetWeaver stack DB available by default, which is called MDO (Manufacturing Data Object). MDO is an internal data storage of SAP MII where customers can store the data for small volume purposes. As SAP is now integrating HANA with MII, in the future it may be possible to store large volumes of data in MDOs.

■ **Note**   *SAP NetWeaver* is a technology platform from SAP that can host most of the SAP business suite products. It's possible to run these products in its web application server called NetWeaver WEBAS (Web Application server).

SAP MII from the Business Perspective

Its scalability, flexibility, low maintenance cost, and multilayered security make SAP MII the most preferred and suitable platform for automation in manufacturing. The following sections explain why SAP MII is best for such business requirements.

Lower Cost for Server Setup and Installation

SAP MII needs to be hosted on NetWeaver and the latest version can be hosted on SAP HANA. If your customer already has NetWeaver, only the SAP MII installation is required. SAP MII does not need to install databases separately for its own standard component because it uses the application database of NetWeaver or HANA. Patch upgrades are possible for free and it's easily installable and available for SAP MII. Overall installation, setup, and maintenance costs are lower than with any other middleware tool.

Low Risk to Business

As SAP MII is compatible and can easily integrate with other SAP ERP modules, standardization with SAP solutions has brought reliability and peace of mind to all the organizations involved in the integration process. The risks and cost of obsolete software and custom integration are no longer concerns to these organizations.

Provision of Vast Scalability Throughout Applications

SAP MII provides the flexibility to expand, integrate, combine, bundle, and layer different functionalities of many applications, as required. The visualization and the user interface development feature of SAP MII can provide a wide range of flexible scalable interfaces to the end user. With the integration feature, SAP MII can connect to many kinds of shopfloor systems. SAP MII is flexible enough to be implemented on large-scale manufacturing systems, rapid manufacturing systems, and small-scale manufacturing systems.

Improved Efficiency

Regardless of the vendors of different systems or software available on the shopfloor layer and ERP layer, it can connect SAP MII to any of them. Thus, implementing it in any scenario makes the process very efficient and reliable. The vendors can leverage the bidirectional integration to all the shopfloor systems supported by SAP MII and can support homegrown solutions on the shopfloor.

Low Total Cost of Ownership

SAP MII can be globally, regionally, and locally implemented. Due to this flexibility in SAP MII, based on customer requirements and budgets, SAP MII can be implemented in the landscape and will still work in the same efficient way.

Customization

As SAP MII is a platform, it is possible to create customer-specific solutions and generate customer-specific reports and frontend applications as per customer requirements.

Smaller Project Teams

Due to its easy code standards, strong logical enhancement, and the flexibility and scalability of the SAP MII application, it can be handled with smaller development teams and project teams, as opposed to any other middleware or reporting tool.

Unified User Maintenance in NetWeaver

No separate user maintenance needed in SAP MII, as it is built on NetWeaver. A single user role can access the SAP MII development platform.

Multilayer Security as Per Customer Requirement

SAP MII can provide multilayer security to any solution. The first layer of security is through project-specific roles, which can be controlled from the NetWeaver User Admin. Apart from that, it is also possible to set strong encryption logic to keep the entire configuration and the data encrypted. SAP MII has custom attributes that can restrict the user interface to a certain user or group. For ECC integration, it is possible to set customer specific encryption to the Java Resource Connector. Another way of securing the solution in SAP MII is to use encoding and decoding while sending the information from MII.

Better Utilization of Human Resources

As SAP MII provides stepwise processing and control at any step or process making direct connection to ERP or shopfloor systems, need for human resources is reduced and the same person can be utilized in more processes. Effort can be channeled to provide greater utilization of manpower.

Guaranteed Message Delivery

One of the more critical risks of the manufacturing industry is production data loss. To prevent this, manufacturing industries are always looking for solutions that can provide guaranteed delivery of data even if the connection is down/interrupted. It is possible to develop a high-scalable solution with SAP MII, which can provide guaranteed delivery.

Provision of Local Survivability

In real manufacturing industries, there may be incidents when the shopfloor is running fine but connectivity is lost with ERP. In such a case, the shopfloor needs to be shut down, which will cause a financial loss to the company. In this case, if SAP MII is working as middleware, SAP MII can buffer the data either in an internal queue or an internal database and keep the shopfloor automation up and running even though the ERP connectivity is down. When the connectivity is re-established, MII can push the data to ERP following the FIFO method.

■ **Note** *FIFO* stands for first in first out, which means products that come in first go out first.

Single User Interface for Manufacturing Employees

SAP MII promotes a single user login facility. When users log on to the SAP MII system, they don't need to separately log on to ECC or the shopfloor. SAP MII maintains a generic user in the backend so that SAP MII can connect to SAP ECC to schedule or confirm orders in ECC.

BI/BW versus MII versus PI

As mentioned, the major requirement of manufacturing is to have a good middleware product that can integrate with any system varying from the shopfloor to ERP. Another requirement is to have a very good reporting solution where the vast reporting needs of the manufacturing system are fulfilled easily.

SAP has a middleware product called SAP PI that integrates ERP with the shopfloor and a reporting product called SAP BI to provide configurable vast reporting. SAP MII can handle both requirements. Sometimes it is not clear which product is best to use. The following section explains when and why to use each particular product.

What Is SAP BI/BW?

BI (Business Intelligence) is an application that provides intelligence based on the series of raw data. BI can provide flexible configurable reporting to the business user and helps you make better business decisions. BI can handle huge volumes of historical data and provide analytics with its high-capacity data processing engine. BI has another component called *Business Warehouse* (BW), which persists all the historical data and helps BI do the analytics based on that.

When Should You Use BI/BW?

- BI is used for cross-functional reporting whereas MII is related to manufacturing domains.

- SAP BI has native connectors to SAP systems, but when it comes to the shopfloor layer, it struggles to extract data due to the special data models. SAP MII overcomes all these problems through its extraction technology specifically designed for the major shopfloor systems, historians, and it follows ISA 95.

- Unlike SAP MII, SAP BI/BW is not capable of easily replicating the SPC/SQC charts, which makes it unsuitable in a manufacturing-specific capability.

- SAP BI/BW cannot provide plant-level value-added metric data at runtime like machine availability, downtime, yields, cycle times, and energy analyses. It cannot integrate directly with production processes like production posting, and goods movement from the shopfloor, which SAP MII can easily provide. Thus, SAP MII also reduces the redundancy in human effort that may happen while entering values in SAP.

- BI is modeled and framed for huge volumes of data whereas MII cannot handle huge volumes of data in a single shot. For MII to handle huge volumes of data, it needs to be scheduled in batches.

- BI can handle Excel files (.xls,.xlsx, and .xlsm) to extract data, whereas MII can't. MII needs custom Java code to extract data from Excel files. If the filename is constant, SAP MII can handle Excel files via the PCo connector.

- BI can generate reports with huge volumes of data very quickly compared to the time SAP MII needs to generate reports with same volume of data. In the future, if HANA integration matures with SAP MII, this execution time constraint will become moot.

- SAP BI is standard reporting tool, so reports and templates are easily customized per customer standards, with no additional coding needed. As SAP MII is a platform, this kind of customizable template needs to be developed from scratch to provide similar functionality to the customer.

What Is SAP PI?

SAP PI enables you to integrate backend systems and applications via the A2A and B2B connector framework. It supports stateful and long-running business logic with a business process engine.

It can only provide integration with ERP to any other multiple legacy system. It follows point-to-point or point-to-many integration. It has no flexibility to integrate with user interfaces.

When Do You Use SAP PI?

- When an enterprise follows a service-oriented architecture and the integration of processes is found to be necessary.

- When a repository is required to store the services, datatypes, or the metadata involved for enterprise services and business processes in the customer landscape.

- When you need to support additional web service standards through UDDI, web service interoperability profiles, addressing, security, reliable messaging, and coordination.

- Whenever there is possibility to have high data volume and critical scenarios of integration to be established between business applications.

What Is SAP MII?

As explained in Chapter 1, SAP MII is a flexible, robust manufacturing platform for developing integration solutions from Level 4 (ERP) to Level 0 (Shopfloor machines). It includes high-end visualization and a browser-independent user interface.

When Do You Use MII?

- You need to analyze and organize datasets from different sources of data.

- You need global operational access across the manufacturing sites.

- You need intelligent applications with drill-down options to view very minute levels of analysis of the datasets across different data points.

- You need to connect the shopfloor or plant machineries to ERP to have real-time data availability using standard SAP connectors.

- Plant personnel need to be able to perform reporting duties (standard, mobile, and ad hoc) along with basic execution duties.

- Plant operations, production, and management users need reports that can be standardized, customized, or mobile-compatible for analyses and monitoring of the different KPIs involved in the manufacturing industry.

BI or PI or MII: Which One to Use

When a customer has the option to use BI, PI, or MII, it can be a difficult decision. This section provides some perspective on which one is better in the manufacturing sector. This section compares BI, PI, and SAP MII.

- To transfer messages and information from the shopfloor to ERP, SAP PI needs to be placed in the local plant. But SAP MII can be placed in the local, regional, or even in global headquarters. SAP MII is more flexible than SAP PI.

- SAP PI is famous for its data routing design and for its guaranteed delivery. You can also develop a similar kind of design in SAP MII easily.

- As SAP PI has a limitation on the shopfloor connectors, there can be inconsistency in message processing. SAP MII has a standard OPC compliance shopfloor connector and SAP PCo for plant connectivity, which means message processing in SAP MII is faster and more consistent.

- Manufacturing shopfloors can vary from site to site and variation is also possible based on the line used at each plant. To process similar data with PI, customization is required on the shopfloor to make the data as per the PI structure. In SAP MII, XML is the backbone of the solution, which means variation in data structure doesn't impact SAP MII very much.

- SAP MII can easily handle all the functionality SAP PI has. SAP MII has a few more features of visualization and data handling over SAP PI. It's best to use BI if the customer data volume is very high and the customer needs a solution where a huge volume of data needs to be transferred from one system to another system. If the customer requires integration and intelligence with a normal volume of data, SAP MII is recommended, as it can provide integration and intelligence with high-end visualization and many other manufacturing benefits.

Summary

This chapter discussed the key challenges in the manufacturing industry and why you should use SAP MII from functional, technical, and business perspectives. You learned when MII is preferred over SAP BI/BW and vice versa. The chapter also explained what PI is, including its advantages and disadvantages and discussed when to choose MII over PI.

In the next chapter, you will learn about some basic building features of SAP MII, including BLS, query templates, visualization, and commonly used action blocks.

CHAPTER 3

■ ■ ■

Basics of SAP MII

Before diving deep into the SAP MII technically and correlating it with the functional requirements, the basic conceptual integral configurations and intelligent development IDE and its functions should be clear to the professionals. This chapter explains the basics of SAP MII, the steps related to its various configurations, and its development components and other basic features.

To work with the technical part of the SAP MII, the important features to know include these:

- Data Services, which are responsible for configuring all the connections to other systems.

- Message Services, which handle message flow in and out through SAP MII.

- The development components, which include logic services, query templates, MDO, visualizations, and other web development components.

Data Services

Data Services provide manufacturing shopfloor connectivity by providing connectors for vendor-specific protocols for plant systems and standard protocols to connect to the relational database. Data connectors come with SAP MII installation that's able to connect to any manufacturing shopfloor system. It also provides different types of configurable data queries (can be configured through SAP MII Workbench) to retrieve or write data to data sources. These data queries can be accessed by HTTP calls or by Java applets from web-based UIs.

Available menu options for Data Services are as follows:

- Data Servers

- Connection Status

- Connections

- Simulator Services

© Suman Mukherjee and Saptaparna Mukherjee (Das) 2017
S. Mukherjee and S. Mukherjee (Das), *SAP MII*, DOI 10.1007/978-1-4842-2814-2_3

- Shared Memory

- Time Periods

- Time Period Schedules

- Data Buffer

Some of these features are described in the following sections.

Data Servers

Data servers are used to configure query templates to query data from different sources. You can browse this data can be in the SAP MII Workbench. See Figure 3-1.

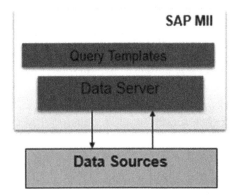

Figure 3-1. *Data server placement in SAP MII*

Server parameters that are common to configure include:

- *Name*: Name of the server provided. It has to be unique.

- *Connector*: To configure the data servers, certain connectors are available: Aggregate, AlarmSuite, DataSource, IDBC, IP21, and IP21OLEDB, InSQL, OLAP, OLEDB Open, Simulator, Universal Data Connector (UDC), Virtual Servers, VirtualAlarm, VirtualIDBC, VirtualOLAP, VirtualTAG, VirtualXML, VirtualXacute, XML, and Xacute.

- *Connector Type*: Type of connection determined by the data source class. The possible connector types are AGG (Aggregate), ALARM, MDO, OLP (OLAP), PCo, SQL, TAG, XCT, XML, and KPIConnector.

- *Enabled*: Indicator used to activate the server. You can check or uncheck it to enable or disable the activation of the server, respectively. If a data server is enabled and you make changes to its parameters, the server is reloaded, and the updated settings are effective immediately.

- *Allow Dynamic Query*: Indicator used to support dynamic queries for users with the Dynamic Query role. When deselected, the data server does not support dynamic queries.

Creating a Connector

Follow these general configuration steps to create a connector:

1. From the left menu, select Data Services ➤ Data Servers, as shown in Figure 3-2.

Figure 3-2. *SAP MII Data Server configuration*

2. Select Create in the next window, as shown in Figure 3-3.

Figure 3-3. *The Create button in the Data Servers configuration*

3. Give it a proper server name (mandatory) to recognize later on and a description (optional). Select the appropriate connector type from the drop-down, as shown in Figure 3-4.

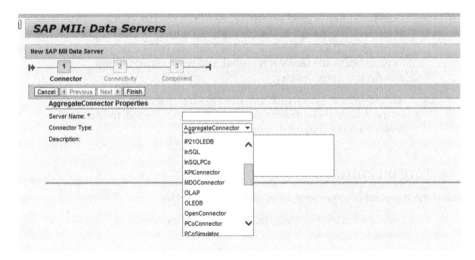

Figure 3-4. *Data Server configuration*

4. Follow the steps for the type of data server you want to create as per your requirements.

5. You can also delete, copy, and edit the selected connector by using the buttons shown in Figure 3-5.

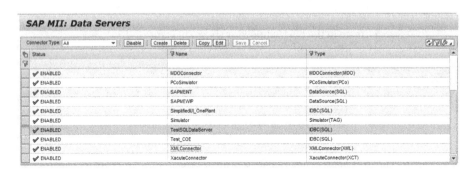

Figure 3-5. *Other buttons in SAP MII Data Servers configuration*

6. Once the data server is selected from the list, details of the connector will be shown and the Usage tab denotes the object names of SAP MII Workbench where the connector is used. See Figure 3-6.

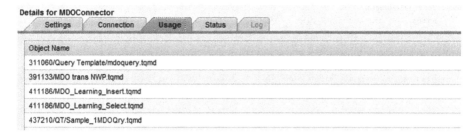

Figure 3-6. *Usage check in the data server*

7. The Status tab shows the status of the connector as Running, Stopped, or Error, as shown in Figure 3-7.

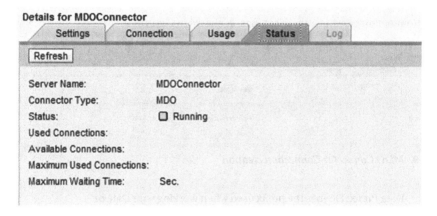

Figure 3-7. *Status check in Data Server*

MDO Connector

A connector used to run queries against manufacturing data objects (MDO).

From Step 2 of the general configuration steps, select the connector as MDOConnector. Once that is created, it will be shown in the Settings tab, as shown in Figure 3-8.

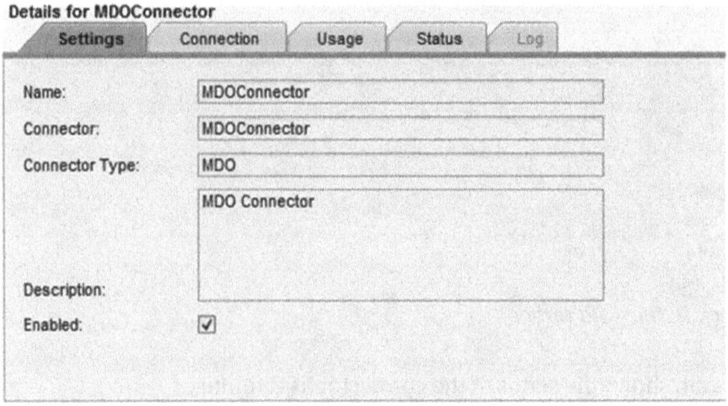

Details for MDOConnector

Settings	Connection	Usage	Status	Log

Name:	MDOConnector
Connector:	MDOConnector
Connector Type:	MDO
Description:	MDO Connector
Enabled:	☑

Figure 3-8. *Configuring the MDO connector*

The Connection tab shows these settings, as shown in Figure 3-9:

Figure 3-9. *MDO Connector Connection creation*

- Data Prefix: Defines the prefix used when working with Date or Time database columns.

- Date Suffix: Defines the suffix used when working with Date or Time database columns.

- Retention Days: Used for data buffering. Number of days the execution attempt remains in the data buffer before being removed.

- Max. Retry Count: Used for data buffering. Number of times the system retries the execution attempt before stopping.

- Retry Interval: Used for data buffering. Number of milliseconds the system waits before retrying the execution attempt.

IDBC (SQL/Oracle) Connector

IDBC Connector provides direct connection to any database to create SQL queries on its table data. The examples of databases are Microsoft SQL server, Oracle database, MaxDB, DB2, and so on.

Properties, UserName, Password, and ServerURL for authentication need to be changed at least while creating a new IDBC Data Server configuration.

The JDBC drivers included with SAP MII are the following:

- *Oracle*: You must use Oracle 7.3.4 or newer (oracle.jdbc.driver. OracleDriver).

- *SQL Server*: You must use SQL Server 6.X, 7.X or 2000 (com.inet. tds.TdsDriver).

- ODBC

From Step 2 of general configuration, select the connector as MDOConnector. After it's created, it appears in Settings tab as shown in Figure 3-10.

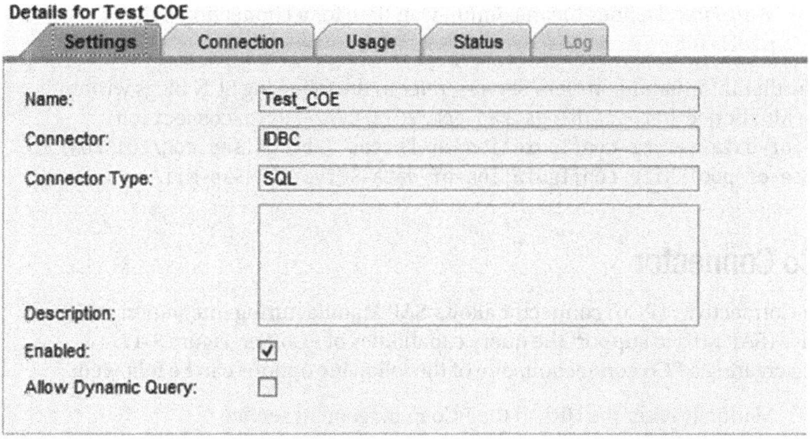

Details for Test_COE

| Settings | Connection | Usage | Status | Log |

Name:	Test_COE
Connector:	IDBC
Connector Type:	SQL
Description:	
Enabled:	☑
Allow Dynamic Query:	☐

Figure 3-10. *The IDBC connector setting*

From the Connection tab, it appears as shown in Figure 3-11.

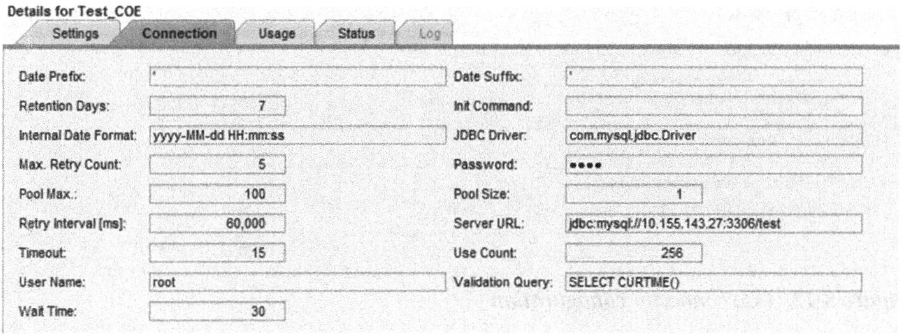

Details for Test_COE

| Settings | Connection | Usage | Status | Log |

Date Prefix:	'	Date Suffix:	'
Retention Days:	7	Init Command:	
Internal Date Format:	yyyy-MM-dd HH:mm:ss	JDBC Driver:	com.mysql.jdbc.Driver
Max. Retry Count:	5	Password:	••••
Pool Max.:	100	Pool Size:	1
Retry Interval [ms]:	60,000	Server URL:	jdbc:mysql://10.155.143.27:3306/test
Timeout:	15	Use Count:	256
User Name:	root	Validation Query:	SELECT CURTIME()
Wait Time:	30		

Figure 3-11. *IDBC Connection configuration*

Here are some additional important connection configuration options available for IDBC connectors:

- *Pool Size*: The connection pool is the total number of threads any DB connection creates so that it can allow that many numbers of parallel DB hits. Pool size indicates the number of connections MII can open at a time in parallel. The default value for the pool size is 1.

- *Pool Max*: Users can set the maximum pool size based on which the DB server allows users to create the pool connection. User can use the same value defined for the DB connection pool size. By defining this in MII, it can also open a maximum of this number of connections at a time. The default value is 100.

- *Wait Time*: Defines the maximum wait time for a connection if the pool is full.

For further information on Data Servers, refer to the following SCN blogs written by Suman Mukherjee: `https://blogs.sap.com/2014/02/24/data-connection-details-for-data-server-configuration/` and `https://blogs.sap.com/2013/03/13/importance-of-pool-size-configuration-of-data-server-in-sap-mii/`.

The PCo Connector

The Plant Connectivity (PCo) connector allows SAP Manufacturing Integration and Intelligence (SAP MII) to support the query capabilities of PCo. See Figure 3-12.

When creating a PCo connection, one of the following options can be followed:

- Manually enter the URL to the PCo management service

- Retrieve the registered PCo instances from the System Landscape Directory (SLD)

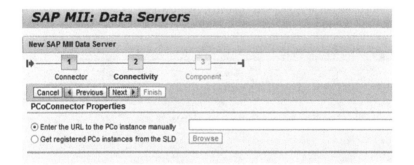

Figure 3-12. *PCo connector configuration*

To configure the PCo connector properties as shown in Figure 3-12, two options are available:

- Option 1: Complete the initial setup of the functional unit SLD using CTC templates. This is a standard procedure of the SAP NetWeaver SLD client configuration. Register the PCo management service in the SLD. After this, follow the instructions below.

- Option 2: If the PCo management Web service interface requires authentication, users are prompted to enter a username and password. After this, follow the instructions below.

To create a PCo data server, you need to go to MII Menu ➤ Data Services ➤ Data Servers. You can choose your connector type as PCoConnector and click on the Create button. You need to provide a unique name for the server.

On the next page, system will ask for the URL to the PCo instance. You need to provide the URL, such as http://<Host>:<Port>/PCoManagement. (Host is the system name where the PCo is installed and Port is the default port 50050 configured in the PCo Management Console).

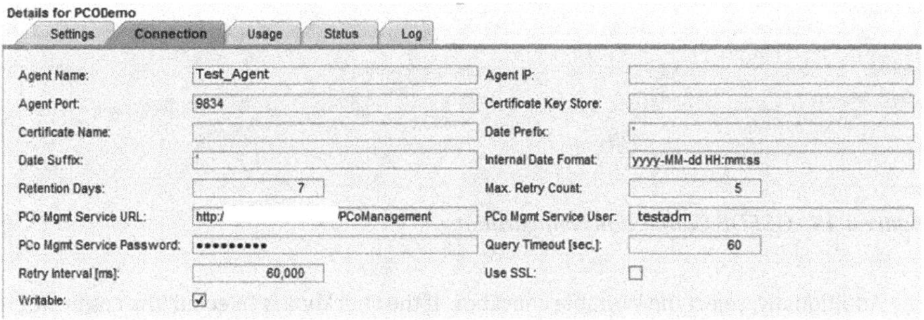

Figure 3-13. *PCo connection configuration*

At the end, you need to provide a user and password.

UDC (OLEDB) Connector

The universal data connector (UDC) is a framework that allows access to SAP Manufacturing Integration and Intelligence (SAP MII) services through proprietary server applications that you develop. The OLEDB Connector is a UDC that allows access to OLE DB data sources. The OLEDB Connector provides OLEDB access to Microsoft-compliant data sources using the PCo server. Tag queries can be created using OLEDB Data Server by selecting the connector as OLEDBConnector. After it is created, it is available in the Settings tab, as shown in Figure 3-14.

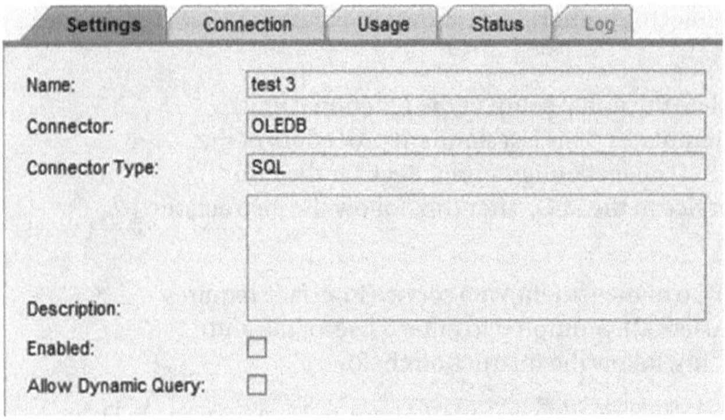

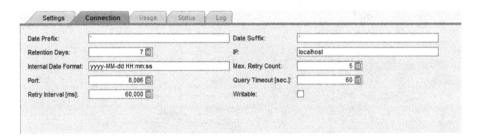

Figure 3-14. *The OLEDB Connector Settings tab*

From the Connection tab, you'll see the settings shown in Figure 3-15.

Figure 3-15. *OLEDB Connection configuration*

Additionally, select the Writable checkbox. If the checkbox is selected, the connector will support writing to the OLEDB agent. If the writable checkbox is not selected, you will not be able to write to the agent, which means the CurrentWrite and HistoryWrite queries will fail.

The XML Connector

The XML Connector can be used to connect to XML-compliant data sources to retrieve the data in SAP MII XML format. A default XML Data Server is available in SAP MII named XMLConnector, although additional instances of XML Data Server can be also be configured. See Figure 3-16.

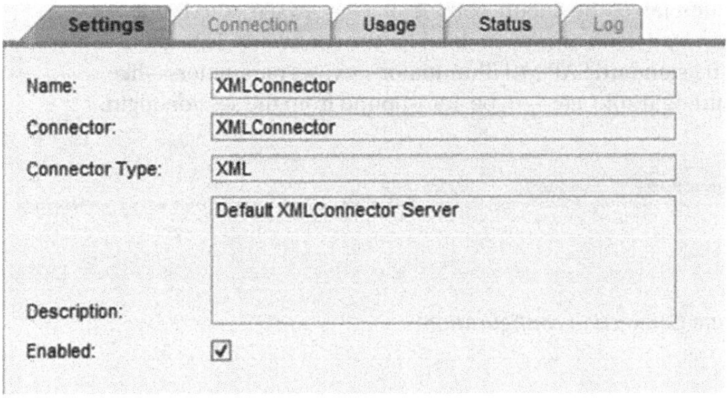

Figure 3-16. *The XML Connector setting*

In the XML Data Server configuration, only the Description property can be edited. Using the XML Data Server, XML queries can be created in SAP MII to retrieve a XML dataset from an URL or a file path in the SAP MII server.

The Xacute Connector

This is an internal system connector used to execute business logic transactions as data queries created using the SAP xMII Workbench, which are called *Xacute queries*. There is a default Xacute Data Server configuration available along with standard installation of SAP MII, named XacuteConnector. Xacute queries can be created using the XacuteConnector Data Server. See Figure 3-17.

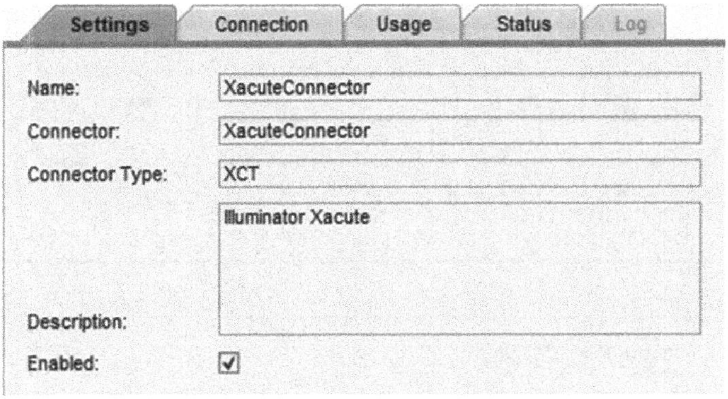

Figure 3-17. *The Xacute Connector Settings screen*

From the Connection tab of the Xacute connector, you can see Auto.Bind (see Figure 3-18). This is by default always enabled for the connector. This feature enables the values of the standard SAP MII illuminator services parameters—like IllumLoginName, IllumLoginRole, etc.—to be auto-bound from the session login.

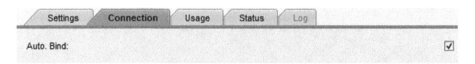

Settings	Connection	Usage	Status	Log

Auto. Bind:	☑

Figure 3-18. *The Xacute Connection configuration*

Connections

Connections are used to create and configure connectivity to other systems. The username and password aliases are defined in the Credential Stores screen and those aliases need to be further assigned during connection configuration. Other than this, the connection specific details like server, port, host, etc. need to be configured. Connection and credential aliases can be further used in the SAP MII action blocks, such as JCo, JRA, Send Mail, etc., instead of providing each configuration details again.

One major benefit of maintaining these aliases is if the connection details are changed, those changes can be directly incorporated into the configurations rather than touching the SAP MII codebase. In production, changing the code again and again is risky, more costly and time consuming, as it involves good amount of testing, documenting, and going through the approval process. See Figure 3-19.

SAP MII: Connections

| Connection Type: Any ▾ | Create | Delete | | Edit | Save | Cancel | Start | Stop |

Connection Name	Connection Type
	JCO
Global_PI	JCO
MailServer	MAIL

Details for

Settings	Usage

Name:	
Description:	S75 010 connection
Server:	ps75d00
Client:	010
System:	01
Pool Size:	10
SSO:	☐
Language:	EN
Use Logon Group:	☐
R/3 Name:	
Logon Group:	

Figure 3-19. *The SAP MII Connections configuration*

The following connection types are possible:

- BC(SAP Business Connector)

- WAS (SAP NetWeaver Application Server)

- JCO (SAP Java Connector)

- FTP (File Transfer Protocol)

- MAIL (E-mail)

- JMS (Java Message Service)

- EJB (Enterprise JavaBeans)

Connection Status

The Connection Status screen displays the status of your enabled database servers. The screen only shows information for IDBC servers that have a connection pool. Most tag-based servers, such as Universal Data Servers (UDS), do not respond to a status check. See Figure 3-20.

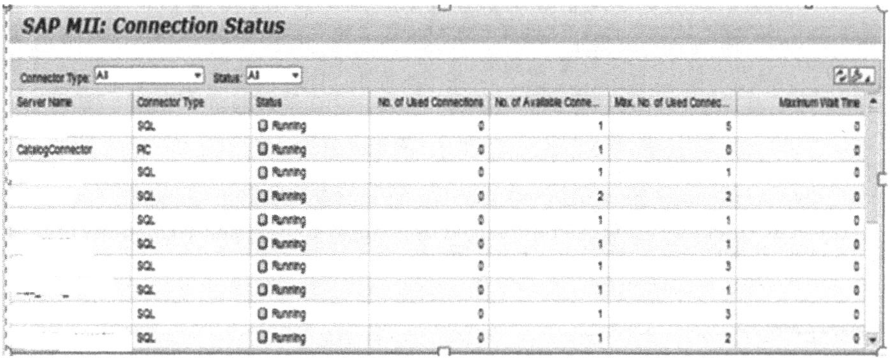

Figure 3-20. The SAP MII Connection Status screen

The status gets updated accordingly as and when a server has zero available connections or has a configuration, network, or communications problem that prevents SAP MII from connecting to the server.

Shared Memory

Shared memory is one of the stronger concepts of variable handling in SAP MII. It's used to store values with some properties that can be retained later. Values can be changed and deleted later. Shared properties are considered one of the temporary data storage properties. Shared properties store the value for one project across all transactions. They work like global data placeholders for particular projects.

Shared properties consist of two parts: default memory and active memory. All the values are stored in the default memory when the variable is created. The same value is copied to the active memory simultaneously. The active memory is always given precedence over the default memory, as the default memory is only used so the variable has some default value. All the business logic accepts the data only from the active memory and it is available to the technical as well as admin user to change if it is required after the copied default value. You must change the default value of a shared property manually in the SAP MII Workbench. Shared properties can be defined in the SharedProperties.mem file of the Meta-inf tab on the SAP MII Workbench.

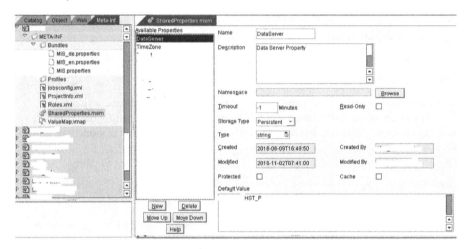

Figure 3-21. *The Default Shared Memory configuration*

The active memory value can be changed by going to Tools ➤ Shared Memory from the SAP MII Workbench, as shown in Figure 3-22.

Shared Memory

Active Properties

CH

Name	Namespace	Description	Type	Storage Type	Last Modified
PI_BOMRead_Na...			string	Persistent	2016-04-28T12:1...
PI_Port		Global PI Port	integer	Persistent	2016-04-28T12:1...
PI_RFCReadText...		Read header text ...	string	Persistent	2016-06-22T09:0...
PI_RFCRead_Na...		PI RFC_READ_T...	string	Persistent	2016-04-28T12:1...
PI_Server		Global PI server n...	string	Persistent	2016-04-28T12:1...
PI_Service_Name		Global PI service ...	string	Persistent	2016-04-28T12:1...
PO_MType_Map		Packaging Materi...	map	Persistent	2016-04-28T12:1...
PO_OType_Map		Packaging order t...	map	Persistent	2016-04-28T12:1...

Refresh Property List

Selected Property Value

Active Memory

PH_CH_XMII_D

Figure 3-22. *The Shared Memory active memory configuration*

The active memory value can also be changed by going to Data Services ➤ Shared Memory of the SAP MII Menu.jsp page.

The Message Services Feature

The Message Service feature integrates enterprise systems with SAP MII. It can be used in SAP MII for receiving enterprise data in the form of asynchronous RFC, ALE/IDoc, or XML messages using HTTP POST. Enterprise systems can also send data. Message listeners can be configured in SAP MII to receive this data. Processing rules then process the data using particular business logic or messages. Messages received by MII using Message Services are stored in the SAP MI database or simply assigned to a category. These messages can be sent to external systems by MII using data services or by compiling them from external systems using web service calls in BLS. Data buffering is also done via Message Listener.

The Message Services on the SAP MII menu page have the features shown in Figure 3-23. These features are discussed in more detail in the following sections.

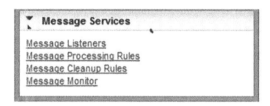

Figure 3-23. *The Message Services menu in SAP MII*

Message Listeners

Message listeners are used to receive web services, RFC (synchronous and asynchronous), or IDOC messages from enterprise systems asynchronously.

To configure an RFC/IDOC (SAPJCo) message listener, click on the Update button in the Message Listeners screen. The selected listener will be updated as per the configuration in NetWeaver. SAP MII Message Listener has three types: IDOC Listeners (10 numbers), RFC Listeners (10 numbers), and SRFC Listeners (10 numbers). See Figure 3-24.

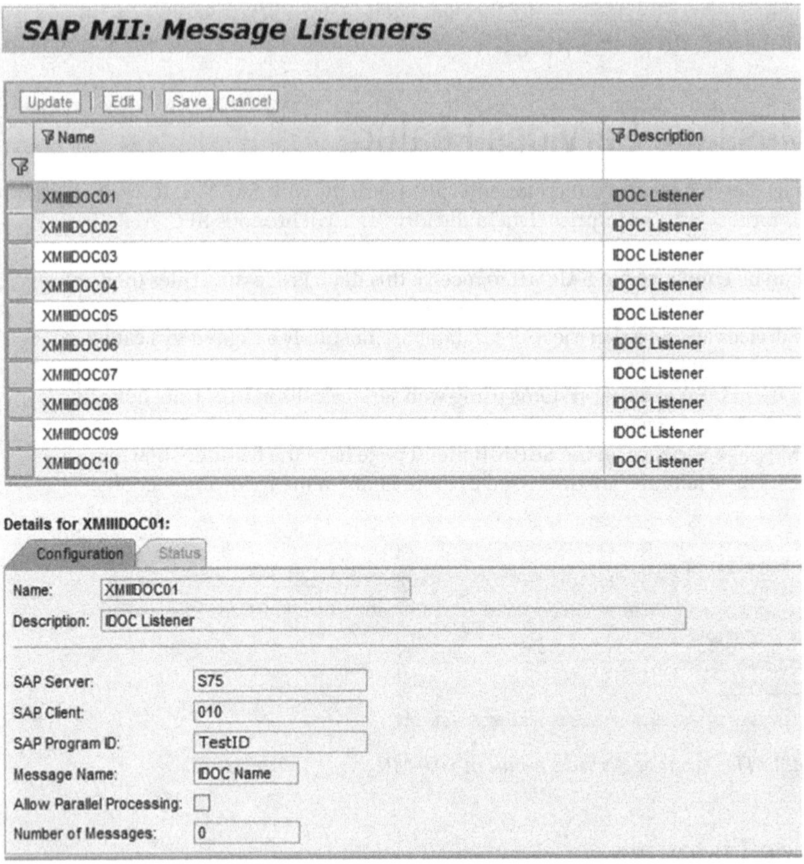

SAP MII: Message Listeners

| Update | Edit | Save | Cancel |

▼ Name	▼ Description
▼	
XMIIDOC01	IDOC Listener
XMIIDOC02	IDOC Listener
XMIIDOC03	IDOC Listener
XMIIDOC04	IDOC Listener
XMIIDOC05	IDOC Listener
XMIIDOC06	IDOC Listener
XMIIDOC07	IDOC Listener
XMIIDOC08	IDOC Listener
XMIIDOC09	IDOC Listener
XMIIDOC10	IDOC Listener

Details for XMIIDOC01:

| Configuration | Status |

Name: XMIIDOC01
Description: IDOC Listener

SAP Server: S75
SAP Client: 010
SAP Program ID: TestID
Message Name: IDOC Name
Allow Parallel Processing: ☐
Number of Messages: 0

Figure 3-24. *The Message Listener configuration in SAP MII*

To complete the Message Listener configuration for IDOC or RFC, it needs to be configured in NetWeaver. The following mandatory properties should be set by the NetWeaver server administrator:

- *ProgramID*: Unique ID and the same as the ID maintained in SAP ERP.

- *MaxReaderThreadCount*: Maximum allowed thread count in SAP ERP.

- *UserName*: Username to log in to the profile of SAP ERP.

- *Password*: User password to connect to the profile in SAP ERP.

- *ServerName*: Server URL used in profile creation in SAP ERP.

- *PortNumber*: Port number used in profile creation in SAP ERP.

- *SAPClient*: Client number used in profile creation in SAP ERP.

The following illuminator service is used for the message listener:
-http://<server>:<port>/XMII/Illuminator?service=WSMessageListener&mode=WSMe
ssageListenerServer&NAME=<UniqueMessageName>

Specify the unique name of the General Properties section. Unchecking the Enabled checkbox allows the user to define a message listener configuration, but not activate it for use.

Any message listener configuration can be enabled or disabled as and when required. The Status property displays the current state of the listener. When a new listener is configured, the default status is always Stopped. In addition, an existing listener can be started or stopped at any point in time. A stopped message listener cannot receive a message from the sender systems.

The Message Processing Rules

The message processing rules are present to determine how a user wants to process incoming remote function calls (RFC), IDocs, and web service messages. Messages are processed based on their type. Processing rules in Message Services are defined to process messages automatically when received by SAP MII from an external sender system. See Figure 3-25.

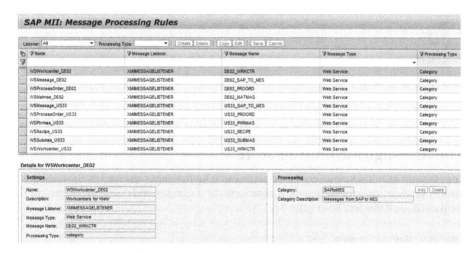

Figure 3-25. *The Message Processing Rules screen*

The Processing Type determines how messages are processed.

- *Transaction based rule*: Messages are immediately passed to a transaction. A business logic transaction is specified as the processing rule.

- *Category based rule*: Only the message is assigned to a category and no automatic processing is done. That is, when a specific message is received by the message listener, it is buffered into the database and the corresponding processing rule is searched. The category is used to logically group messages for ad hoc processing.

The Message Cleanup Rules

This is configured to delete buffered messages based on various conditions. The Message Cleanup screen shows a list of message cleanup rules, where you can run message cleanup rules, enable or disable message cleanup rules, and delete them as required. See Figure 3-26.

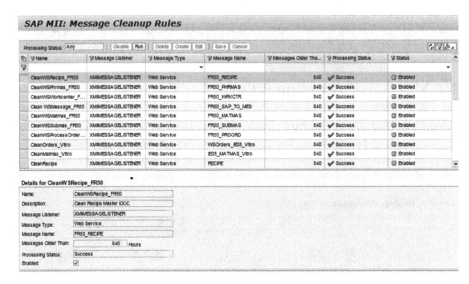

Figure 3-26. *The Message Clean Up Rule configuration screen*

The Message Monitor Feature

The Message Monitor feature enables you to search for messages received by the message listener services, view message details, reprocess the messages, and delete messages from the databases, if needed. See Figure 3-27.

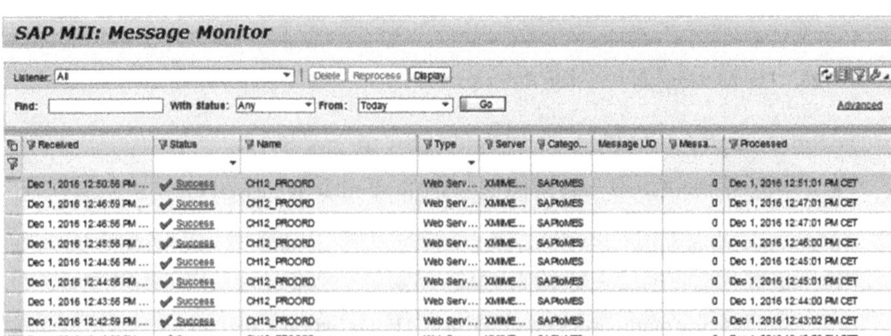

Figure 3-27. *The Message Monitor in SAP MII*

Message Services: Quality of Services

This function can be used to provide quality of service for clients in plant systems, SAP ERP, and PI. Messages can be processed in two ways.

Exactly Once (EO)

Exactly Once processes a message just one time. For RFC and IDocs, messages with the same transaction ID are rejected from message processing and then the message is stored as a duplicate in the MII system.

For HTTP messages, messageUID is used to determine if the message ID is a duplicate. The messageUID can be passed in an URL or can be created using the XPATH. The complete URL for EO support is as follows:

```
http://<server>:<port>/XMII/Illuminator?service=WSMessageListener&mode=WSMess
ageListenerServer&NAME=<UniqueMessageName>&MESSAGEUID=<UniqueMessageUID>
```

Exactly Once In Order (EOIO)

Exactly Once in Order processes messages sequentially exactly once in a queue. SAP MII processes the messages based on the sequence of the messages as sent by the client or the sender system.

Sequence numbers are sent along with the message to SAP MII. To process messages in EOIO format, EO must be supported that is, messageUID must exist.

The complete URL with sequence and message numbers is:

```
http://<server>:<port>/XMII/Illuminator?service=WSMessageListener&mode=WSMes
sageListenerServer&NAME=<UniqueMessageName>&MESSAGEUID=<UniqueMessageUID>&SE
QUENCENAME=<SequenceName>&MESSAGENUMBER=<MessageNumber>
```

Content Development

Content development is the main feature of SAP MII in which developer can develop the SAP MII solution. This section of the menu consists the IDEs for SAP MII. The following components of this menu are discussed in this section:

- NWDI Configuration
- Workbench
- Tools & Archive
- Self Service Composition Environment

NWDI Configuration

In the Content Development ➤ NWDI Configuration menu, specify the Development Track name present in NWDI to be used for the SAP MII development objects. All Workbench projects are created as Development Components (DC) in the same development track under a specific Software Component Version (SWCV).

The Development Track and SWCV are created in the DTR in NWDI, as shown in Figure 3-28.

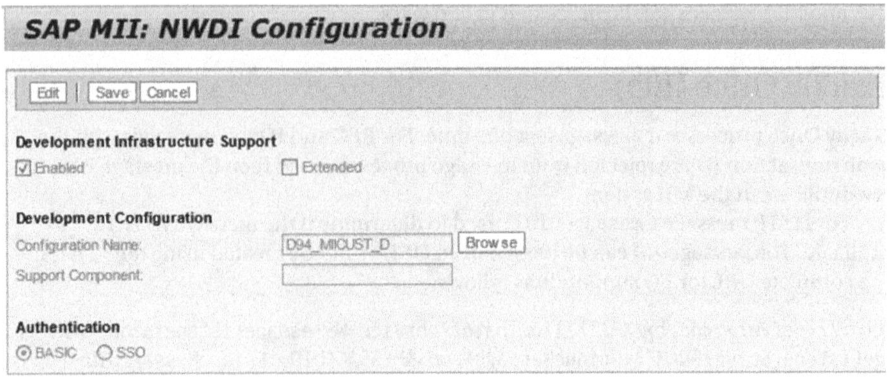

SAP MII: NWDI Configuration

| Edit | | Save | Cancel |

Development Infrastructure Support
☑ Enabled   ☐ Extended

Development Configuration
Configuration Name: [D94_MIICUST_D]   [Browse]
Support Component: [   ]

Authentication
⊙ BASIC   ○ SSO

Figure 3-28. *The NWDI Configuration*

■ **Note**   The DTR of the NWDI provides a versioned storage of the source files in a database. As part of the NWDI, the DTR runs as a service on the AS Java. It is seamlessly integrated into all development processes: as a developer, you can access it using the SAP NetWeaver Developer Studio, and the Component Build Service (CBS) retrieves the source files directly from the DTR. The objects in the DTR are mainly managed directly in the Change Management Service (CMS).

To be able to develop your own application, developers need to create their own software component (SC) in the System Landscape Directory (SLD). Developers have to do this before starting to develop their software. The software component is the standard delivery unit for application. The Configuration Wizard creates a default SC as a post-installation action. If a different SC is required or if the Configuration Wizard does not perform this step, a system administrator or quality manager creates the software components (SCs).

During development work, the developers add new development components to this SC.

Development Components (DCs) are the reusable building blocks for software components. A DC is a named container for arbitrary objects, e.g. Java source files, JSPs, dictionary definitions, deployment descriptors, etc. These contained objects are not directly visible to other components, i.e. the DC acts as a black box. The developers have to explicitly define "public parts" if they want some of these objects to be visible from the outside. A public part has a name and a purpose and contains a list of objects called *entities*.

The SAP MII Workbench

SAP MII Workbench is an IDE (Integrated Development environment) for developing and managing SAP MII development objects.

In Workbench, multiple MII related objects can be developed in their respective sections. You can develop these objects in Workbench:

- BLS (Business Logic Service)

- Query template

- Display template

- MDO object

- Web page

The SAP MII Workbench has a few sections in it. Let's go through it for a better understanding. Figure 3-29 shows the full SAP MII Workbench with callouts marking its many functions.

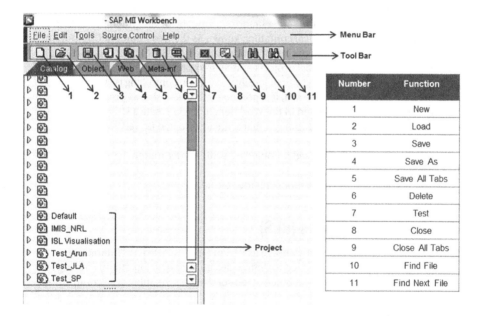

Figure 3-29. *The SAP MII Workbench*

At the top of the IDE, there is a menu bar, which enables you to navigate throughout the IDE. Apart from that menu, there are a few standard features under Tools, like global variable declaration and active shared memory handling.

Just below the menu bar, one more bar is available. It helps you create new objects and templates as well as save those components. Apart from that, you can execute the developed content to do a sanity check or unit test while developing.

Below the bar, on the left side, there is one section consisting of four tabs. This is actually the placeholder of developmental components. It shows the hierarchical structures of the development components.

The first tab called Catalog is where business logic, query template, and display template information can be saved.

The second tab is Object and it's where developers can create their own objects for MDO, KPI, and Alert. Developers can define their object models and specifications in this section based on the development component.

The third tab is Web. This is where web coding, like HTML, IRPT, UI5, HTML5, JavaScript, and CSS, is stored. Apart from the UI components, txt, image, pdf, and XML files can also be stored on the Web tab.

The last tab is called Meta-Inf. This is where key configuration can be saved, like shared memory, project specific shared memory, roles, etc. In other words, it stores the project's metadata.

On the top-left side of SAP MII server, you see all the four tabs. Below that server, one hierarchy is maintained based on certain predefined layers. There should be one project that needs to be created under the server before starting the development. This project is the unique placeholder or logical container, known as the Development Component (DC) for the development elements for an entire solution. In SAP MII, it is possible to create two types of projects—Local projects and Shared projects.

Local projects are created and stored locally. No version controlling is available for that.

If NWDI is connected to SAP MII, it is possible to create a shared project. Basically, when a project is created in the Workbench, it will create a DC (Development Component) for the software component that's already created in NetWeaver for the specific SAP MII.

The left-bottom section is used for object-specific configuration. It populates only when some objects are selected.

The entire right section is for modeling the solution.

Business Logic Services (BLS)

Business logic services, commonly known as BLS in SAP MII, is a IDE (Interactive development environment) provided to define, design, and develop manufacturing logic. A BLS consists of a variety of action blocks, web services, a scheduler, data connectors, a logic editor, and more.

BLS transactions are like MII transactions that are graphically modeled and executable and are stored as XML in SAP MII. The internal MII content is executed at runtime by the BLS engine. See Figure 3-30.

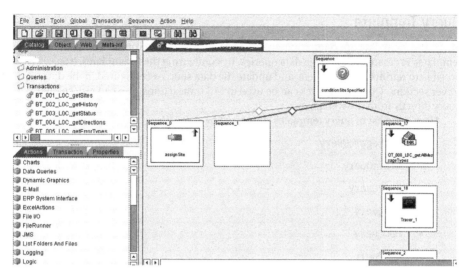

Figure 3-30. *Business Logic Services in SAP MII*

Together, these functionalities provide all of the necessary tools for defining and running business logic associated with customer-specific applications. SAP MII Business Logic Service's broad range of functionality means it can be applied in far-ranging applications, including:

- Key performance indicator (KPI) handling

- Alerts and events generation

- Data extract/transform/load (ETL)

- Application-to-application integration, including two-way ERP integration

- Dynamic content delivery of reports, graphics, and dashboard images

- Complex manipulation and transformation of data from multiple sources

- Relating and combining data from multiple sources

- Operational workflows

- Automated or manual data collection

- Production execution: tracking, routing, and monitoring

Query Template

This is the main data querying component in SAP MII. SAP MII Workbench has a few templates to create and manage data queries. By configuring these templates, it is possible to retrieve, insert, delete, and update the data sources configured in the data server sections. Query templates can be used in MII transactions; you can also call the query directly from the web pages.

Here is the list of query templates supported by SAP MII:

- AggregateQuery

- AlarmQuery

- OLAPQuery

- PCoQuery

- MDOQuery

- SQLQuery

- TagQuery

- XacuteQuery

- XMLQuery

- CatalogQuery

- KPIQuery

Among them, the mostly used queries are SQL Query, MDO Query, PCo Query, and Tag Query to fetch the data from disparate external source systems except MDO. Xacute Query and XML Query are the most used options for internal queries. Xacute Query is used to call transactions on the web page. XML query is used to handle XML related calls and illuminator service calls from transaction. See Figure 3-31.

Figure 3-31. The SAP MII Query Template

MDO Object

Manufacturing Data Object (MDO) is a newly added layer in SAP MII. It is an innovative concept introduced for data acquisition in SAP MII. MDO acts as a data storage permanently or temporarily within MII. MDO can put any data object into its namespace. It mainly uses the SAP MII standard database, which is the NetWeaver database, to store the data so it is somehow a good replacement of custom database for a small-scale project. MDO has flexibility to move with the same structure and namespace when the project is moving from one system to another. Apart from object maintenance, MDO has the data querying capability to retrieve, store, update, and delete the data from any layer of data source, from plant to ERP. See Figure 3-32.

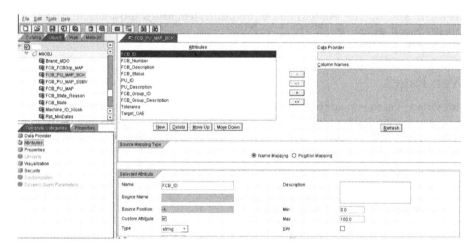

Figure 3-32. *The SAP MII MDO (Manufacturing Data Object) Object Creation screen*

There are three types of MDOs available in SAP MII. They are:

- *Persistent*: Used to store and persist the data permanently.

- *On-Demand*: It is kind of a virtual table, which exists at the time of execution instance.

- *Joined*: This is a joint of two persistent MDOs.

The Visualization Services

Visualization refers to displaying a set of data so that the data points can be easily analyzed and studied in a user friendly way. The representation of data is very interactive and intelligent through various reports, dashboards, interactive presentation apps (mobile or web), etc.

Like many other platforms, SAP MII lets users create dashboard objects and web pages that can be used in various kinds of applications.

For SAP MII, visualization services are divided into Dynamic Page Generator and Web Page services.

Dynamic Page Generator

This is used to create SAP MII-based HTML page content or chart servlet URL. This can be accomplished by selecting an appropriate display template and query template and various other properties related to dimensions and other configurations.

This consists of various display template components that are available in SAP MII, like ichart, igrid, ispc, etc. For the new UI5, the display template is also available in SAP MII, like 15grid, i5chart, etc.

Web Pages

This service is used to create rich, flexible, user friendly user interface for various customer-specific dashboards. Web pages generation in SAP MII supports various UI technologies like IRPT, HTML, HTML5, UI5, etc. and supports various scripting languages like JavaScript, CSS, etc. See Figure 3-33.

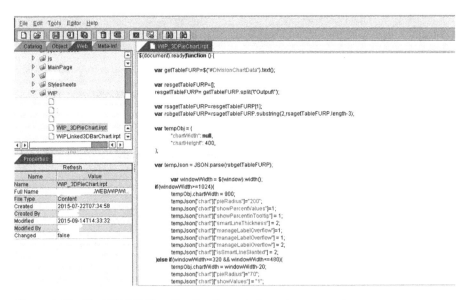

Figure 3-33. *The SAP MII Visualization through the web page service*

Animated Graphics

Animated objects are the customized User Interface (UI) widgets for applications such as digital cockpits or dashboards, label generation, specialized UI, and report components, which you can use without applets or other controls.

These objects are created in the SAP MII Workbench and are based on Scalable Vector Graphics (SVG), an XML-based format for representing vector drawings. See Figure 3-34.

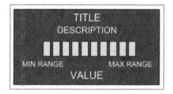

Figure 3-34. *An example of using animated graphics in SAP MII*

SVG files and animated objects are transformed into image files using SVG Renderer and Animation Renderer actions under Business Logic Transactions in the SAP MII Workbench.

Self-Service Composition Environment

SAP MII Self-Service Composition Environment is a SAP UI5-based tool that enables users to create dashboards by dragging and dropping MII objects. It can be used by business and technical users as well.

SSCE has a powerful drag-and-drop environment in SAP MII to create dashboards using any SAP MII content (query templates, display templates, MDO/KPI objects, and resource files), UI elements, and tags from the Plant Information Catalog (PIC). Configured tags from the PIC can be positioned on images. It is possible to configure condition specific colors, graphics, and icons. It also gives you the option to create displays using different layouts of SSCE.

The Save option is also available for the created dashboard to be used later. Customization options are also available for the dashboard by adding the saved content to the navigation tree. One of the important parts of SSCE is to secure the dashboards by assigning roles.

The SAP MII Self-Service Composition Environment is divided into the following components:

- *My Dashboards Tab*: A single screen wherein users can find all their dashboards and navigation links. See Figure 3-35.

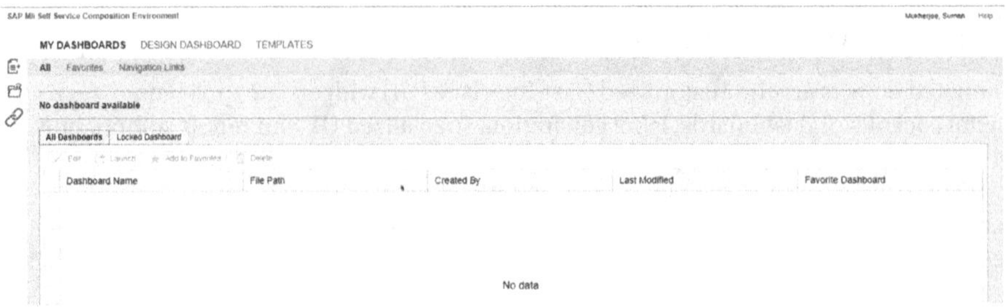

Figure 3-35. *The My Dashboard in SSCE*

- *Design Dashboard Tab*: A screen where the logged-in user can design/create a dashboard, as shown in Figure 3-36.

- *Left Side Toolbar*: Contains icons to trigger all the actions that could be performed in the Self-Service Composition Environment. See Figure 3-36.

Figure 3-36. *The Design Dashboard and the left-side toolbar*

- *Right Side Pane Bar*: Contains multiple tabs, first of which is the MII objects that could be integrated with any SAP MII content like query or display template in the layouts to create dashboards. The second one is the UI elements that contain all the available UI designing controls like Button, Dropdown, Textbox, Radio button, checkbox, etc. You need to drag and drop it into the layout to design your own dashboard. Similarly, PIC and Clipboard is used to embed the PIC hierarchy and to refer to the clipboard content used in the dashboard design. See Figure 3-37.

Figure 3-37. *The Design Dashboard right side menu*

- *Layout Toolbar*: The toolbar just above the layout contains a few actions that could be performed while any MII element is embedded in the dashboard and the basic configuration needs to be changed. See Figure 3-38.

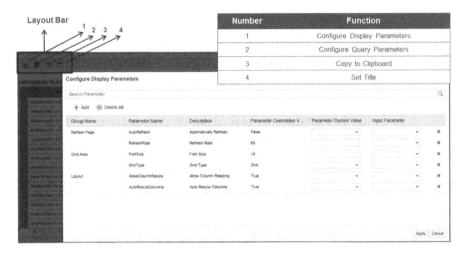

Figure 3-38. *The Layout bar in the Design Dashboard*

Summary

In this chapter, you learned about the basic building features of SAP MII in detail, including its development configurations. In the upcoming chapters, you'll read about the functional concepts in the manufacturing industries and their associated domains.

To start with, the next chapter discussed the discrete manufacturing industry, the requirement of SAP MII in this industry, and how SAP MII provides a solution to this industry.

CHAPTER 4

■ ■ ■

Implementation of SAP MII in Discrete Manufacturing Industries

This chapter provides an overview of discrete manufacturing and industries that fall under it. It also explains how MII fulfills the need of such industries. It explains how the SAP MII and its related modules can be used to fill the gap of information flow between management and production.

Industries with Discrete Manufacturing

As explained in the last chapter, discrete manufacturing consists of the produced components that are easily identifiable and can be disassembled to reverse the process and get the main supplied input component we began with. Various industries come under this manufacturing sector, including automobile, aviation, power generation, mining, etc.

The following sections describe some of the discrete manufacturing sectors mentioned here.

Automobile Manufacturing

Automobile manufacturing is one of the more conventional manufacturing industries. Just like with any other manufacturing sector, there are many process steps involved in the automobile sector. Assembly is one of the key process steps in this sector. With most manufacturing companies, parts, engines, and other components (windshields, tires, etc.) are manufactured by subsidiary companies; few companies prefer to manufacture these components in-house.

© Suman Mukherjee and Saptaparna Mukherjee (Das) 2017
S. Mukherjee and S. Mukherjee (Das), *SAP MII*, DOI 10.1007/978-1-4842-2814-2_4

In the automobile industry, the first automation assembly line was introduced by Henry Ford in 1908. Before that, components of the vehicle were made in very small number and involved specialized craftsmen. Assembly line automation introduced duplication of components using a semi-automatic robot. But still it could not help much with the assembling process, as it took the same amount of time for the multiple expert human fitters to assemble the parts that were being automated by robots.

The assembly process was then split into different operations and one fitter became responsible for one operation, and so on. That reduced the assembly time by about 8.5 hours but the process again was revised, and the concept of the operational stand came into the picture. As per this new concept, complete assembling was moved into stands for each operation and the vehicle chassis placed into a movable conveyor belt. This change helped the assembling process a lot by reducing the assembling time drastically from hours to a few minutes. With this new process, fitters could work in their own assigned stand and performed the same operation repeatedly. The assembling vehicle automatically moved from one stand to another using a conveyor belt. Later, the complete assembling process was split into bigger sections but the operations concept remained as same. Those sections are:

- **Chassis**: This is the backbone of any vehicle and the main component of the assembly process. The chassis holds the complete body of the vehicle and is the strongest part of a vehicle. Each chassis has a specific number associated with it that acts as a unique identification number for the vehicle (this is called the Vehicle Identification Number or VIN). It is mainly a casted frame which is welded and bolted to other components. The chassis is the beginning component of any assembly process. First, it is placed in the conveyor belt, then the other components are added to it, like wheel base, gear box, fuel tank, etc.

- **Body Assembling**: Body assembly handles the upper part of the vehicle. This assembly starts with molded aluminum sheet with the shape of the vehicle. Later, door pillar, roof, and floor pane are fitted with welding and bolting in the main body. Each stand/station handles a specific fitting operation.

- **PaintShop**: This is one of the most important sections in the assembly line. In the early days, the complete painting process was manual but now it is fully automated using robots. Before starting the painting, the body is coated with electrostatically charged coating then after drying, multiple top coats are sprayed on it.

- **Interior Assembly**: After the painting of the body, interior assembling is initiated. Here, the interior components, like steering wheels, windshields, flooring, wiring, etc. are fitted into the body.

- **Final Assembly**: In this section, the chassis is finally bonded to the body of the vehicle. Two separate assembly lines are merged in this step. The body fits into the chassis and the engine assembly and wheel assembly are completed in this area.

- **Quality Control**: One of the most critical parts of vehicle assembly is quality control. Quality control is associated with each operation of the assembly. It starts with the chassis and ends with shipping. For each operation, separate quality inspection needs to be carried out. Repairing and changing is required as per the result.

Automobile assembling is done with thousands of components. These components are received from vendors and need to pass the quality testing. Each component needs to be SPC approved. See Figure 4-1.

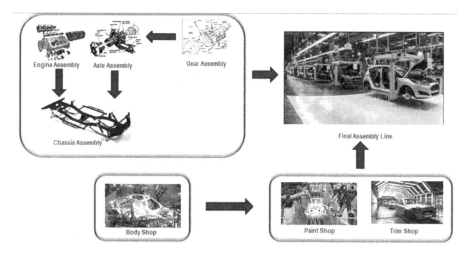

Figure 4-1. *Automobile manufacturing process*

Requirements of SAP MII in Automobile Industries

After the concept of automation entered the manufacturing processes of the automobile industry, many systems got involved in different layers. The top layer is for planning and the bottom layer is the plant automation, which is directly involved with the plant robots and machines of the stations/stands. In most industries, the layer planning is done using ERP and the shopfloor automations are handled by MES. MES can be homegrown, handled by a third party, or be SAP's own MES product (SAP ME). Currently, there is a gap among the ERP planning and the shopfloor automation. This is one of the major requirements that calls for a solution that will be able to fill this gap and SAP MII has the capability to do so.

When shopfloor automation is in place and the fitters are working on their assigned stand, a good warehouse is required in parallel to continue seamless production in the assembly line. Seamless production occurs when the fitters find there is a lack of material and the warehouse is immediately able to supply them the quantity they need; otherwise, production is blocked and the production completion will be delayed.

A real-time sync between the planning system and the warehouse is also required. For example, vehicle wheels come from a secondary vendor. If the company gets an order to assemble five cars, that means they need 20 wheels in place to complete the order. But in the wheel assembling stand, they have just five wheels ready, so in this case, the organization needs to check the available stock in the warehouse to complete this order. If the warehouse has fewer than 15 wheels, the system should be intelligent enough to create another order for the vendor to deliver more wheels to the organization in time. This kind of real-time integration is always required to complete orders in time with good results.

Quality control is one of the biggest challenges for any automobile company. If any of the quality parameters fails during any of the assembling steps, then the steps must be repeated or the material must be scrapped, which is a complete waste of time, manpower, and material. So, quality control should be a mandatory requirement in every operation. Thus, only after closing the issue in a particular operation, it should be allowed to move the assembly to the next stand. Proper SPC analysis is required in the quality step for each process to catch such issues. Hence, in parallel to quality control, integration of the production line with ERP planning is also required so that the production time can be adjusted accordingly at the time of order creation.

As the assembling process is automated, the plant maintenance also needs to be integrated with the ERP and thus should also be automated. This helps reduce scheduled or unscheduled downtime of any line of any machine to a great extent.

To summarize, the requirements of SAP MII in the automobile industry are the following:

- Integration of shopfloor and ERP with SAP MII to provide real-time updates to both the sides.

- Integration of shopfloor and other legacy systems with SAP MII to provide supportive data like components in operations, 3D modeling, design, etc.

- Seamless integration of the warehouse with SAP MII so that assembly is always up and running.

- Connectivity of assembly lines with quality modules to maintain proper quality control through SAP MII custom applications.

- Proper integration of the production line with the plant maintenance module through SAP MII to reduce the downtime and increase the efficiency of the production.

- Creation of various dashboards and analytical reports like SPC analysis, YTD/YTM reports, material movement report, and order status report, through SAP MII to provide better visibility and status of the production.

Achieving the Solution with SAP MII

The automobile industry follows the layered architecture model, where the topmost layer is ERP for planning, PM, and QM and the bottom layer are the shopfloor machines. One automated MES layer is required to connect the shopfloor machines and middleware systems. SAP MII, being an intelligent and integrated platform, is one of the best solutions in manufacturing automobile industries. MII can fulfill these requirements by developing custom solutions on SAP MII to handle the automated MES requirement without any other SAP product involved.

Another SAP product, SAP ME can be used on the shopfloor directly as MES. To integrate SAP ME with ERP, it has a component termed SAP MEINT, which leverages SAP MII's integration capability. SAP ME also has a standard dashboard (i.e., the Production Operator Dashboard—POD) and a custom dashboard development feature, which leverages the SAP MII intelligence capability.

As per this industry, monitoring orders is one of the most important requirements. To achieve this, SAP MII can connect to ERP using its message services and thus can receive the production order related IDOCs (LOIPRO) and its related master data IDOCs—MATMAS (Material Master) and CLFMAS (Classification Master)—from ERP. MII can schedule to start processing on the received order IDOCs and master data IDOCs using its "processing rule" feature. SAP MII can manipulate the order messages and enhance it as per the MES requirements using the material details, descriptions, and material classification details. If the shopfloor uses any kind of other legacy information like design, 3D modeling, or engineering data, then MII can incorporate this information with the order data based on the operations, sub-operations, and components, and can prepare the final message required in MES or at the shopfloor level.

It is also possible to design a custom report to monitor the order status, such as when the order was received, when was it processed, and when it was sent to MES. This includes granularity such as if the order is in the queue or processed in any of the steps, or if it is failed or even reprocessed in any other steps. A proper audit trail is also possible to maintain proper tracking on the order—such as whether it is processing automatically or manual interventions are required to process or re-process a message. An activity log is also available to give a clear view to the higher management about a particular order, such as the components consumed, the engineering models used, and which subcomponent is managed properly inside the order or which one has failed. This order status report can provide a transparent view of the end-to-end order process flow, along with acknowledgments to ERP once the order is received and to certain user groups once the order is successfully released or cancelled.

Warehouse management is one of the key requirements of the automobile industry. Here, ERP needs to be integrated with warehouse management systems. It also must be connected to the assembly line to fulfill the demand. A transfer order needs to be created in ERP for material moving from the receiving end to the warehouse or from the warehouse to the assembly line. Similar to a production order, a transfer order also can be monitored and analyzed using SAP MII. Providing guaranteed delivery in any direction is possible using SAP MII.

Along with order handling, integration with a quality module for quality control is another important industry requirement. As mentioned, SAP MII has a standard capability to connect to any of the ERP modules through IDOC or RFC. In ERP, quality management is directly related to planning. ERP has a standard module (i.e., the Quality Management—QM) to manage the quality notifications. Whenever any operation is completed, the shopfloor triggers one quality notification to ERP to carry out the necessary quality checks. Once the required quality check is done by the quality inspection team, they will update or close the notification with proper reason. If the quality inspection is successful, the notification is closed, but if any issue is found in the inspection, it is sent to be fixed with the same status updated for the notification.

The same product is tested again once the rework is done and the status is finally updated accordingly (either successful or scrapped). SAP MII can replicate the complex ERP screens or modules in a more simplified way in its own portal. It helps the quality and production teams manage the notifications easily and with minimum user interactions. No separate user training is required to understand the quality module as is required during ERP operations. SAP MII can also generate the quality report based on the actual production rate and the planned production rate with good quantity and scrap, which helps maintain the ISO standard for the industry.

Similar to the QM module, plant maintenance is another important area involved in this industry. Automated assembly line consists of multiple machineries and sensors and there are possibilities of breakdown or malfunction of the equipment. It's also sometimes necessary to take the line down for maintenance. Also, considering the regional holidays or natural calamities and disasters, the systems in the plant could be shut down. All these reasons affect the production as well as the delivery of the final product in a bad way.

Higher management also feels the need to monitor these kinds of situations and consider these at the time of planning. In ERP like with the QM module, the plant maintenance module is present to handle the planning more efficiently. It is possible to integrate the plant maintenance module to MII using IDOC and RFC, so SAP MII can create any breakdown, scheduled downtime, unscheduled downtime, break, shutdown, or changeover notifications. It's easily possible from MII to develop an easy and user-friendly screen with minimum user interactions like date, notification type, reason, and username. Using the notification management, it is possible to create custom reports of the downtime with good analytics and generate efficiency and availability reports, which help maintain the ISO standard.

On the shopfloor, operators and production users manually draw charts and graphs on the blackboard and conduct meetings to detect any abnormal happenings on a particular day, or over the week, month, or year. These kind of detections leave chance for human error via calculations or data analyses mistakes. To reduce all chance of human errors, these calculations and analyses can be provided by SAP MII through SPC, Year to Date (YTD), and Year to Month (YTM) charts automated with user filter selections via an interactive user interface.

Aviation and Defense Airspace

Aviation is one of the oldest industries in the manufacturing world. Aviation can be broadly divided in two areas: public aviation and defense aviation. Public aviation is mainly related to airplanes and defense aviation is related to fighters, launchers, missiles, etc. Like the automobile industry, the aviation industry states that assembly is one of the most important parts. Here, the process starts with the design phase, where designing the product is done and later on the design needs to be tested in a rigorous scientific setting to ensure it is foolproof. Once the design is finalized and approved, it is passed to the production units. The production unit starts with the collection of materials components and subcomponents. In production units the main structure of the plane body, wings, etc. are produced. Once quality testing is done, the product moves to the final assembly section. In this section, the body is attached to the wings. Interior assembling of the plane, wheel fitting, fuel tank fitting, and finally engine establishment is done.

Once the full assembly is done, it passes through painting and heatproof coating. Once that's done, it is tested. Testing is the most critical and crucial section of the aviation industry. Testing is an ongoing process throughout the assembly. Every component, such as an engine wheel, needs clearance from testing and needs to go through a rigorous testing for final clearance. The final testing process is field testing, where the planes are tested with multiple critical conditions processes, such as low temperature fly, high temperature fly, runway submerge, low visibility, etc. This process checks the survival capability and various parameters of the product. Once final clearance is given from the field testing, the plane is delivered to the customer.

Requirements of SAP MII in Aviation Industries

In the aviation industry, one of most important requirements is information security. As the manufacturing is involved in human life and government confidentiality, so in the solution, high-end security measures are required. Integration of assembly lines with various information and production systems is another very important requirement in this industry. Integration with planning is required to get the exact visibility for material movement because in this industry, the semi-finished product of the current process is the raw material for the next process. For instance, a semi-finished product of the production process is the body and wings of the plane and that is the main row material for the next step, which is final assembly. Validation and verification in the process is another important requirement. As this is one of the most secure and critical industries, only certified professionals can work with this process.

To summarize, the main requirements are as follows:

- Multi-layer security in the solution.

- Integration with the planning, material management, and shopfloor layers.

- Validation and verification based on certification.

Achieving the Solution with SAP MII

As the aviation industry is more secure, process-oriented, and sophisticated, its shopfloor automation is far more advanced. Although the processes are operation-oriented, the validations are more complex in this industry. To handle such complex manufacturing operations, a high-end integrated MES solution that's capable of managing fabrication, assembling, and final installation of parts together from a single interface is expected. SAP ME is capable of handling such discrete manufacturing execution requirements with flexibility to connect across multiple systems and machineries. It can also provide a configurable dashboard to handle various visualization requirements. SAP CAMS is mostly used for such industries due to the fact that it can cover most of the requirements of this industry as standard features.

■ **Note** SAP Complex Assembly Manufacturing Solution (CAMS) for Defense and Security allows planners and design engineers to define the manufacturing and installation or assembly processes for the machining or fabricating parts, subassemblies, major assemblies, final line installation, and tooling, as well as define the quality assurance process. The suite also include a comprehensive manufacturing shopfloor management application that delivers complete visibility of the entire shopfloor to manufacturing management, shopfloor supervisors, and shopfloor operators and mechanics.

For more information, visit: http://help.sap.com/cams72?current=cams72.

SAP MII can be used as an integrator in this industry. If SAP ME or SAP CAMS is used in this industry for the shopfloor automated MES solutions, then SAP MII can work with SAP MEINT or SAP CAMSINT, which is solely responsible for integration between the shopfloor and the ERP modules using IDOC or RFC. Integration with any other legacy system is also possible in SAP MII. Data enhancement by adding more granular details of component is also possible in SAP MII. For SAP MEINT and CAMSINT, SAP MII works as per this flow:

ERP to ME/CAMS

1. Messages come from ERP to SAP MII in the form of IDOC in SAP MII Message services.

2. The messages are picked up from the message service and are processed in SAP MII based on the workflow configuration to ME/CAMS. Standard workflows are available in MEINT/ CAMSINT. It is also possible to customize workflow as per the requirements in all four steps of the workflow.

3. Messages are pushed to MES using a service transaction.

ME/MES to ERP

1. Messages come from ME/CAMS in the form of an RFC call and will pass to ERP.

2. The messages are picked up and processed based on the workflow configuration to ERP. Standard workflows are available in MEINT/CAMSINT. It is also possible to customize workflow as per the requirements in the steps of the workflow.

3. Messages are pushed to ERP using a service transaction.

Apart from the workflow, it is also possible to add new logic/functionality/validation in ME/CAMS solution using an activity hook.

As aviation is a very secure industry, multilayer security is required. SAP ME or SAP CAMS has a multi-layer security feature. Both products use LDAP for user authentication and it is possible to create functionality-specific roles to restrict access to each page of the solution. Apart from that in SAP MII, it is possible to put role-specific restrictions in multiple sections of the same pages using custom attributes.

The aviation industry is the most sophisticated and secured, so validation and verification of specific skills are required. Considering this, in SAP ME and in SAP CAMS, it is possible to handle user certification for operation configuration even at the activity level. Thus, when users are working on that particular operation, the system will allow them to confirm the operation only if they have a valid certificate for that particular work. HR integration with SAP ME or SAP CAMS is also available to get this kind of user-specific information.

Power Generation and Mining

Power generation and mining is another important area for monitoring. Although it is not related to manufacturing directly, an automated monitoring system is always preferred over manual monitoring, which is prone to human error.

With current modern power generation techniques, lots of sensors, PLCs, and automated machines are involved, so it is very important to monitor all those components continuously. With other methods of power generation like wind power and tidal power generation, you must be able to get real-time information about the weather, such as air flow, humidity, rainfall, cloud formations, etc. Then the system must be able to move the face of the windmill or the propeller of the tidal power in the proper direction or perhaps even shut down the mills when necessary.

Similarly, for thermal and nuclear power, the boiler temperature and the core temperature are critical parameters related to control and monitoring. For thermal power, the fuel valve and coal chute control are other factors to monitor. With hydro power generation, water level monitoring in the storage and the turbine speed are the major control criteria.

Requirements of SAP MII in Power Generation and Mining

Modern-day mining is mostly done using automated boring and digging machines, and those machines are controlled from the earth and work under the ground. It is important for the mining organizations to trace the positions of these machines in real-time to ensure that they are digging in permitted levels. They also need to be able to monitor the status of the equipment to determine when maintenance is required on these machines. The major monitoring criteria for the mining industry are the position of those machines, the status of the equipment, and the performance and efficiency analytics based on the position measured from time to time.

All this monitoring information must be captured in real-time or near to real-time. It is also important to predict future events based on historical data after performing predictive analyses. For example, once the boiler temperature reaches the threshold and stays at that same temperature for more than five minutes as an example (this time can vary as per the thermal plant operation team), historical statistics predict that the boiler wall may crack. Thus, a predictive warning will be issued before this incident happens so that the operation team can take preventive measures manually. There could instead be an automated system that closes the fuel line valve and stops the fuel supply to the boiler.

Achieving the Solution with SAP MII

In power generations and mining, the equipment is controlled by PLCs or SCADA or historian systems. SAP MII has the best capability to connect to those systems using SAP PCo (a freely distributable component with SAP MII package) and it can monitor those devices in real-time. It is also possible to set up the triggering logic in PCo so that whenever the conditions are satisfied, the notifications can be easily triggered to MII and then MII can automatically perform the next course of action.

As per current feature, SAP MII can connect and leverage HANA's in-memory processing and predictive analyses capability from MII by exposing HANA's services to SAP MII. Hence, now it is very easy to do predictive analyses based on the historical data from MII.

Business predictions like deciding when to control the power generation by predicting from the historical data available to avoid wasting generated power is also possible using SAP MII analytics.

Equipment status monitoring, downtime monitoring, work shift details, machine overview details, etc. are also possible using SAP MII, as it can connect to any shopfloor systems, MES, database, or any planning system and MII can work as a perfect middleware among those.

In the past few years, it had been a trend in the industry to have all the information handy in one place even if the employee is travelling or is visiting some other department and not present in real-time production through mobility devices like iPhone, iPad, Windows tablet, etc. It is also imperative to send notifications from production for incidents via email or SMS to the respective and responsible groups. SAP MII provides a very rich and easily interactive user interface to these users and it's compatible with the mobility devices to view all the information even when the users are not present in production unit. Also, SAP MII is capable of giving user kiosk-mode frontend applications. Further, SAP MII is capable of triggering emails and SMS to the required group for any kind of incidents happening on the shopfloor.

Summary

In this chapter, you learned about the basic functionalities of different manufacturing sectors involved in discrete manufacturing processes, such as the automobile, aviation, and airspace defense industries, as well as power generation and mining. You learned about the possible scenarios where automation is preferred and how SAP MII can fill the gap.

In the next chapter, you learn about the process manufacturing. You will learn about the types of industry involved in manufacturing. You will also learn how SAP MII helps to fulfill the requirement in these industries.

CHAPTER 5

SAP MII Implementation in Process Manufacturing

This chapter provides an overview of process manufacturing and the industries that fall under this kind of manufacturing. It also explains how SAP MII and its related modules can be used to provide solutions to those industries.

Process Manufacturing

Process manufacturing is slightly more complex than discrete manufacturing. It involves the conversion or transformation of raw materials to produce the final product. It is not possible to separate the materials involved into different processes, in order to arrive at the original raw materials. This process depends on several key factors like the proportion of raw materials (percentage), the base preparation time (blending, mixing, cooking, etc.), mold or container handling, bottling or filling management, packaging or sealing management, quality and waste management, and warehouse management. As the base material preparation is done by blending, mixing, purifying, and cooking, or other relevant methods, the measurements and the percentage of raw materials are maintained in the planning systems and depend on the batch size, which is termed as the control recipe. The control recipe and the corresponding formulas are maintained in the planning process. In this industry, manufacturing is done based on market research, without any "customer demand". After the product is manufactured and released into the market, a market survey is conducted and, based on the survey, the product is again enhanced and released to the market. This is the main difference between the process and discrete industries. Process manufacturing is common in the pharmaceutical, consumer packaged goods, and oil and gas manufacturing industries.

Oil and Gas Manufacturing

From the time when the humans learned to use the machines and motors to ease their daily lives, the concept of fuel was introduced. Fuel was required to run the motors and machines. Initially, machines ran on steam, but to produce that steam, either coal or oil was burned. Oil was used indirectly to produce the steam. After the invention of the

© Suman Mukherjee and Saptaparna Mukherjee (Das) 2017
S. Mukherjee and S. Mukherjee (Das), *SAP MII*, DOI 10.1007/978-1-4842-2814-2_5

combustion mechanism, steam engines were replaced and these new machineries could run directly on oils. With the innovations in engines, machines, and automation, oil and its biproducts are one of the mandatory requirements for modern civilization.

Petrol, diesel, and kerosene are the three main products used for modern transportation and utilities. Natural gas is one of the essential products for daily life as well as for industrial use. Other products like lubricants, chemical additives, glycerin, and other cosmetic products are also derived from such oils. All these products are sub-products of crude oil, which is drilled from the earth.

Crude oil cannot be used directly because of its various contaminants. The oil and gas industries follow various processes to clean the crude oil so it's usable.

Generally, the following two processes are used to extract and process crude oil (see Figure 5-1):

- Oil upstream

- Oil downstream

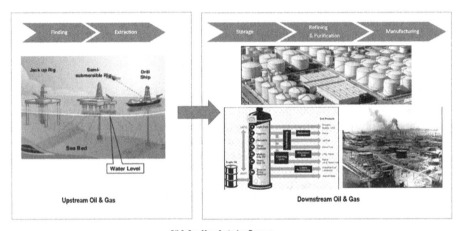

Figure 5-1. Oil and gas manufacturing process

Oil Upstream

The term *oil upstream* is mainly related to extracting crude oil from under the earth. In this process, the focus is to find the crude oil and extract it; it does not involve the purification process. The different extraction steps or processes are directly linked to the oil upstream.

In the petrochemical industries, the search of underground oil is done during the upstream process. Locating the crude oil is not enough; after it is found, it's brought up to the surface. The oil rigs and the wells are set up in the oil field to carry out the oil extraction work. Once the extraction is done, it is supplied to the purification plant for refining.

Requirement of SAP MII in Oil Upstream

Oil rigs and wells are not necessarily located in the same region or geographical area. The oil industry personnel must get all the information from the oil rigs collectively at a single place, i.e., in one user interface application. They need all the required information to be in one place for analysis at the same time.

The information they need is of the following kinds:

- Oil rigs are movable and thus the exact coordinates of the oil rig are very important. Operators need to drill exactly at the correct position to extract the crude oil.

- Sea weather is also an important information that should be available. Weather conditions affect the correct course of action to be taken.

- It's also important to know the status of the oil rig, whether it's down, running ,or in an ideal state. Based on this status, it is easy to determine the crude oil production rate, the volume of crude oil extracted, and other critical attributes involved in the process. It's important to know the status of the equipment involved in processes in order to monitor malfunctions or downtimes of the equipment. Higher management expects that if there is an issue, it will be immediately recognized and resolved as soon as possible.

- Business stakeholders and management people want an analytical view of the information from the different oil rigs in drill-down mode. From the same dashboard or report, they should be able to drill down from the highest geographical view (such as the Asian region, European region, etc.) to a more granular geographical view (such as each unit of a rig placed in some location of Asia), depending on their need to analyze and monitor the data.

- As this is a highly hazardous, risky, and accident-prone industry, an advanced alarming mechanism must be in place. It is also expected that the mechanism will predict potential accidents by analyzing historical data. Based on that analysis, it can then trigger some early alarm or alert to avoid the incident.

Solution with SAP MII

As SAP MII is a composite application platform, it can provide custom applications with a user interface that includes all the information in a single interface. SAP MII can integrate with Google Maps API to provide a real-time view of Google Maps with all the coordinates. As SAP MII has built-in connectors to connect to automated Level 0 and Level 1 systems, it can connect to different PLCs, SCADA, and historians, and can fetch real-time time-series data. Further, SAP MII has built-in alarming mechanisms using SAP PCo. SAP MII can also connect to the alarm suite directly, so it is possible to do the predictive analysis in SAP MII using SAP HANA and then trigger the rig's alarm directly.

Oil Downstream

Oil downstream is mainly concerned with purification of the extracted crude oil. The crude oil is processed and refined until the finished product is achieved. During the downstream process, the manufactured crude oil is converted into other products and then sold to the end customers.

This process starts by transferring the crude oil from the rig to the first refinery through the pipelines and then to the surface. In the refineries, the contaminants are separated from the crude oil and the crude oil passes through multiple separation processes to get the first level of purified oil, which is diesel. The diesel is further refined to get the next level of purified oil, which is petrol. Kerosene is the most refined oil, and it's achieved at the final level in the refining process. In the intermediary separation processes, multiple biproducts are also extracted, including like petroleum jelly, lubricating oil, etc. To get the final industrialized biproducts, further processing is required. Sometimes those biproducts are transferred to secondary refineries through pipelines or on vessels.

There are some general steps that are followed during the purification process.

First, the crude material is stored in a tank or vessel. Processing is done through multilevel heat treatment or by blending in chemicals that purify the material or the biproducts. Once the final product is ready, the oil is again stored in a storage tank for further supply. The biproducts are moved to a packaging section into drums with unique identification numbers. Once the drumming process is done, the packaging section packages them together depending on the batch requirements. Finally, the packaged product is moved to the warehouse for final shipment to the market.

During this process, quality assurance is always front of mind. During the blending process, the blending ratio is finalized for further manufacturing based on the quality report of the initial batch. Similarly, during the drumming process, either further purification is required or the product is ready for drumming, depending on what the quality report says. The quality report determines the results based on the samples collected from the production units and the samples collected based on batches. Every organization has certain fixed sample sizes defined for each batch to determine the quality results of the batch.

Generally, natural gas also follows this similar process.

Requirement of SAP MII in Oil Downstream

Most of these steps (materials, warehouse/tank sales, quality assurance, etc.) are managed by the SAP ERP system (SAP ECC). The purification process is managed by Wonderware systems, SCADA, DCS, Historians, or LIMS, depending on the organization's landscape. The disconnection among all these different systems and the lack of automation between the different processes demands a system that can connect everything. Process order and worklist reports, for example, must be presented with real-time data. These reports show if the order status was released in ECC, or if the order was completed in ECC or technically completed. These reports include data such as auto or manual batch creation, batch status tracking, GI (goods issue) or GR (goods receipt) done, activity across all the processes, which helps during an audit, and event logging and monitoring.

Capturing the data from these different systems is a requirement in oil downstream, because it enables the production users to analyze and monitor the performance and status of the site at a more granular level. Tanks and vessels must also be leveled automatically to reduce spilling materials while loading. Plant maintenance and quality management must be integrated in order to decrease the downtime of the site and to improve the quality and reduce rework.

Solutions with SAP MII

SAP MII can integrate with SAP ECC and can support bidirectional flow of information. Thus operators on the shopfloor can immediately connect to real-time production data. As SAP MII can integrate with SAP ECC using SAP MII, it is possible to provide a custom, user-friendly frontend with minimum user interaction to replicate the ECC processes. The alarm system to check and control the tank or vessel levels while loading the material can also be achieved by SAP MII as it is capable of generating alarms and notifications. SAP MII can connect to a weighing system to determine first and second level weights as defined by the process and help with tank-to-tank or tank-to-vessel transfer processes. SAP MII can integrate with MES like Wonderware, Rockwell, etc., and historians through web services and SAP PCo. It can connect to the LIMS database easily to capture the specific gravity of the material. SAP MII has a PIC feature that creates the hierarchy of the ERP workflow. PM and QM level integrations are also easily possible with SAP MII, as explained in the previous chapter.

CPG Manufacturing

CPG stands for *consumer packaged goods*, which means the goods are directly consumable by the end consumers and are delivered in a packaged form. These industries include food and beverages like soft drinks, chocolate, ice cream, as well as daily life products like toothpaste, creams, toiletries, and so on. In general, from a consumer perspective, CPG products are defined as goods that are used often and need to be replaced frequently. From a manufacturing perspective, consumer products are manufactured in bulk and the production happens without any consumer-specific demand. Sometimes people think that CPG is itself retail. The main difference between CPG and retail is that CPG manufactures the consumable products and delivers them to retail companies and retail companies sell those products to the consumers: So to summarize, CPG is involved in the manufacturing of products and moving the products through wholesale businesses to the retailer. Retailers sell the CPG product to the consumers.

In CPG, the manufacturing process depends on the product. To generalize, the process steps can be explained as follows.

Raw Material Loading and Weighing

The first steps in CPG manufacturing is raw material loading, weighing, and assignment to the kitchen. During this process, the raw material requirements to create the base product is collected from the receiving station or warehouse and then, based on the production batch size, it is weighed, separated, and placed in the respective individual sections. During chocolate manufacturing, for example, the raw materials like cocoa powder, milk, butter, and sugar are weighed. These materials are not necessarily produced by the manufacturing company, and could be imported from other vendor organizations. For example, some chocolate companies purchase cocoa powder from vendors and some prepare the power as a sub-process by roasting and grinding the beans to get the powder.

Preparation of the Base Material

The next step is to prepare the base material. To do so, all the raw material assigned to the batch is collected and placed in a mixing machine to get the final base product. This process can continue for a long time. Materials are sometimes added simultaneously; in other cases, they must be added sequentially based on time. The mixing and timing is determined by the company's secret procedure, from which the exact quantity or timing is already defined. For example, during chocolate preparation, liquid chocolate is the base material. To prepare the liquid, the cocoa powder, sugar, and milk are mixed to produce a smooth paste. Then cocoa butter, which is extracted from the cocoa bean, is mixed with this paste.

Preparation of Molds

Mold preparation is a parallel step to base material preparation. The mold is required to hold the base material. For example, for chocolate, plastic molds are prepared with the shape and size of the chocolate bars. For soft drinks, molds are basically the plastic and metal bottles that vary in size as per the content capacity. For fruit juice, the molds are basically the laminated pet packets. The molds can be prepared by the CPG manufacturing company itself or by other companies and then purchased by the CPG company.

Filling the Material

The base material is moved to the filling line through pipes to complete the filling process. Filling depends on various manufacturing products. At the time of filling, a few important parameters must be maintained properly. For example, during chocolate manufacturing, the chocolate must be maintained at a certain temperature to retain to its liquid form. The molds are filled with liquid chocolate. Similarly for manufacturing of soft drinks, a certain pressure is required to maintain the aeration of the liquid. During the manufacturing of ice cream, a subzero temperature is needed to keep the ice cream intact and avoid melting.

Once the filling is completed, some sub-processes must be completed. For example, for chocolate and ice cream manufacturing, toppings and paper sealing are added. For soft drinks, ketchup, fruit juice, and other products that use bottles and cans, capping and sealing is required. During cooling, all these products are passed through a refrigeration process to normalize the temperature. Sometimes they are cooled at more than the normal room temperature to give them an accurate shape and proper rigidity. For example, chocolates need to be cooled to give them a solid hard shape so that they can be separated at a later stage. Similarly, for other product types, cooling is required to increase the lifespan of the product (for prolonged shelf life of the product).

Delensing/Separation Process

Delensing or separation is the next step in CPG manufacturing. This involves separating the product form the molding case. The *delensing* term is mostly suited to the chocolate manufacturing industries, as once the chocolate is ready, it is removed from the plastic molds, which are used with the next production batch. Separation describes most CPG production models, because at the time of filling, the products are set in a tray with a fixed number and the plate is called a cassette. For example, in ice cream manufacturing, all the cones and cups are set in a cassette and once the filling and cooling are completed, the cones and cups are removed from the cassettes. This is the separation process. Once the separation is completed, you have the final product.

Packaging the Products

Packaging is the next step. In this step, the final manufactured product is packaged. Individual products are packaged first. For example, individual chocolates, ice cream bars, soft drink bottles or cans are packed and then moved to the next line for boxing up. Labeling and printing is one of the important sub-processes in this step. In this sub-process, the manufacturing date, batch number, lot number, expiration date, and sometimes a barcode are printed on each label and then the corresponding label is pasted on the product.

Final Boxing

The final step is boxing or final packaging. During this step, the entire individual product is packaged or boxed as per the lot size. The lot size is defined in the planning system per batch, For example, one box of chocolates can contain 10, 12, or 15 individual chocolates, and that exact number must be determined in the planning system first. Sometimes this final packaging is also associated with another process, such as cartoning. Cartoning refers to packaging multiple boxes into a single carton.

Quality Control

Quality control is one of the major steps in CPG and it's associated with every step or process under it. During the first step, raw material loading, weight measurement, and assignment to the kitchen, every material is tested in the quality lab for expiration, density, color etc. In the base material manufacturing step, while mixing, samples from the mixture are checked to ensure proper mixing of the components—color, fragrance, taste, etc. During the molding step, molds are checked for length, width, logo position, logo impression quality, aging of the mold, and magnetic testing for contaminations that may be in the base material. For ketchups, soft drinks, etc., where bottles and cans are used, these bottles and cans are checked and tested for no leakage, no harmful chemical or bacteria, flotation of those elements and de-shaping. In the filling step, after filling is done, the quality testing happens using ultraviolet, magnetic, and vibration tests for removing air bubbles or any metal contaminations in that liquid.

Another important quality test is done during this step, which is called the goodwill quantity check. For example, suppose it is decided to have 200 grams of a product per bottle of the product. As per company policy, while automatically filling, they can fill more than the decided quantity, but it is not a good practice to fill lesser than the decided quantity.

The additional weight added per can, bottle, or cup is called the goodwill quantity, meaning Goodwill Quantity (per bottle/per cup/per can) = Actual Quantity - Planned Quantity. In capping and sealing sub-process, the capped and sealed bottle samples are collected from the lines to check the cap position and if the container is air tight and sealed.

During the cooling process, the check is required for the temperature decided to be maintained and after cooling process, the sample product is again checked if it is properly chilled or not as required. For example, after cooling process, chocolate samples are collected and cut in the middle to check if they are chilled thoroughly and there is no melted portion within the chocolate. In the delensing step, each individual product is visually checked manually (sometimes with camera), and there should not be any broken item or improperly filled item. Another test is done by physically tasting the product. Random samples are collected in the current production line. For example, are the raisins, nuts, chocochips, or toppings present in the chocolate or not. The testers taste the sample to give it a go-ahead, verifying the taste of the product. In the packaging step, they check if the product is wrapped properly with proper sealing and verify that the critical information, such as batch number, lot number, manufacturing date, expiry date, etc. are printed on each sample as desired. Figure 5-2 shows this overall process.

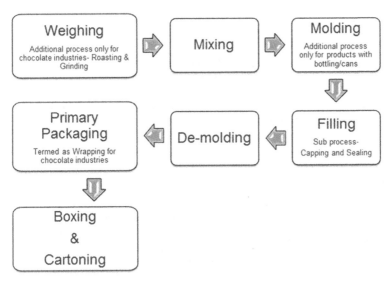

Figure 5-2. The CPG manufacturing industry process

Requirement of SAP MII in CPG

CPG sectors require analytical reports and intelligent integration across different systems. As in CPG manufacturing, multiple sensors, sensing machines, and PLCs are involved. The manufacturing time is very fast and all the analytics need to be done on real-time data, so intelligent integration is the major demand in the CPG sector. Multiple SCADA and historians are also involved in the landscape, so the system must integrate with these systems to get historical data. Downtime of the machines involved is another key risk factor for this sector as it may incur a huge loss for the company. Quality procurement is also an important requirement in this sector. As automation is involved in modern CPG sectors, integration with the planning and material management module is also very important in order to reduce the production timeline and to increase the production rate, thus making delivery faster. Analytical reports play a major role in production performance monitoring. OEE (Overall Equipment Effectiveness) reporting is one of the key reports that helps the industry maintain ISO standards. Apart from this, critical quality reports for waste management, re-work management, and quality notification management are also required. Material distribution, order status, and product movement reports help workers understand the movement of material or final product as a part of supply chain monitoring. Other than the analytical reports, status reports are also important. These include machine status reports, line status reports, resource availability reports, production score boards, KIOSK views, etc. These provide a look at the current situation and productivity of the site.

Solution with SAP MII

SAP MII can address all the requirements of CPG manufacturing. The main solution for the CPG is intelligent integration and smart reporting. SAP MII can provide both. From an integration perspective, SAP MII can connect directly to PLCs, sensors, SCADA, and historians through SAP PCo, UDC, and OPC connectors to fetch real-time and historical data. SAP MII can provide all the status reports like machine status, line status, availability reports, etc. SAP MII can integrate with SAP ECC to provide real-time order status reports and material management reports, as those are part of the ERP planning. SAP MII has great flexibility with charting libraries and can easily provide the desired charts required by clients. As OEE reporting is one of the important and critical requirements of CPG industries, it can be handled in two ways—either by using SAP MII and putting all the OEE derived in SAP MII using custom logic or by using the new product of SAP called SAP OEE. PM and QM level integrations are also easily possible with SAP MII, as explained in the last chapter.

Pharmaceutical Manufacturing

The pharmaceutical industry consists of manufacturing products that help in the healing process of living beings. It produces medication for disease. All the drugs being released to the market must comply to rules set by WHO (the World Health Organization), the FDA (Food and Drug Administration in the US), or the MHRA (Medicine and Healthcare Regulatory Agency).

The pharmaceutical industry is categorized into a few divisions, such as lifesaving drugs including tablets, capsules, syrups, and other injections; life support devices like pacemakers, hearing aids, and stent ICU equipment; optical parts, like spectacles, lenses, eye drops, etc., and medical devices like blood sugar measuring kits, RNA, DNA and protein analyses kit, etc. Manufacturing processes are different for each division and are often company secrets and dependent on research and patents.

As an example, we discuss contact lens manufacturing. Lens manufacturing involves two processes—mold creation and polishing and finishing. The mold creation process is an old process where the molds are created from plastic and then filled with liquid gel material to form the lens. The polishing and finishing technique is a more modernized process to create contact lenses. The gel that manufactures the lens is solidified as a cylindrical rod called a plasma stick. Then these rods are cut into small pieces and polished on both the sides. Both process are explained in detail next.

Molding Process

During mold creation, molds are manufactured from plastics; raw plastics are loaded into the machines and then melted. After that, two molds are manufactured for one lens with this liquefied plastic. One is called the front curve mold and the other one is called the base curve mold. Both the molds have to be manufactured as per FDA (Food and Drug Administration) approved power prediction. Both the front and base molds are affixed together and the gaps between both the molds are filled with lens manufacturing gel. These gel-filled molds pass through a few sub-process like vibration and ultraviolet checks to ensure there are no air bubbles. There are several other sub-processes that test the quality and authenticity of the molded lens and these processes come under the organization's quality policy.

Finishing Process

The molds are further de-molded to get the final product, which is the actual lens. The lenses are coated with multiple chemical components like nitrogen, carbon, oxygen, etc. to provide extra protection to the end consumer's eye. After this, the lenses are again passed through many quality checks.

Lens Manufacturing in Modernized Integrated Process

In the polishing and finishing lens manufacturing process, once the plasma sticks are ready and cut into pieces, each small piece is placed into an automated polishing machine. In these machines, the pieces of plasma gel are polished and the final lenses are manufactured. The target powers of the lens are fed into the polishing machine so that it can polish the lens piece to the desired level only.

Quality Control

During the lens manufacturing process, several critical attributes and parameters are involved and need to be checked periodically. Critical parameters are based on the power of the lens. In the mold creation process, critical attributes and parameters are measured in two stages. The first measurement is of critical parameters like predict power, predict center thickness, predict diameter, and predict radius. These are measured in the plastic mold. This stage is called *predict* because from the mold all these results are predicted to get the actual measurement. The second measurement is of critical attributes like actual power, actual cylinder, actual ion permeability, actual center thickness, actual coating thickness, actual diameter, actual axes, vacuum testing, etc. They measured on the actual manufactured lens after the de-lensing process. See Figure 5-3.

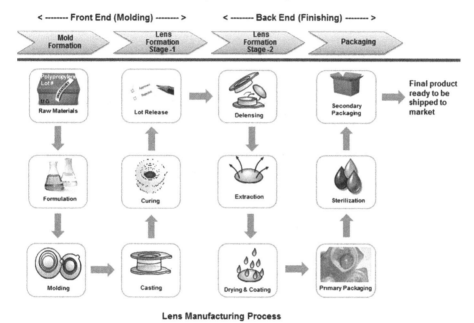

Figure 5-3. *Lens manufacturing process*

Requirement of SAP MII in Pharmaceutical Industries

The pharmaceutical industry's major requirement scenarios involve integration and reporting. For the integration requirements, SAP ECC and machine integration is the most important one. Quality control is done through a series of machine tests and by visual manual inspections. For visual inspection, the manual form is filled and maintained but it is very problematic to keep all the paper records intact. One major critical requirement of the pharmaceutical industry is to track everything, starting from receiving the raw materials until the expiration of the product, because it's directly linked to human life. Most companies keep complete records for a few years even after the expiration of the product for legal reasons, so that any time if anyone wants to check the record of a particular product, everything can be back-tracked.

From a reporting perspective, the product handbook is one of the most critical reporting requirements. It contains the complete record of the product, such as the components used and in what percentage, the expiration date of the raw materials, source of the raw materials, batch number, patient ID, patient approval authority and date, manufacturing time of the drugs, manufacturing conditions and parameters, actual results of the parameters, quality inspection record, storing parameter details, assigned batch details, and more. These details are captured with the exact timestamp and auditing information.

As security and safety is another major concern in this industry, resource availability, process certification of the resource, compliance verification, and machine availability are also important required reports. As explained, the pharmaceutical industry has to deal with a huge volume of data and it needs to keep the data for a long time, so a proper data persistence mechanism with a proper archiving and backup plan is important.

Solution with SAP MII

If we consider the integration requirement of pharmaceutical industries, SAP MII can provide the best solution for it. SAP MII has standard connectors available to connect to SAP ECC and can directly fetch data from ECC using push and pull methods. Master data and planning data can be pushed to MII from ECC and MII can store that data and provide rich analytics it. SAP MII can integrate with the shopfloor machines directly using the standard PCo connector. So using SAP MII, it is possible to get the machine data directly in real-time. As visual inspection is an important requirement, SAP MII can integrate with CSV and Excel files directly to read and store the data. SAP MII can provide custom screens for the inspection form to the end users so that they can log the inspection report directly to the SAP MII screens.

Common custom reports used in the pharmaceutical industry include the yield report, the actual versus planned quantity report, delayed versus on-time schedule report, machine overview report, trending report, production rate report, delta report for quality parameters and attributes for individual processes, historical report, machine status capturing the different status of the equipment throughout a selected period, and audit reports (who, when, what, why, and where). These reports are easily created by using SAP MII to gather all the related data from various integrated systems. Similarly, SAP MII can build the product reports to provide complete visibility of individual manufactured product and can provide digital copies of the report, which are easier to store than paper printouts.

Dealing with the high volume of data is another important requirement of pharmaceutical industries, and there are multiple ways to fulfill this requirement using SAP MII. As SAP MII can be hosted on SAP HANA now, this can be one of the great solutions for this requirement. SAP MII can leverage the in-memory processing capability of SAP HANA and can store the data in HANA DB. It will make the process faster. Apart from this, SAP MII can go with the traditional way to store the data in any relational database and can generate all the required reports.

Another approach is to use BI. In this case, SAP MII can work as an integrator to move the data to the BI data pool. SAP MII is also capable of statistical calculations like mean, average, and standard deviation, which are critical process parameters and critical quality attributes. Due to its flexibility to connect to any legacy system and any SAP system, SAP MII makes it very easy to represent near-to real-time data within a reasonable time period.

Summary

In this chapter, you learned the basic functionalities of different manufacturing sectors involved in process manufacturing, including the pharmaceutical, consumer packaged goods, oil and gas manufacturing industries, and the possible scenarios where automation is preferred. You learned how SAP MII is capable of providing great solutions to all the needs of these industries.

The next chapter explains the various processes and ideas upon integrating SAP MII with ERP, as well as various legacy systems and the shopfloor system with SAP's other products.

CHAPTER 6

Integration with SAP MII

Integration with various systems is one of the key features of SAP MII; this chapter discusses SAP MII's possible integration areas. It also explains the steps needed to create integration with various systems from SAP MII. The steps of integration with SAP ECC, databases, other legacy systems using HTTP and web service protocols, and other standard connectors like e-mail, FTP etc., are explained in this chapter. Along with that, using SAP MII as an integrator for other SAP manufacturing products such as SAP ME and SAP OEE is also explained.

SAP MII:

- Can integrate with databases like SQL and Oracle.

- Can integrate with SAP Enterprise planning, i.e., SAP ECC.

- Can integrate with SMTP, which enables it to send e-mails.

- Can integrate with any other legacy systems that support HTTP POST service, web service, etc.

- Can integrate with file transfer protocol and, using its own standard file handling business logic, can connect to local folders and shared network folders to exchange files.

- Is used by SAP manufacturing products like SAP OEE and SAP ME as their integration platforms.

Integrating SAP MII with Databases

By using SAP MII, it is possible to connect to databases of different applications to fetch data. To achieve this, you have to first configure the data server to connect to the database. Once that is done, the database can be accessed from the SAP MII Workbench where the query templates can be created. These query templates execute MII specific query editor operations like INSERT, UPDATE, DELETE, and SELECT. First, the data server section explains the different data servers that MII supports. In the second section, the query templates are described. These query templates can be used in SAP MII transactions inside any nested logic as the data provider.

© Suman Mukherjee and Saptaparna Mukherjee (Das) 2017
S. Mukherjee and S. Mukherjee (Das), *SAP MII*, DOI 10.1007/978-1-4842-2814-2_6

Data Servers

SAP provides connectivity to various data sources or data servers from which data can be fetched, pushed, and updated. This bi-directional flow of data can be configured in the SAP Data Servers configuration feature. Various connectors are already configured in SAP MII and other third-party vendors can be configured by providing appropriate Database Driver JARs (visit https://blogs.sap.com/2014/02/24/data-connection-details-for-data-server-configuration/ for more information about the appropriate DB drivers and download links) and connection properties. These data servers are used while configuring query templates. See Figure 6-1.

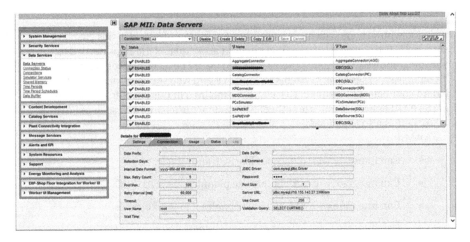

Figure 6-1. The SAP MII Data Servers screen

Query Templates

Query templates are configured from the SAP MII Workbench with a query. Queries can be used to read, write, update, or delete data from the data source. Here are the SAP MII query template types:

- Aggregate
- Alarm
- OLAP
- MDO
- KPI Framework
- SQL

- Tag
- Xacute
- XML
- PCo
- Catalog

The most frequently used and important query templates are explained in the following sections.

Configuring SQL Query Templates

The SQL query is used with SQL-oriented connectors, such as the IDBC connector. It is used to retrieve and update data from connected databases.

Follow these steps to configure a SQL query template:

1. From the Catalog tab, select Project, then right-click and select New. Choose a query type, such as SQL Query. See Figure 6-2.

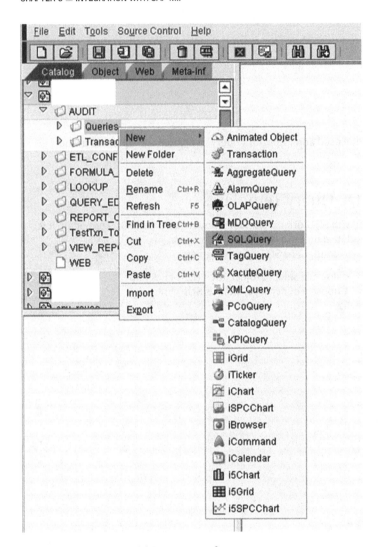

Figure 6-2. Creating a SQL query template

2. Select a server from the list of available servers. This list is generated from the data servers configured in the SAP MII Admin menu. See Figure 6-3.

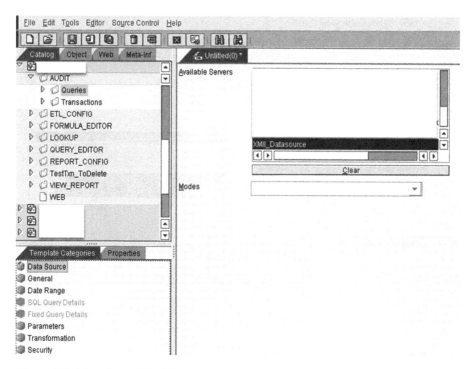

Figure 6-3. *Choosing a SQL data server*

3. Select a mode for the query from the Modes list. Different types of connectors will have different modes available. See Figure 6-4.

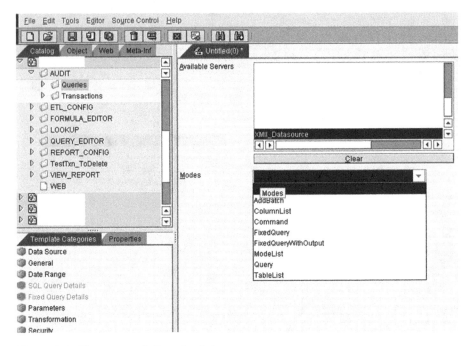

Figure 6-4. *Choose a mode from the data server*

SQL connectors have the following modes:

- *ColumnList*: Used to retrieve a list of columns for a specific table in the selected database.

- *Command*: Used when no result is expected from the query. INSERT, UPDATE, and DELETE queries can be used in this mode.

- *FixedQuery*: Complex SELECT queries are written using this mode. Database specific queries and stored procedures can be invoked using this mode through query statements, parameters, and filter conditions.

- *FixedQueryWithOutput*: Used to execute a Oracle stored procedure that returns a reference as output.

- *ModeList*: All the modes that are available for SQL will be given as output.

- *Query*: Used to create a query by configuring different parts of the query through selection.

- *TableList*: Returns a list of all tables in the selected database.

From the modes defined here, the following are the most commonly used modes for SAP MII application development. Once Query mode is selected, the query needs to be defined, as shown in Figure 6-5.

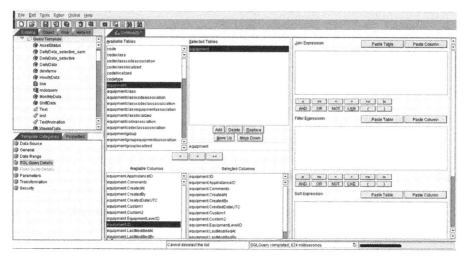

Figure 6-5. *Query Mode screen*

If fixed query mode is selected, then the user needs to write the SELECT statement manually, as shown in Figure 6-6.

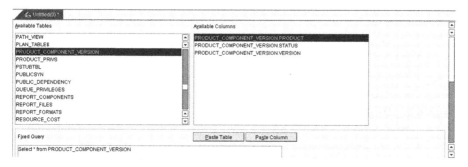

Figure 6-6. *Fixed Query Mode screen*

If command query mode is selected, the user needs to write the UPDATE/INSERT/ DELETE statement manually, as shown in Figure 6-7.

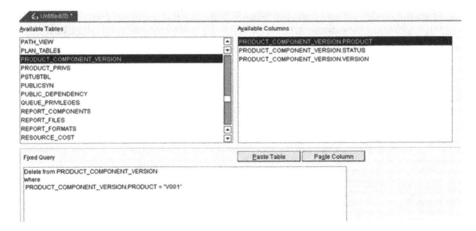

Figure 6-7. *Command Query Mode screen*

The various template categories for the SQL query are shown in Figure 6-8 and explained here:

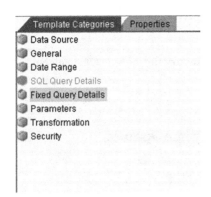

Figure 6-8. *SQL Template Categories*

- *Data Source*: Used to choose the source of data for the query. The appropriate server and mode is then selected.

- *General*: Resultset for queries can be configured using different properties:

  - *RowCount*: Maximum number of rows returned from the query

  - *NumberFormat*: Numeric format for data values

  - *CacheDuration*: Amount of time queries are kept in the cache

- *Date Range*: The Date Range screen is used to assign parameters for time-sensitive queries. In tag and alarm queries, the date filter is applied to the Time column. In a SQL query, the date filter is applied to the DateColumn.

- *SQL Query Details*: This is used to configure the query. The table list and column list is displayed and the query can be formulated here if Query mode is selected.

- *Fixed Query Details*: This is used to configure the query if a mode other than Query mode is selected.

- *Parameters*: Used to provide test parameters to query for testing purposes.

- *Transformation*: Used to provide an XSL to transform the query output according to the solution's requirements.

- *Security*: You use the Security screen to assign roles with read or write permissions.

To test the query formed and its resultant dataset, execute the query shown in Figure 6-9.

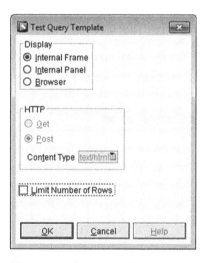

Figure 6-9. *Query template execution options*

The display options for the Query template execution results are:

- *Internal frame*: This is an internal frame in the SAP MII Workbench environment that displays the query result, as shown in Figure 6-10.

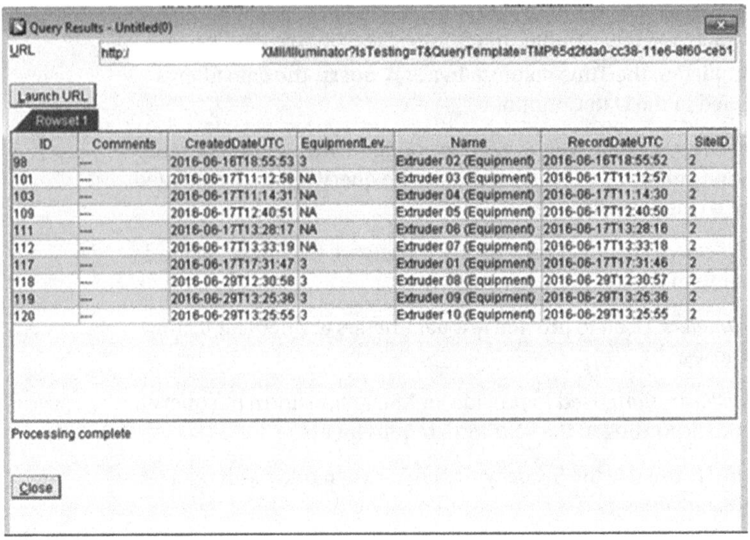

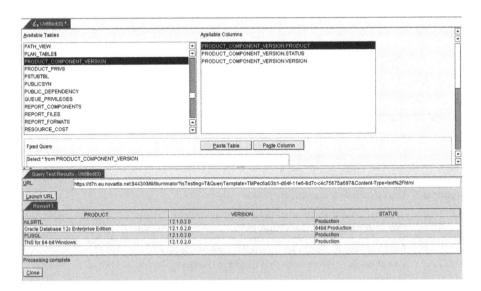

Figure 6-10. Internal Frame Query execution mode

- *Internal panel*: This is an internal panel that appears just below but inside of the query panel and displays the query result, as shown in Figure 6-11.

Figure 6-11. Internal Panel Query execution mode

- *Browser*: Here, you can select the type as text/html, text/xml, or text/csv, as shown in Figure 6-12.

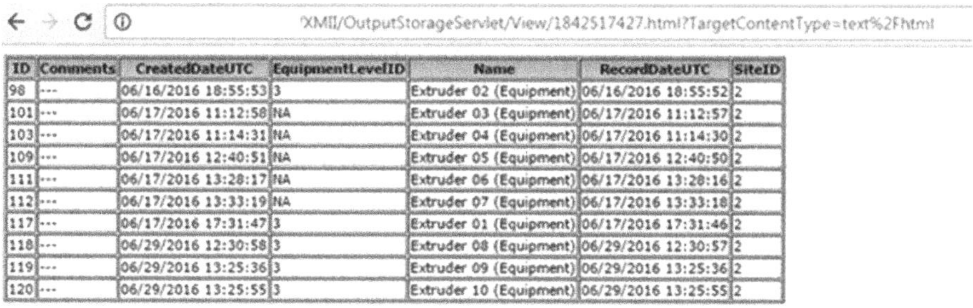

ID	Comments	CreatedDateUTC	EquipmentLevelID	Name	RecordDateUTC	SiteID
98	---	06/16/2016 18:55:53	3	Extruder 02 (Equipment)	06/16/2016 18:55:52	2
101	---	06/17/2016 11:12:58	NA	Extruder 03 (Equipment)	06/17/2016 11:12:57	2
103	---	06/17/2016 11:14:31	NA	Extruder 04 (Equipment)	06/17/2016 11:14:30	2
109	---	06/17/2016 12:40:51	NA	Extruder 05 (Equipment)	06/17/2016 12:40:50	2
111	---	06/17/2016 13:28:17	NA	Extruder 06 (Equipment)	06/17/2016 13:28:16	2
112	---	06/17/2016 13:33:19	NA	Extruder 07 (Equipment)	06/17/2016 13:33:18	2
117	---	06/17/2016 17:31:47	3	Extruder 01 (Equipment)	06/17/2016 17:31:46	2
118	---	06/29/2016 12:30:58	3	Extruder 08 (Equipment)	06/29/2016 12:30:57	2
119	---	06/29/2016 13:25:36	3	Extruder 09 (Equipment)	06/29/2016 13:25:36	2
120	---	06/29/2016 13:25:55	3	Extruder 10 (Equipment)	06/29/2016 13:25:55	2

Figure 6-12. *Browser Query execution mode*

SAP MII uses a particular XML structure to display the result. It includes rowsets, columns, and iterating rows. Row nodes contain the data from the resultant query. Figure 6-13 shows the query result in XML format.


```
▼<Rowsets CachedTime="" DateCreated="2016-12-27T20:01:44" EndDate="2016-12-27T20:01:44" StartDate="2016-12-27T19:01:44" Version="15.1 SP3 Patch 0 (Nov 7, 2016)">
  ▼<Rowset>
    ▼<Columns>
        <Column Description="ID" MaxRange="1" MinRange="0" Name="ID" SQLDataType="-5" SourceColumn="ID"/>
        <Column Description="Comments" MaxRange="1" MinRange="0" Name="Comments" SQLDataType="12" SourceColumn="Comments"/>
        <Column Description="CreatedDateUTC" MaxRange="1" MinRange="0" Name="CreatedDateUTC" SQLDataType="93" SourceColumn="CreatedDateUTC"/>
        <Column Description="EquipmentLevelID" MaxRange="1" MinRange="0" Name="EquipmentLevelID" SQLDataType="-5" SourceColumn="EquipmentLevelID"/>
        <Column Description="Name" MaxRange="1" MinRange="0" Name="Name" SQLDataType="12" SourceColumn="Name"/>
        <Column Description="RecordDateUTC" MaxRange="1" MinRange="0" Name="RecordDateUTC" SQLDataType="93" SourceColumn="RecordDateUTC"/>
        <Column Description="SiteID" MaxRange="1" MinRange="0" Name="SiteID" SQLDataType="-5" SourceColumn="SiteID"/>
      </Columns>
    ▼<Row>
        <ID>98</ID>
        <Comments>---</Comments>
        <CreatedDateUTC>2016-06-16T18:55:53</CreatedDateUTC>
        <EquipmentLevelID>3</EquipmentLevelID>
        <Name>Extruder 02 (Equipment)</Name>
        <RecordDateUTC>2016-06-16T18:55:52</RecordDateUTC>
        <SiteID>2</SiteID>
      </Row>
    ▼<Row>
        <ID>101</ID>
        <Comments>---</Comments>
        <CreatedDateUTC>2016-06-17T11:12:58</CreatedDateUTC>
        <EquipmentLevelID>NA</EquipmentLevelID>
        <Name>Extruder 03 (Equipment)</Name>
        <RecordDateUTC>2016-06-17T11:12:57</RecordDateUTC>
        <SiteID>2</SiteID>
      </Row>
    ▶<Row>...</Row>
    ▶<Row>...</Row>
    ▶<Row>...</Row>
    ▶<Row>...</Row>
    ▶<Row>...</Row>
    ▶<Row>...</Row>
    ▶<Row>...</Row>
    ▶<Row>...</Row>
    </Rowset>
  </Rowsets>
```


Figure 6-13. *Standard XML Query template result output*

URL Format for Queries

SAP MII queries can be used as standalone services in the WEB v2.0 REST interface. The result is available as XML, which is in the standard SAP MII format:

```
http://<servername>/XMII/Illuminator?QueryTemplate=<Project>/<Path>/
<TemplateName>
```

The MDO Query Template

The MDO Query template queries the data in an MDO. When configuring an MDO Query, the MDO Type Connector is used. It is associated with retrieving or updating data in an MDO. The MDO Query can also be used to join results from two different MDOs. The results of an MDO Query are shown in an XML document using the standard SAP MII structure.

Follow these steps to configure an MDO query template:

1. In Catalog tab, select any project, right-click, and then select New ➤ MDOQuery, as shown in Figure 6-14.

Figure 6-14. Creating an MDO Query template

2. Select a server from the list of available servers, as shown in Figure 6-15.

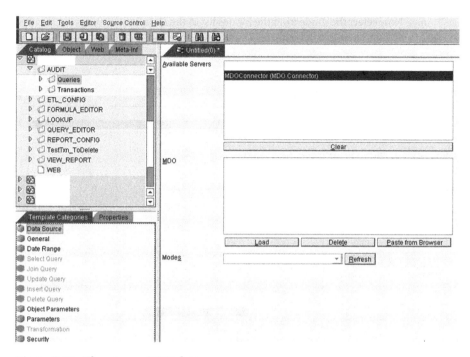

Figure 6-15. *Choosing an MDO data server*

3. Click on Load from the MDO section and select the MDO
    object to work on, as shown in Figure 6-16.

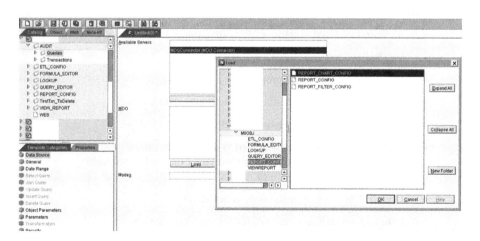

Figure 6-16. *Loading the MDO object*

4. Now select the mode from the Modes list in the Data Server screen, as shown in Figure 6-17.

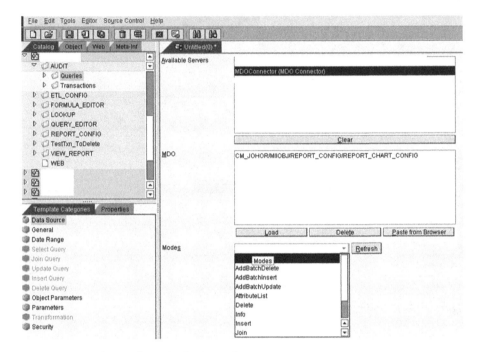

Figure 6-17. *Selecting the MDO Query mode*

The following modes are available:

- *AttributeList*: Used to retrieve MDO attributes and configurations.

- *Delete*: Used to delete the data stored in MDO.

- *Info*: Used to fetch MDO properties.

- *Insert*: Used to insert data for MDO without a data provider.

- *ModeList*: Used to retrieve list of available modes in MDO.

- *Select*: Used to fetch data persisted in the MDO in case of persistence MDO and for on-demand MDO, data is fetched from the backend.

- *Update*: Used to update the data in the MDO.

- *Join*: Returns data as result of a JOIN on selected MDOs. Depending on the type of JOIN, the data will be returned.

5. Depending on the mode selected, the Query can be defined. The following query options are available for selected modes:

- *Select Query*: If the mode selected is the Select type, the MDO will be configured in a Select query. The attributes can be selected from the list of available attributes for the MDO. If you choose Select mode, the screen in Figure 6-18 appears.

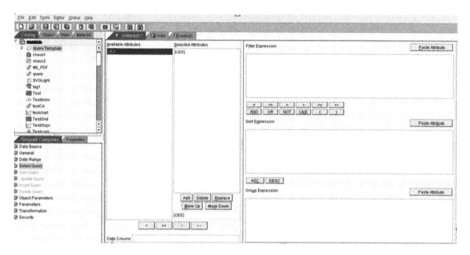

Figure 6-18. *The Select Query Mode screen*

- *Join Query*: If the mode selected is the JOIN type, the MDO will be configured in a JOIN query. It uses two or more persistent MDOs. Two types of joins can be applied—inner join and left outer join—and based on the type of join, the result will be fetched. See Figure 6-19.

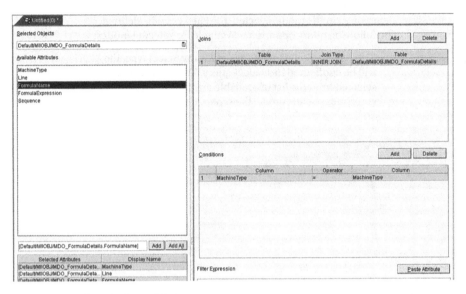

Figure 6-19. *The Join Query Mode screen*

- *Update Query*: If the mode selected is the UPDATE type, the MDO will be configured in an UPDATE query. This is used to update the listed attributes of the MDO. See Figure 6-20.

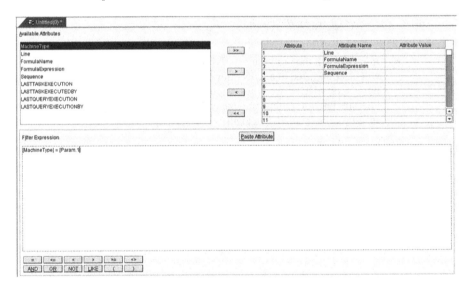

Figure 6-20. *The Update Query Mode screen*

- *Insert Query*: If the mode selected is an INSERT type, the MDO will be configured in an INSERT query. This is used to insert the data in MDO without a data provider, as shown in Figure 6-21.

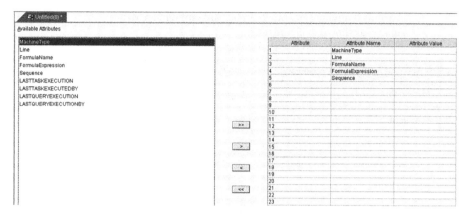

Figure 6-21. *The Insert Query Mode screen*

- *Delete Query*: If the mode selected is the DELETE type, the MDO query will be configured in a DELETE query. This is used to delete data from the MDO, as shown in Figure 6-22.

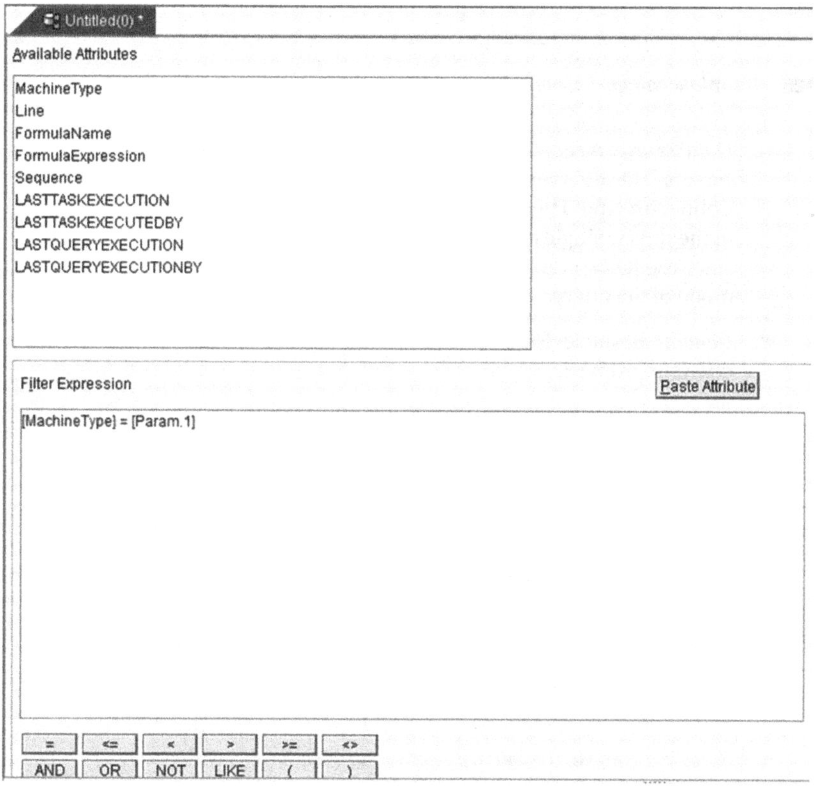

Figure 6-22. *The Delete Query mode screen*

123

6. Various template categories can be configured in an MDO query, as shown in Figure 6-23.

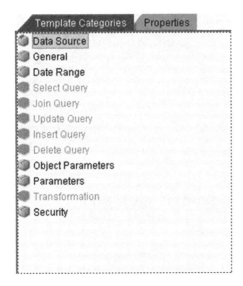

Figure 6-23. *Template categories in an MDO query*

- *Data Source*: A server is selected from the list of available servers. These servers are configured with the MDO Connector type. Then, it loads the MDO(s) that are required in the query. Single or multiple MDOs can be configured since the JOIN query can be configured. Then it selects the mode of the query.

- *General*: Resultset for queries can be configured using different properties:

  - *RowCount*: Maximum number of rows returned from the query

  - *NumberFormat*: Numeric format for data values

  - *CacheDuration*: Amount of time queries are kept in the cache

- *Date Range*: The Date Range screen is used to assign parameters for time-sensitive queries. In tag and alarm queries, the date filter is applied to the Time column. In a SQL query, the date filter is applied to the DateColumn.

- *Parameters*: Used to provide values for parameters used in a query.

- *Security*: You use the Security screen to assign roles with read or write permissions on the MDO.

7. Test and execute the query result. See Figure 6-24.

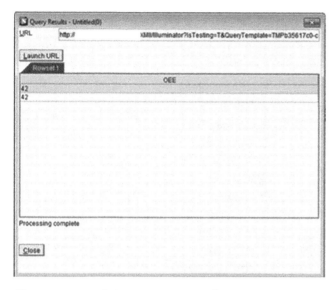

Figure 6-24. *MDO Query execution result screen*

The PCo Query Template

The PCo Query template can be used to connect to a SAP PCo server and fetch details from it using PCo tags and by writing simple SQL query statement. This query template supports the PCo connector.

Follow these steps to configure a PCo query template:

1. From the Catalog tab, select a project, then right-click and select New ➤ PCoQuery, as shown in Figure 6-25.

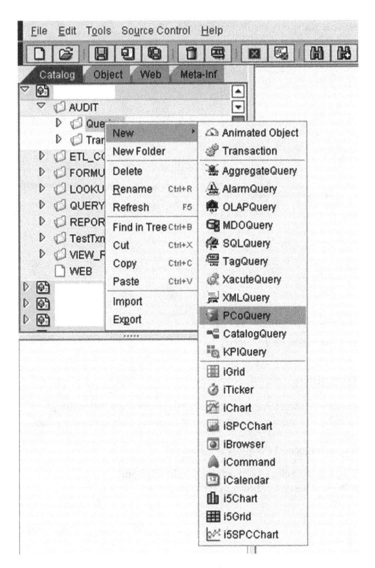

Figure 6-25. *Creating a PCo query template*

2. Select a server from the list of available servers from the data source screen, as shown in Figure 6-26.

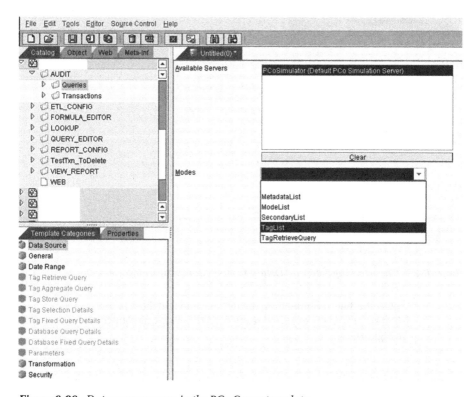

Figure 6-26. *Data source screen in the PCo Query template*

3. After TagList is selected, double-click on the Tag Selection details from the Template Categories tab, as shown in Figure 6-27.

Figure 6-27. *Choosing Tag Selection Details from the Template Categories tab*

Select the Tags required from the left side and add them to the right side to get the expected result from those tags, as shown in Figure 6-28.

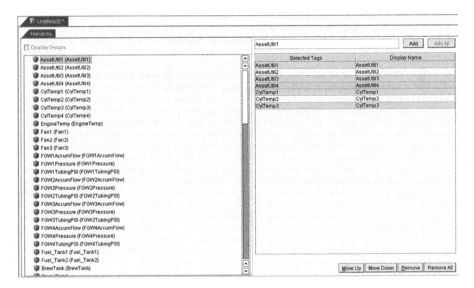

Figure 6-28. *Configuring tags in the Tag Selection Details screen*

4. Test and execute the query result, as shown in Figure 6-29.

TagName	Description	Source	NativeSource
AssetUtil1	AssetUtil1	AssetUtil1	AssetUtil1
AssetUtil2	AssetUtil2	AssetUtil2	AssetUtil2
AssetUtil3	AssetUtil3	AssetUtil3	AssetUtil3
AssetUtil4	AssetUtil4	AssetUtil4	AssetUtil4
CylTemp1	CylTemp1	CylTemp1	CylTemp1
CylTemp2	CylTemp2	CylTemp2	CylTemp2
CylTemp3	CylTemp3	CylTemp3	CylTemp3
CylTemp4	CylTemp4	CylTemp4	CylTemp4
EngineTemp	EngineTemp	EngineTemp	EngineTemp
Fan1	Fan1	Fan1	Fan1
Fan2	Fan2	Fan2	Fan2
Fan3	Fan3	Fan3	Fan3
FGW1AccumFlow	FGW1AccumFlow	FGW1AccumFlow	FGW1AccumFlow
FGW1Pressure	FGW1Pressure	FGW1Pressure	FGW1Pressure
FGW1TubingPSI	FGW1TubingPSI	FGW1TubingPSI	FGW1TubingPSI
FGW2AccumFlow	FGW2AccumFlow	FGW2AccumFlow	FGW2AccumFlow
FGW2Pressure	FGW2Pressure	FGW2Pressure	FGW2Pressure
FGW2TubingPSI	FGW2TubingPSI	FGW2TubingPSI	FGW2TubingPSI
FGW3AccumFlow	FGW3AccumFlow	FGW3AccumFlow	FGW3AccumFlow
FGW3Pressure	FGW3Pressure	FGW3Pressure	FGW3Pressure
FGW3TubingPSI	FGW3TubingPSI	FGW3TubingPSI	FGW3TubingPSI

Figure 6-29. *Tag selection mode query result*

The XML Query Template

This query template uses the XML connector by default. The query template can return an XML output from any URLs provided to it. For example, if an illuminator service needs to be executed using certain logic, the illuminator URL can be configured in the XML query template to return the XML output and this XML can be further used in business logic transactions. See Figure 6-30.

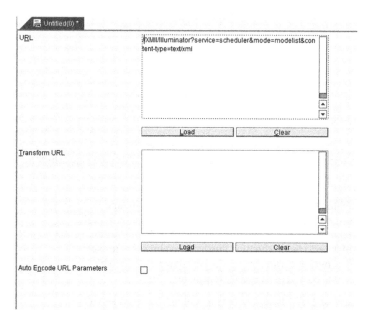

Figure 6-30. *Providing an XML Query template URL*

■ **Note** In the XML Query template while providing the URL, it is best not to use the host and port URL because during migration or any change to the host or server, you would need to change this manually in the code. It's better to use // instead of the host and port for the external URL. For the internal URL, where the object is being called from the Web tab in the MII Workbench, it is best to use `web://` or `server://`.

The Xacute Query Template

This query template uses the Xacute connector to connect to any business logic transactions that are called directly from the UI. It can only execute with standard BLS XMLoutput as an input to it, as shown in Figure 6-31.


```
▼<Rowsets CachedTime="" DateCreated="2016-12-27T20:01:44" EndDate="2016-12-27T20:01:44" StartDate="2016-12-27T19:01:44" Version="15.1 SP3 Patch 0 (Nov 7, 2016)">
  ▼<Rowset>
    ▼<Columns>
        <Column Description="ID" MaxRange="1" MinRange="0" Name="ID" SQLDataType="-5" SourceColumn="ID"/>
        <Column Description="Comments" MaxRange="1" MinRange="0" Name="Comments" SQLDataType="12" SourceColumn="Comments"/>
        <Column Description="CreatedDateUTC" MaxRange="1" MinRange="0" Name="CreatedDateUTC" SQLDataType="93" SourceColumn="CreatedDateUTC"/>
        <Column Description="EquipmentLevelID" MaxRange="1" MinRange="0" Name="EquipmentLevelID" SQLDataType="-5" SourceColumn="EquipmentLevelID"/>
        <Column Description="Name" MaxRange="1" MinRange="0" Name="Name" SQLDataType="12" SourceColumn="Name"/>
        <Column Description="RecordDateUTC" MaxRange="1" MinRange="0" Name="RecordDateUTC" SQLDataType="93" SourceColumn="RecordDateUTC"/>
        <Column Description="SiteID" MaxRange="1" MinRange="0" Name="SiteID" SQLDataType="-5" SourceColumn="SiteID"/>
      </Columns>
    ▼<Row>
        <ID>98</ID>
        <Comments>---</Comments>
        <CreatedDateUTC>2016-06-16T18:55:53</CreatedDateUTC>
        <EquipmentLevelID>3</EquipmentLevelID>
        <Name>Extruder 02 (Equipment)</Name>
        <RecordDateUTC>2016-06-16T18:55:52</RecordDateUTC>
        <SiteID>2</SiteID>
      </Row>
    ▼<Row>
        <ID>101</ID>
        <Comments>---</Comments>
        <CreatedDateUTC>2016-06-17T11:12:58</CreatedDateUTC>
        <EquipmentLevelID>NA</EquipmentLevelID>
        <Name>Extruder 03 (Equipment)</Name>
        <RecordDateUTC>2016-06-17T11:12:57</RecordDateUTC>
        <SiteID>2</SiteID>
      </Row>
    ►<Row>...</Row>
    ►<Row>...</Row>
    ►<Row>...</Row>
    ►<Row>...</Row>
    ►<Row>...</Row>
    ►<Row>...</Row>
    ►<Row>...</Row>
    ►<Row>...</Row>
    </Rowset>
</Rowsets>
```


Figure 6-31. *SAP MII BLS standard XML output*

The Xacute Query template has following mode options available (see Figure 6-32):

- *ModeList*: Retrieves a list of available modes in MDO.
- *Query*: Provides a link to the BLS and to define the input and output parameters for the result of the query template. By default, the output parameter is * in the drop-down for multiple output type variables declared in the BLS. Further, developers can select the particular output variable from the BLS that are need to be shown from the output of the query template.
- *TargetFolderList*: Lists all the folders present on the target server.

- *TransactionFolderList*: Lists all the transaction folders paths present on the target server.

- *TransactionInputList*: Provides input details of the business transaction.

- *TransactionList*: Lists all the transaction objects and their path.

- *TransactionOutputList*: Gives the output details of the business transaction.

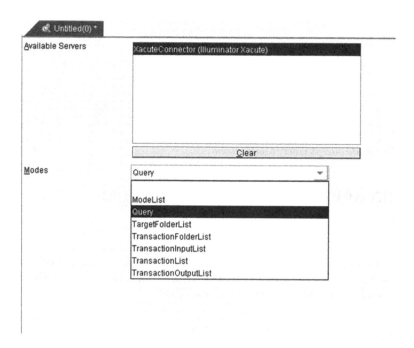

Figure 6-32. *The Xacute Query modes*

The most common mode used is Query mode. If query mode is selected, you'll see the screen shown in Figure 6-33.

131

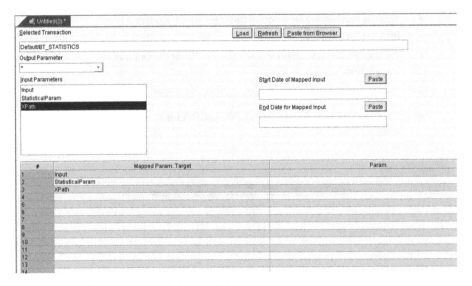

Figure 6-33. *The Xacute query's Query Mode screen*

Integrating SAP MII Using Business Logic Services

Before working on integrations with these various systems, MII developers need to have a good basic understanding of SAP MII business logic services, know how to develop the BLS, and know the most commonly used action blocks required for creating the BLS. The most commonly used integration scenarios are then explained.

What Are Business Logic Services?

SAP Manufacturing Integration and Intelligence is a platform provided by SAP mainly for integration with the Manufacturing Execution System and Enterprise System. It acts as middleware for integration. Apart from this, SAP MII can also be used as a platform for customized integration. With the help of the latest SAP UI technology (UI5), MII acts as the backend platform for placing logic to provide data to the frontend SAP UI5, which displays data in a user-friendly and presentable way.

For this environment, the logic development is very generic with drag-and-drop coding and is called MII transaction or Business Logic Services (BLS). BLS is a diagrammatic way of writing logic, in which the logic is formed with certain blocks known as *action blocks* in MII. They have unique functionality and pertain to a single business requirement. The blocks follow a left-to-right execution flow.

In a SAP MII transaction, any kind of business logic can be implemented. It can either have a logic to query database for INSERT, UPDATE, and DELETE operations or can have logic for integration with SAP ECC, SAP ME, or SAP OEE systems. Even HTTP

POSTs, web services, e-mail, FTP, and message queuing integration are possible, as long as you have the appropriate connector for the specific system.

Moreover, SAP MII transaction action blocks have two sections—one is for configuration and the other is the link editor, which has editor functions and operator sections for the logic to be modified. Apart from the SAP MII standard action blocks, it gives users the flexibility to add custom action blocks, which can be added from System Resources ➤ Custom Action in the SAP MII admin page. Adding custom actions requires a couple of setups, like BLSSDK and MII Jar files for the custom action need to be implemented properly. This involves a wide range of flexibility among users to develop logic based on the technical requirements of the manufacturing applications.

SAP MII Transaction can be executed manually for testing the logic manually from the SAP MII Workbench. Apart from this standard way, there are various other approaches, as follows:

- On a scheduled basis, using SAP MII scheduler based on some logical condition or event

- Web pages via external URN (Runner Service or Illuminator Service using Xacute Query) or Web Service (SOAP) request

- From another SAP MII Transaction synchronously or asynchronously

Architecture-wise, SAP Transaction uses the XML and web service frameworks. Web Service/SOAP requests and XML data structure can be exposed with proper functionality. Web server has the engine installed on it and rest of the editors are dynamically loaded from the SAP MII BLS menu on independent machines with the proper JRE setup. Web server stores a SAP MII transaction as XML along with the other configurations, like the global properties, schemas, etc.

Creating a BLS

SAP MII Transaction can be created in the SAP MII Workbench, but the SAP MII Workbench must first be opened.

1. Choose MII Admin ➤ Content Development ➤ Workbench ➤ File ➤ New ➤ Transaction, as shown in Figure 6-34.

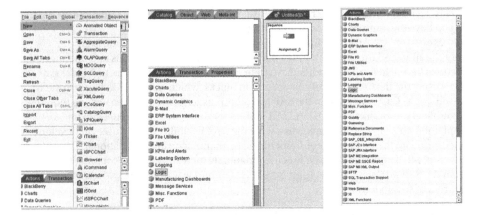

Figure 6-34. Basic components for creating a SAP MII BLS (transaction)

These show the basic SAP MII transaction creation components. The extreme right figure has all the folders under which all the possible actions are categorized. These actions are the building blocks of the logic involved in creating a transaction. Any logic requires basic input or output parameter to work with it. In a similar way, the SAP MII Transaction also has some parameters (see Figure 6-35). There are three types of parameters:

- *Global*: Global for all projects.

- *Transaction:* Specific to a transaction, mainly used for input and the output.

- *Local:* Local to a transaction. Parameters used internally for a logic to be executed.

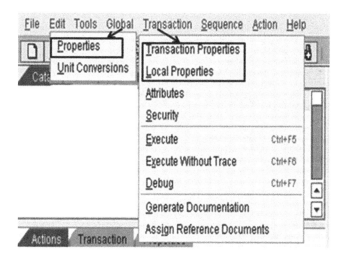

Figure 6-35. *Available properties for creating variables in SAP MII BLS*

Common Action Blocks

To elaborate on the functionalities of SAP MII Transaction, action blocks come into the picture as they are the building blocks of any SAP MII logic (BLS). There are many actions available for each category. The charts category includes the display analytics action, the data queries category includes the query action blocks, the logging category includes actions to log the data at any breakpoint, the logic category includes the basic logic to be implemented, etc.

Logic

This folder has the logical action blocks, which are required for the main logic implementation. Assignment action block is for assigning a data value from the previous output to any local or transaction variable. Switch case action block is used to switch to multiple logic as per the switching condition. It has for loop or repeater or iterator action block to loop over the XML nodes as required. It also includes action blocks that are required for handling exceptions, like exception enablers and throw and catch blocks. Figure 6-36 shows a glimpse of the action blocks available in the Logic folder.

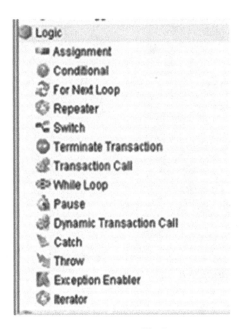

Figure 6-36. Logic action blocks

Each action expects different inputs and provides different outputs as per its execution.

- *Assignment action*: This action block is used to assign values to transaction properties. This action does not need to be configured nor need the input field to be filled up. Rather, you can assign a property in this action or include an editor operator or functions to modify them. See Figure 6-37.

Figure 6-37. *Assignment action block*

There are different Link Interaction and Link types available during configuration of an action block. Refer to Figure 6-38 for more detail.

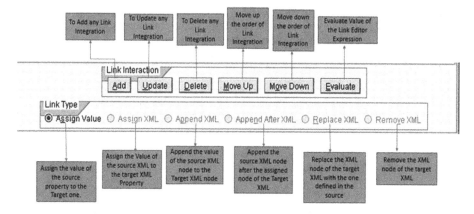

Figure 6-38. *Configure Link options in any action block*

- *Condition action*: This action is used to evaluate any number of conditions as configured and then navigate the logic toward true or false, as per the executed logic. See Figure 6-39.

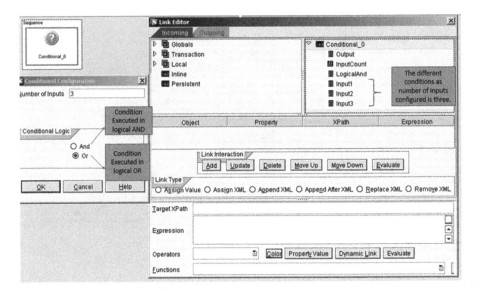

Figure 6-39. *Condition action block*

- *Repeater action block*: This action block is used to repeat on the XML node, the input we provide as the XPATH, which is repeating in the XML. The output fetches the value of the child nodes while repeating on the particular node. See Figure 6-40.

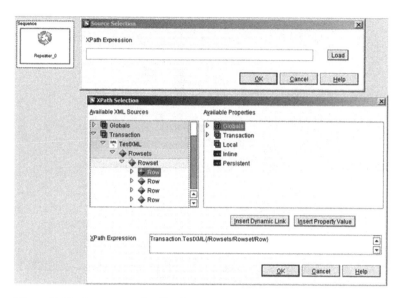

Figure 6-40. *Repeater action block*

- *For Next Loop action block*: This is used to execute a series of action blocks a specified number of times. It is similar to the for keyword in common programming languages. See Figure 6-41.

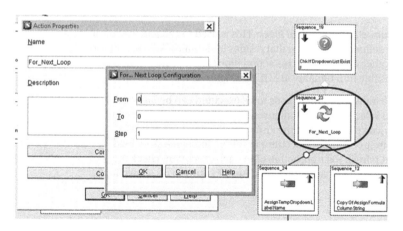

Figure 6-41. *For Next Loop action block*

- *Switch action block*: This is used to control execution flows in BLS transactions based on a variable, which can be a property of another action block, transaction properties, and local properties. See Figure 6-42.

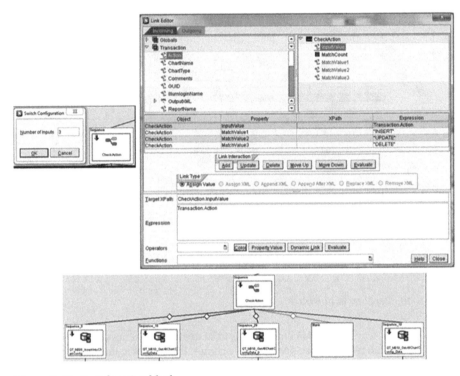

Figure 6-42. *Switch action block*

- *Transaction Call action block*: This is used to call and execute a predefined transaction that resides in the same MII server from another transaction. This action block allows you to create some reusable functionality in MII. See Figure 6-43.

  The transaction that needs to be executed can be browsed and selected in the configuration screen for the field called Transaction Name or the entire transaction path can also be mapped in the link editor of this action block. To reload and refresh the transaction after each execution, check the box called Reload Transaction After Execution, as shown in Figure 6-43.

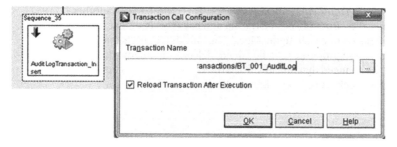

Figure 6-43. *Transaction Call action block*

By setting up the Async property to true or false, BLS can be called asynchronously or synchronously, respectively. See Figure 6-44.

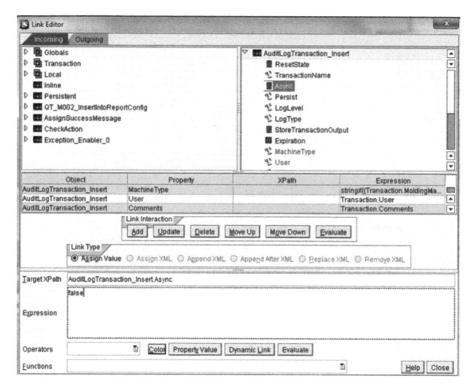

Figure 6-44. *Setting the Async property of the Transaction Call action block*

- *Dynamic Transaction call action block*: This is used to call another transaction from the nested transaction call. This is similar to the Transaction Call Action block. The only difference is that the transaction properties can be added, deleted, and mapped. Fields can be changed dynamically when the Dynamic Transaction call action block is used. See Figure 6-45.

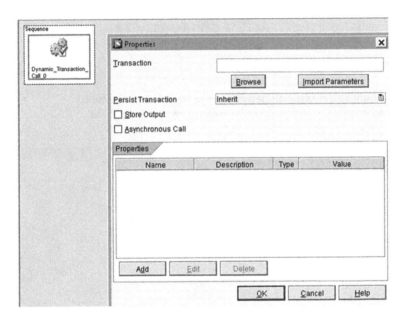

Figure 6-45. *Dynamic Transaction action block*

- *Iterator action block*: This is used to repeat the data of a list variable. It is like repeater but the repeater repeats in the XML node whereas this repeats on the list variable. It expects a list type variable for its input, as shown in Figure 6-46.

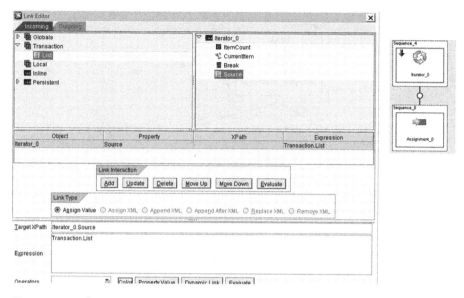

Figure 6-46. *The Iterator action block*

- *Exception Enabler action block*: Enables logging any kind of exception during the execution of the business logic. This action is used to indicate to the developer that the exception handling model has changed during runtime.

- *Throw action block*: This throws any kind of error that has occurred due to some exception that the developer wants to log. This is used to put the transaction in an exception state, which causes all actions to be skipped until a Catch action or until the end of the transaction is reached.

- *Catch action block*: This catches an error at any point of execution. When a transaction is in the exception state, the transaction skips all actions until the Catch action is reached, or until the transaction finishes.

Conceptually, exception handling is similar to any other object oriented programming exception handling concept. See Figure 6-47.

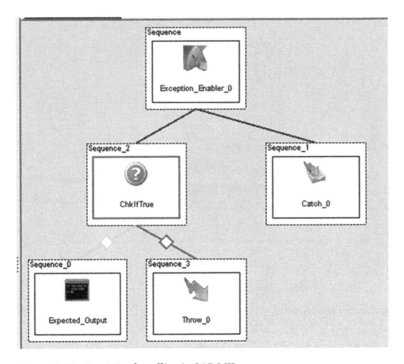

Figure 6-47. *Exception handling in SAP MII*

The Logging Action Blocks

This category has actions that are used to log in between the logic of BLS. Refer to Figure 6-48 for the action blocks available under Logging.

Figure 6-48. *Logging action blocks*

There are three main actions. The first of these is the Tracer action block, which is used to debug BLS transactions by displaying any message or value in the trace window while running the BLS transaction from the Workbench. See Figure 6-49.

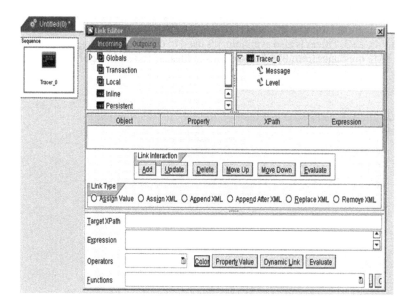

Figure 6-49. *Tracer action block*

The Message action block provides a relevant message to the MII developer during debugging. The Level action block provides the option to define the trace level during debugging, as shown in Figure 6-50.

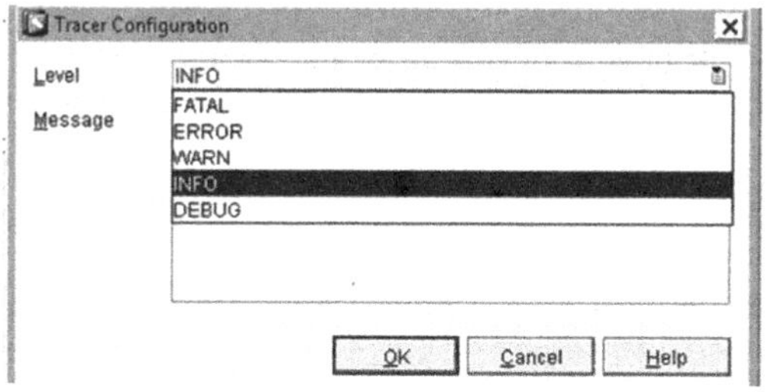

Figure 6-50. *Level types in Tracer*

INFO gives the information related to the parameters used in the action block. FATAL only returns the relevant message if a fatal error is caught during execution of the BLS. WARN only returns warning information that occurred during execution of the BLS. DEBUG returns the intermediate debugging step details of the action blocks during execution of the BLS. ERROR returns any error messages that occurred during the execution of the BLS. By default, the INFO level type is selected.

Apart from this, XML Tracer is also available. It's used to create custom log or trace files to log only XML messages from BLS transactions in files, as shown in Figure 6-51.

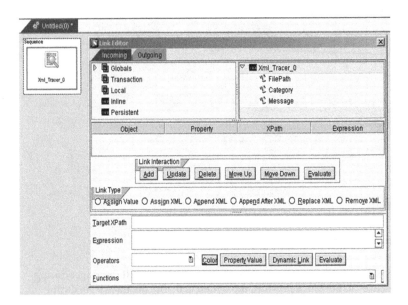

Figure 6-51. *XML Tracer action block*

The FilePath option provides the web file path where the developer wants the XML tracer to be written. The Message option provides the relevant message that needs to be written in the file.

Event Logger is available to trace message logging in the NetWeaver log, as shown in Figure 6-52.

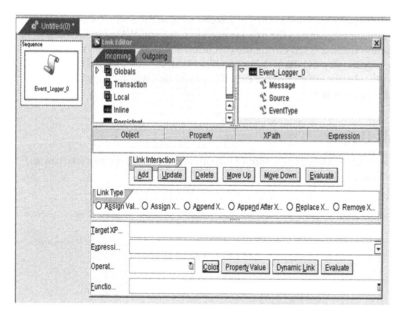

Figure 6-52. *Event Logger action block*

- *Message*: Provide the relevant message that needs to be written in the NetWeaver log.

- *Source*: Defines the logging source information like any unique identification so that developers can search the logging information using that keyword in the log viewer of the NetWeaver. By default, the source is defined as UserEvent.

- *EventType*: Defines the type of the event that you want to log in NetWeaver, as shown in Figure 6-53.

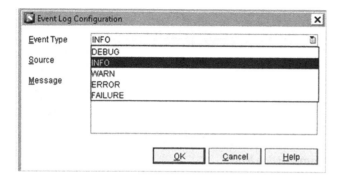

Figure 6-53. *Event types in Event Logger*

INFO gives information related to the parameters used in the action block. FAILURE returns the relevant message only if the exception type is "failure". WARN returns the warning information that occurred during the execution of the BLS. DEBUG returns intermediate debugging step details of the action blocks during execution of the BLS. ERROR returns the relevant error message only if the exception type is "error". By default, the INFO level type is selected.

SAP MII XML Output

SAP MII works with XML. XML has a standard format, which follows the rowsets/rowset/ row format. See Figure 6-54.

```
- <Rowsets DateCreated="2003-07-23T10:45:17" StartDate="2003-07-23T11:00:00" EndDate="2003-07-23T12:00:00" Version="10.0">
  - <Rowset>
    - <Columns>
        <Column Name="Name" SourceColumn="Name" Description="Employee Name" SQLDataType="1" MinRange="0" MaxRange="0" />
        <Column Name="ID" SourceColumn="ID" Description="Employee ID" SQLDataType="5" MinRange="0" MaxRange="3" />
      </Columns>
    - <Row>
        <Name>John Smith</Name>
        <ID>1</ID>
      </Row>
    </Rowset>
  </Rowsets>
```

Figure 6-54. SAP MII XML output action block: standard output XML

These action blocks (shown in Figure 6-55) make creating a SAP MII specific standard XML much easier:

Figure 6-55. SAP MII XML Output action blocks

- *Document action block*: The main action block that defines the XML structure where the columns are assigned to its probable datatype, length of datatype, etc. See Figure 6-56.

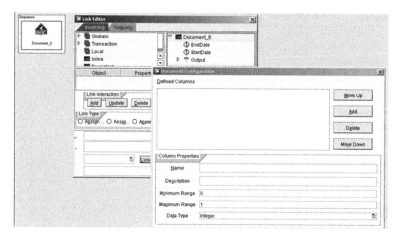

Figure 6-56. *Document action block*

- *Rowset action block*: Adds a Rowset element in a XML document defined by the Document action block.

- *Column action block*: Adds a new column definition under the rowset in a XML document defined by the Document action block. See Figure 6-57.

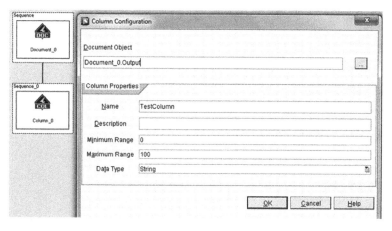

Figure 6-57. *Column action block*

- *Row action block*: Adds data rows as <Row> elements and their children in a XML document defined by the Document action block. See Figure 6-58.

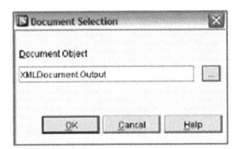

Figure 6-58. *Row action block configuration*

The Data Queries Template

The Data Queries template has all the query type action blocks that you can create from the Query template feature in SAP MII. This includes SQL, MDO, and many more, as shown in Figure 6-59.

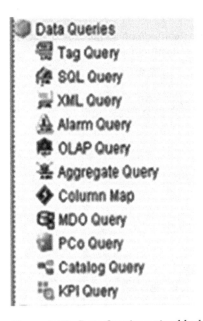

Figure 6-59. *Data Queries action blocks*

To add and configure this action, first of all, a blank sequence is chosen and the desired action is double-clicked or dragged over the sequence. An an example, consider SQL Query Data Queries. The SQL query would be dragged and dropped on the blank sequence. You can also select the blank sequence and double-click on the Query action block. See Figure 6-60.

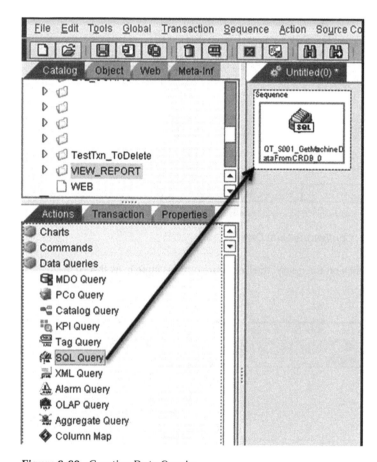

Figure 6-60. *Creating Data Queries*

For this action to be configured, you have two options. You can choose the Configure Objects option by directly double-clicking on the specific query action block, as shown in Figure 6-61.

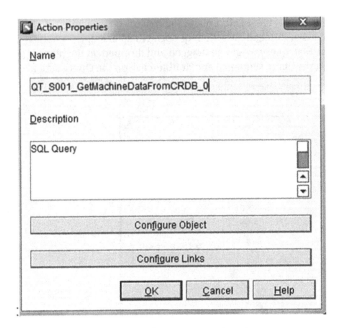

Figure 6-61. *Option 1: Configuring Data Queries*

When you right-click on the query, the Configure options appear, as shown in Figure 6-62.

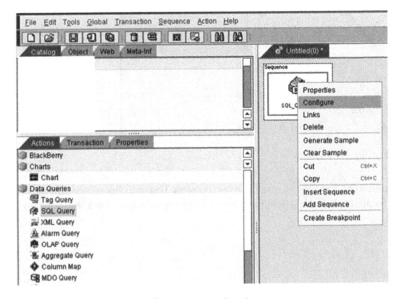

Figure 6-62. *Option 2: Configuring Data Queries*

Next, a screen appears to configure the query (refer to Figure 6-63) and when you click on the Load button, a list of queries appears from which the required query can be selected.

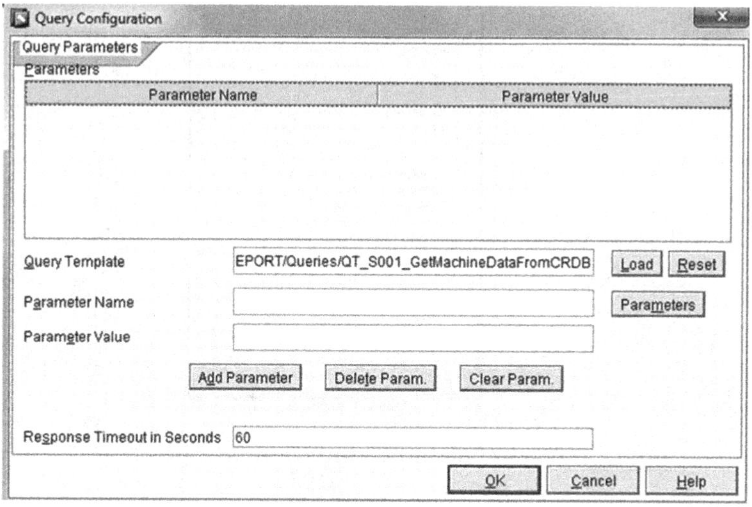

Figure 6-63. *Query Configuration screen*

Once the query object is configured, click on Links (see Figure 6-62) or click on Configure Links (see Figure 6-61), as shown in Figure 6-64.

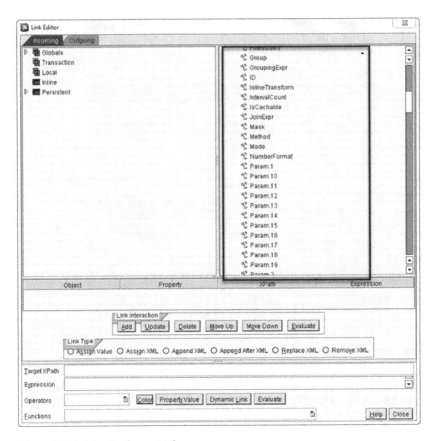

Figure 6-64. The Configure Links screen

Linking helps dynamically assign the query parameters as required during the runtime execution of the BLS. Apart from that, it is also possible to create a dynamic query statement and link it to "Query" and then assign a mode of the query as per the mode list available against the query template.

Users can create filter expressions (`FilterExpr`), join expressions (`JoinExpr`), and group expressions (`GroupingExpr`) dynamically so that the logic can reduce the hardcoded or static values and query expression. This makes the logic call a fewer number of action blocks because the same query template can be reused by passing dynamic parameters. This in turn helps the logic be optimized and efficient.

For example, say you want to query a table named `User`, which consists of the ID, name, country, address, contact_no, and e-mail table columns. There are two ways you can retrieve data from the table:

- Retrieve the data for the country of India only.

- Retrieve the data with an ID from 12 to 99; the name is blank.

To handle both scenarios, instead of writing two SQL query templates, you can use a single query template while passing the expressions dynamically.

The query template is created in Fixed Query mode and saved. Then the query statement mentioned next needs to be linked to the Query parameter dynamically from the Configure Links screen.

```
Statement : Scenario 1 : SELECT * FROM User WHERE User.country = 'India'
        Scenario 2 :SELECT* FROM User WHERE User.ID BETWEEN 12 AND 99 AND
        User.name IS NULL
```

When the query template is created with Query mode and saved, the following configurations need to be maintained from the Configure Links screen:

1. The User table needs to be linked to the Tables parameter.

2. The respective column names (comma-separated column names) need to be linked to the Columns parameter, like ID, name, country, address, contact_no, and e-mail.

3. The filter criteria needs to be linked to FilterExpr. In scenario 1, it will be User.country = 'India' and in scenario 2, it will be User.ID BETWEEN 12 AND 99 AND User.name IS NULL.

Like with SQL queries, a similar approach is possible and beneficial for code optimization.

Integrating SAP MII with ERP (SAP ECC)

As explained in the beginning, ECC integration is one of the major requirements of the manufacturing shopfloor and middleware. The following section explains why this integration is needed and how to create seamless integration using SAP MII.

Why Do We Need ERP (SAP ECC) in the Manufacturing Industry?

As explained earlier, ERP is the Enterprise Planning System, meaning the business planning from higher authorities are done in ERP. As with other industries, manufacturing follows a few standard steps to work. These steps are planning, orders as per demand, BOM (Bill of Materials) creation based on the order created and, in parallel, the master data management is also required to maintain material classification, routing, workcenter etc. After this, the order details are passed along with the BOM and master data to the shopfloor production and to the warehouse. This ensures that the transfer of material from the warehouse and the production execution process on the shopfloor happens correctly.

The operations, components, and steps need to be followed as defined in the BOM and the master data. Once the manufacturing process is complete, the produced quantity, including good quantity and waste, are updated in the ERP. The cost analysis and the shipment handling information needs to be passed to the shopfloor from the ERP. Once the shipping is complete, this same information needs to be updated in the ERP.

To complete this manufacturing cycle, collaboration is required among the various modules, including PP (Production Planning), MM (Material Management), Finance and accounting (FICO), Supply Chain, Shipping, Sales, Warehouse Management, and more, in ERP. SAP ECC is a product by SAP that integrates all these modules internally as a package of ERP.

Integrating SAP ECC with the Shopfloor

Another integration requirement is to fill the gap between ECC and shopfloor manufacturing so as to pass the planning information in real-time. SAP MII can integrate both of these and pass the data bi-directionally in real-time. SAP MII provides a few extra layers of security in terms of access restrictions, encryptions, etc. and intelligence like reporting, real-time status monitoring, acknowledgment handling, and more.

Integrating SAP MII with SAP ECC

SAP MII can integrate with SAP ECC in two ways (see Figure 6-65):

- *Using IDOC*: IDOC is an intermediary document of SAP that's used to transfer data between two SAP systems or from one SAP system to another non-SAP system. IDOC generates an enhanced XML structure based on the IDOC type to be consumed by the system. SAP MII has a standard feature available to consume IDOC XML and process it as required.

- *Using RFC (BAPI)*: BAPI includes the standard or customized function modules in SAP ECC. Function modules are procedures defined in the SAP system. They are used to expose the SAP data to a non-SAP system. Whenever a function module is enabled as a remotely accessible function module, it's called BAPI (Business API).

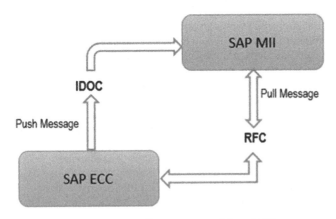

Figure 6-65. *Information flow between ECC and MII*

Integrating SAP ECC and MII Using IDoc

SAP ECC can push the message through IDoc to MII but, before receiving the message in SAP MII, a few configurations need to be done at the MII end. Follow these steps:

1. Configure the message listener in NetWeaver. The listener holds the configuration of the ECC ends, such as unique program ID, client, host, etc. SAP MII has 10 dedicated IDoc listeners. To configure it, go to http://<host>:<port>/nwa.

2. Navigate to Configuration Management ➤ Infrastructure ➤ Application Resources, as shown in Figure 6-66.

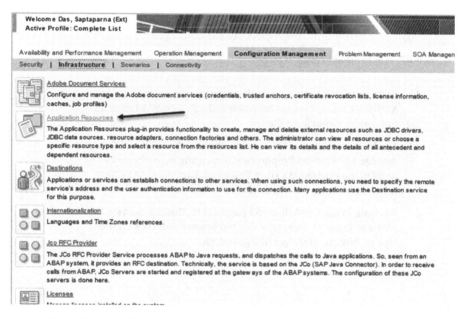

Figure 6-66. *Configuration management*

3. Click on the Application Resources link to get the screen shown in Figure 6-67.

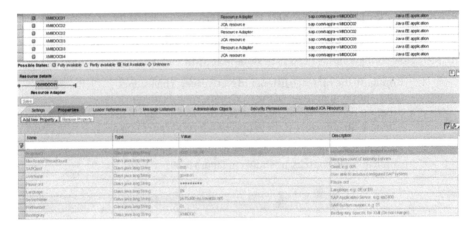

Figure 6-67. *Application Resources screen*

4. In the resource name, put the listener's name, such as XMIIIDOC01 and press Enter. Select the Resource Adapter for the configuration from the list.

5. The bottom section of the screen will show the details of the listener. Click on the Properties tab to configure it. You need to fill in the ProgramID, User, Password, Language, SAPClient, ServerName, and portNo fields.

6. Navigate to the SAP MII menu page. Go to Message Service ➤ Message Listener. Select the desired listener and click on the Update button, as shown in Figure 6-68.

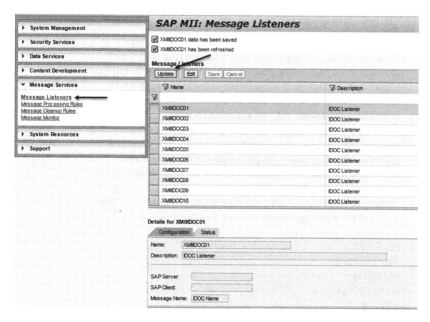

Figure 6-68. *Message listeners*

Using these steps, IDoc messages can be received and further stored in the internal table of SAP MII. Now you need to know how to process the IDoc message. To do so, another configuration is required, called *processing rules* (see Figure 6-69).

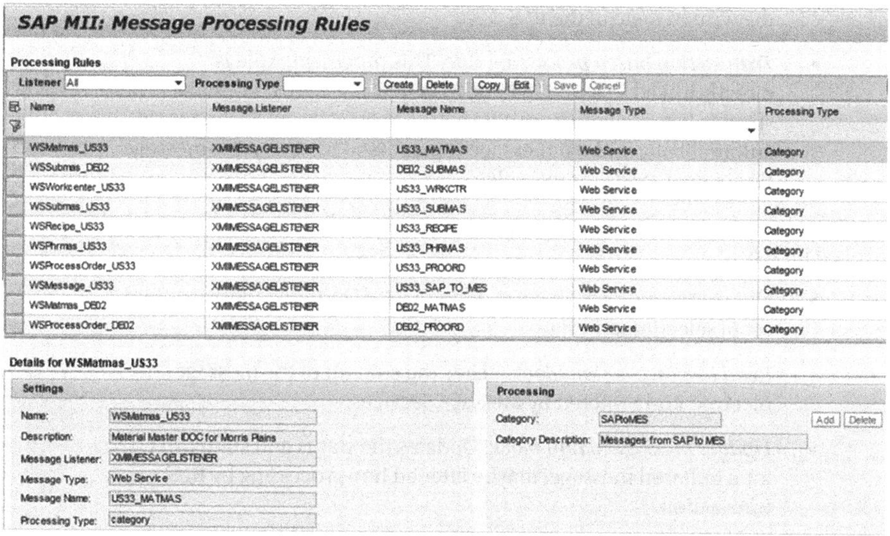

Figure 6-69. *Message processing rules*

In SAP MII, two types of processing rules can be defined:

- *Category based processing rule*: Defines a unique category for a message type. The benefit of using this rule is that each message from ECC being pushed to MII is tagged with a unique identification ID, which helps to recall the message from MII logic anytime. There is no need to store the message separately in another database. Only the message ID needs to be stored and can be used to recall the message. Another benefit of using this rule is that the status of each message can be identified and monitored uniquely, as processing of this rule is not automatic and the developer can define the logic based on the status categorized to determine when to pick the message, the frequency of picking it, and the priority of message types. The status of the message needs to be updated as follows:

```
RECEIVED=1
PROCESSED=2
FAILED=3
NORULEDEFINED=4
RUNNING=5
CATEGORIZED=6
```

  where the numbers are used in the MII logic to represent the respective status.

  Generally, to handle a category based processing rule, one scheduler must be scheduled with a MII transaction that can periodically check for any new message in the queue based on the written logic in the BLS.

- *Transaction based processing rule*: This processing rule is directly linked to a BLS. Whenever a new message comes to a specific listener with a specific message type, the BLS is triggered automatically and the message is processed instantly. No message ID concept exists for this rule.

To handle the category-based message processing, these action blocks need to be invoked in BLS:

- *Query Messages action block*: Finds a list of buffered messages by a set of selection criteria.

- *Read Message action block*: Reads the content of the messages received and buffered by Message Services.

- *Update Message action block*: Updates the status and status text for a buffered message, maybe after ad hoc processing by BLS transaction.

- *Delete Message action block*: Deletes a buffered message from the SAP MII database. Like the Read Message and Update Message action blocks, this action block also has no object configuration and only the MessageId needs to be specified in its link configuration.

- *Post Message action block*: Posts the message directly in the same MII server instance.

Integrating SAP ECC and MII Using RFCs (BAPI)

SAP MII BLS offers some powerful action blocks to connect to the SAP ECC to retrieve or write data that comes from the shopfloor. This integration with ECC is provided by SAP JCo or JRA actions to execute the BAPI to connect to SAP systems. See Figure 6-70.

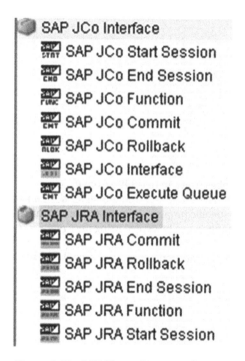

Figure 6-70. SAP JCo and JRA Interface action blocks

To configure a SAP server alias, an alias editor needs to be opened using the SAP MII Data Services ➤ Connections menu option, as shown in Figure 6-71.

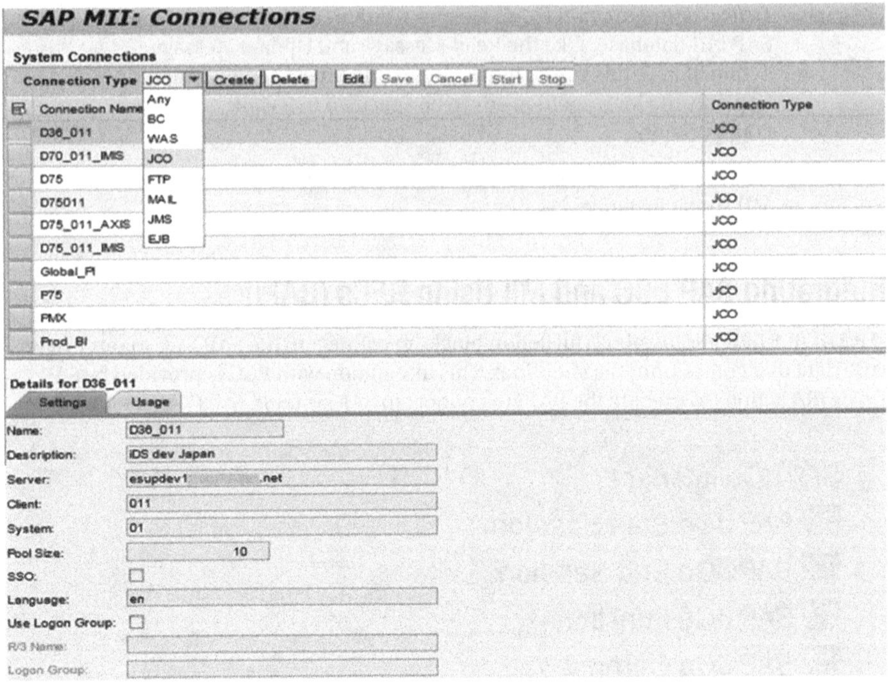

Figure 6-71. *MII Connections screen*

Click on the Create button to create a new alias. You can select JCo from the drop-down. You must specify a unique name, an optional description, and the server hostname or IP address. You must also specify connector-specific properties for the server for which the configuration is created. An existing configuration can be copied using the Copy button and deleted using the Delete button.

Next, you create credential access to the SAP connection being created, as shown in Figure 6-72.

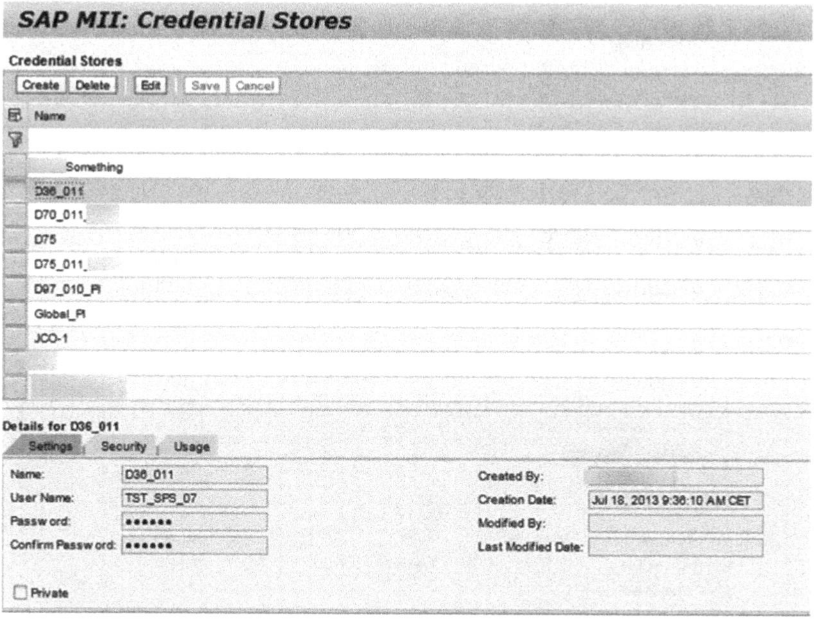

Figure 6-72. *Credential Stores*

Both the JRA and JCo action blocks in SAP MII can connect to SAP ECC through BAPI, but as the SAP JCo action block is more commonly used, we only explain that one in this chapter.

SAP JCo Interface Action Block

The action block that's most commonly used to call the BAPI is the JCo Interface action block without any session handling. The SAP JCo Interface action is used to create a connection to the SAP Java Connector (JCo) interface from the ERP server and create a Remote Function Call (RFC) request to execute the BAPI. See Figure 6-73.

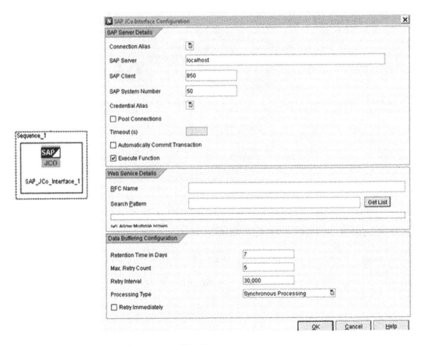

Figure 6-73. JCo Interface action block

The following options must be filled in:

- *Connection Alias*: From this drop-down, you can choose the SAP connection that was created in Step 1. The SAP server, client, and system number will then be auto populated.

- *Credential Alias*: You can choose the specific credential being set up against the connection.

- *RFC Name*: This can be searched using search pattern options and then you can select the desired BAPI from the list.

Web Service Details		
RFC Name		
Search Pattern	BAPI_PROC*	Get List
BAPI_PROCCOMP_READMULTIPLE		
BAPI_PROCDIA_READMULTIPLE		
BAPI_PROCDIA_USED_IN_PROCVAR		

Figure 6-74. Configuring BAPI in the JCo action block

These options must be configured to execute the BAPI and further process in BLS. BAPI can also be called by using the SAP JCo Function action block, but it works with session handling logic (i.e., the SAP Start Session and SAP End Session action blocks).

Integrating SAP MII with an SMTP Server

Simple Mail Transfer Protocol (SMTP) is basically an Internet standard for electronic mail transmission. The following section provides details on how SMTP can be used with SAP MII.

SMTP server can be configured from the SAP MII menu by choosing Connections, as shown in Figure 6-75.

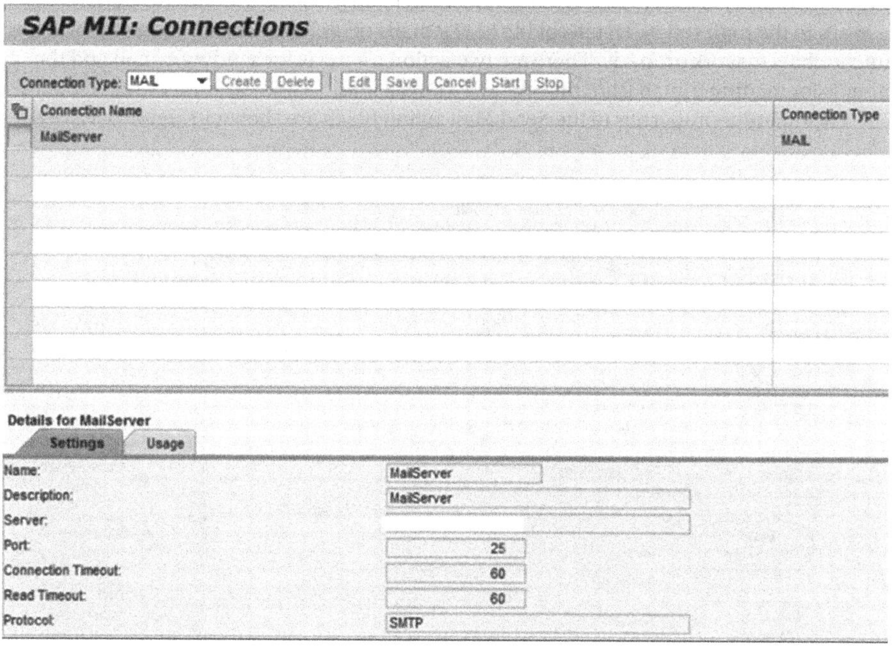

Figure 6-75. *SMTP server connection configuration*

Credentials can be maintained from the credential store similarly as explained for the JCo connection type. This is to facilitate sending e-mail to recipients as per requirements in case any notification must be sent. To fulfill this requirement, SAP MII includes action blocks under the E-mail category, as shown in Figure 6-76.

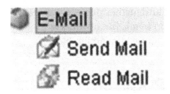

Figure 6-76. *E-Mail action blocks*

This sends an e-mail to recipients mentioned through the SMTP server. The configuration required to carry out this action has to be preconfigured in the connection section and the same can be selected while configuring the e-mail action block in the SAP MII transaction. To configure this action block, a couple of configurations in the SAP MII admin are mandatory. One is the connection details and the other is the credentials to log in to the mail server. Details of the SMTP mail server must also be accessed for this functionality to work properly. There are two actions—one is for sending e-mail and the other is for reading E-mail from the SAP MII Transaction.

The different properties of the Send Mail action block are shown in Figure 6-77.

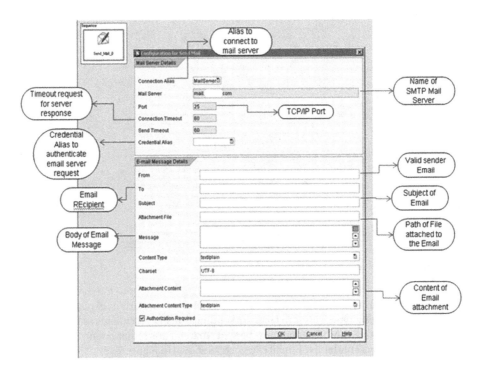

Figure 6-77. *The Send Mail action block*

Similarly, Read Mail also has different properties that need to be set up before using the action block to read the mails. The configurations are similar to Send Mail and are shown in Figure 6-78.

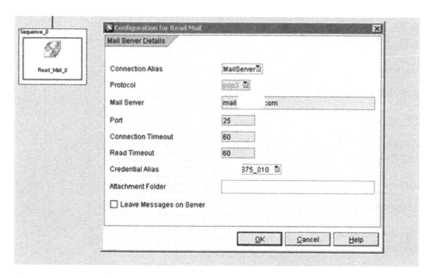

Figure 6-78. *Read Mail action block*

Integrating SAP MII with Web Protocols

SAP MII can be integrated with other legacy systems using standard web protocols like Web Services and HTTP POST. SAP MII has built-in action blocks dedicated to call web services and can also post messages to the server instance.

Web Service Action Block

This executes a web service using its WSDL URL by sending and receiving SOAP messages. The Web Service action block needs to be configured with information like WSDL, authentication, and connection details. See Figure 6-79.

Figure 6-79. *Web Service configuration wizard*

Follow these steps to configure a web service action block:

1. Once the WSDL is entered in the URL field of the configuration wizard, click the Next button.

2. Based on the requirement, the authentication and connection details will be set.

3. In the next view, the required port needs to be selected from the available ports. See Figure 6-80.

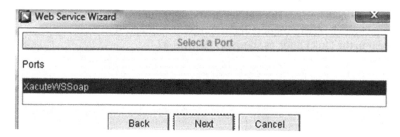

Figure 6-80. *Port selection in Web Service*

4. After selecting the port in the next view, Operation needs to be selected, as shown in Figure 6-81.

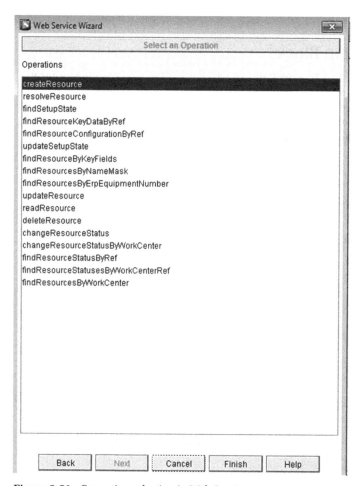

Figure 6-81. *Operation selection in Web Service*

5. Click the Finish button. The web service configuration is now done. The web service request and response structure will appear in the Link Editor, as shown in Figure 6-82.

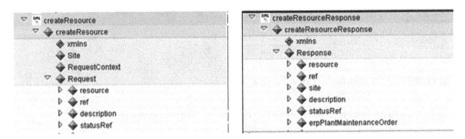

Figure 6-82. *Web Service request and response structure*

HTTP Post Action Block

HTTP Stands for Hyper Text Transfer Protocol, which is used as an application protocol between collaborative, distributed information systems.

Launch the Workbench from the SAP MII portal. In the bottom-left corner, on the Action tab, there is a action menu item called Web. All the HTTP action blocks are available under it, as shown in Figure 6-83.

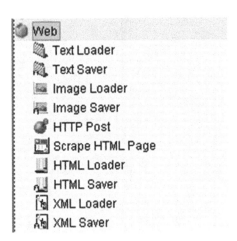

Figure 6-83. *Web action blocks*

The HTTP Post action block can perform the following functionalities (see Figure 6-84):

- Post a document to a specific URL and process it

- Call a web service where valid WSDL definition is not available

- Read information from an RSS feed

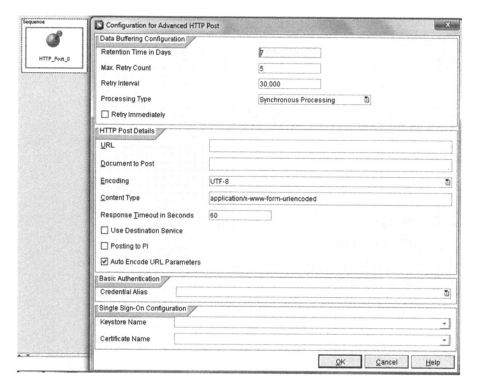

Figure 6-84. *HTTP Post action block*

Available properties are as follows:

- *URL*: URL where the document need to be send.

- *Post Data*: Document to be posted

-, *UserName*: Credential to access the URL

- *User Password*: Credential to access the URL

- *Content Type*: Depends on the document and the type accepted by the URL

- ReturnAsString: Stores return result as a string

- *ReturnAsXML*: Stores the XML if resultant XML is expected

- *UseDestinationService*: Forced to use the specified destination service

Integrating SAP MII with File Systems

The File I/O folder contains all the action blocks that deal with file input and output (see Figure 6-85). Using these set of action blocks, you can write and delete files and create directories in the Workbench. There are action blocks for reading files from external sources using the File Transfer Protocol. Flat file and advanced flat file parsers are actions that parse flat files, where CSV input can be parsed into XML with different structures.

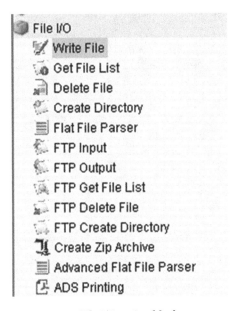

Figure 6-85. *File I/O action blocks*

Get File List Action Block

This action block retrieves a list of files under a specified folder. The Folder path can be from the network shared drive, from a local drive folder (where the MII server is installed), or from the web tab of MII Workbench needs to be specified. If a particular file type needs to be fetched, then the mask feature is there to provide the specific file extension. SAP MII takes the following file types: .csv, .txt, and .xml (or any kind of flat file). See Figure 6-86.

Figure 6-86. *Get File List Action Block*

Write File Action Block

Among all the actions in this set, this is the most common action block and is used quite frequently. This action can be used to write a file that either creates a new file and writes in it or appends in an existing file. The link editor and configuration screen have the following properties. The path to be provided is the link of the text file, as shown in Figure 6-87.

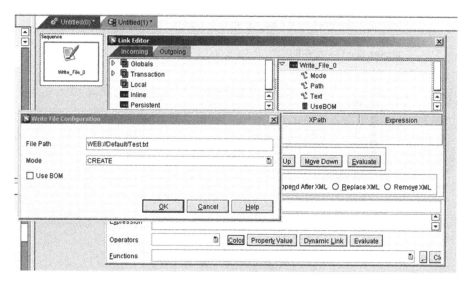

Figure 6-87. *Write File action block*

The web folder path is provided as `WEB://<ProjectName>/<FileName>`. The mode has to be either CREATE or APPEND as per the file. The available text is the text to be written in the file and path has the file path.

When the write file action block is executed, the file is generally created under the Web tab of the Workbench in the specified path defined in the configuration. MES works only with file systems, in which case the write file action block is used to write the file in the MES destination folder. The Use BOM checkbox allows you to write a byte order mark for UTF-8 in front of the file and is applicable only when the file is created. BOM is required for certain programs like Microsoft Excel to recognize a UTF-8 CSV file containing Unicode characters.

The Write File action block is also used to trace the business logic value when the value is required to be traced at runtime directly. In this case, the developer can place the write action block in the respective BLS with the variable defined in configure links to trace the value as desired for debugging. Thus during execution from the frontend, when the control comes to the BLS where the write action block was placed, it executes the block. The developer then can check the exact value being passed from the frontend to the BLS. It helps to analyze the logic if you find any bugs in the code.

- *Delete File action block*: It takes the fully qualified path to delete the specified file.

- *Flat File Parser action block*: It takes as input a Comma Separated Values (CSV) file and converts it to the SAP MII XML format of /rowsets/rowset/row. To use this action block, you have to load a text file loader before calling the flat file parser. The string content of the text loader also needs to be mapped to the input of flat file parser. See Figure 6-88.

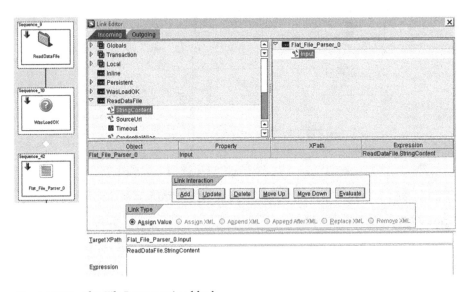

Figure 6-88. *Flat File Parser action block*

- *Advanced Flat File Parser action block*: This is the advanced version of the flat file parser action block. Developers can define additional features while parsing a flat file. You can provide the document configuration to define column properties. The Has Columns checkbox is by default disabled if the columns are not defined. If those are not defined, you can check it. Once it's checked, it means that while generating the output XML, the action block will use the first row or the input data to generate the columns. Otherwise, it will generate columns by string as the datatype. If auto expand is selected, then additional columns defined will be added; otherwise, they will be truncated while generating output. The end of line character lets you specify a character that will act as an end of line character; by default, a line feed or carriage return is treated as the end of line character. Comma is the default delimiter, but you can provide a particular delimiter that will split the different data values within a flat file row and put them in the XML document.

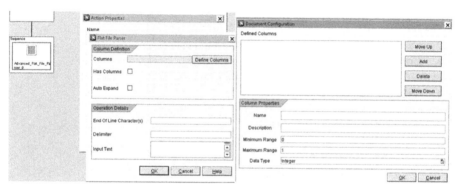

Figure 6-89. *Advanced Flat File Parser Action block*

- *FTP action blocks*: FTP transfers file between devices on a network. To use FTP, SAP MII has some built-in action blocks dedicated to FTP integration. The FTP connection must first be created before you use the FTP action blocks in BLS.

Creating a FTP Connection

File Transfer Protocol (FTP) is a standard network protocol that's used to transfer files from a server to a client using the client-server architecture. Although it is not used much anymore due to poor security, it is still sometimes used for internal file transfers within the same server on a closed, secured network. Follow these steps to create the FTP connection in SAP MII:

1. In the SAP MII portal, navigate to Data Services ➤ Connections, as shown in Figure 6-90.

Figure 6-90. *Data Services Connections selection*

> 2. On the Connections page, Click on Create, as shown in Figure 6-91.

Figure 6-91. *Create SAP MII Connections*

> A popup to create the connection appears.

3. Provide a name for the connection. Select FTP for the connection type and click on OK. See Figure 6-92.

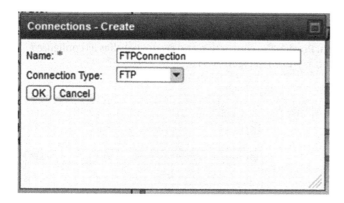

Figure 6-92. *Creating an FTP connection*

4. Now provide the server IP and port of the destination system and save, as shown in Figure 6-93.

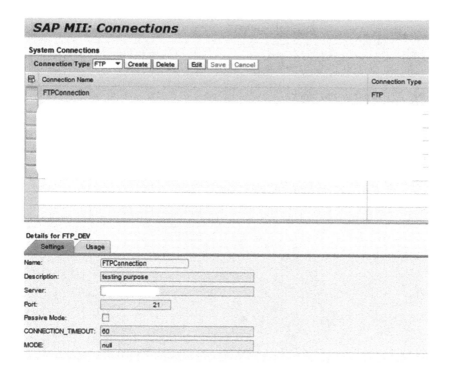

Figure 6-93. *FTP Connections configuration*

The FTP connection is created now.

5. Use the Connection alias in the configuration link of the FTP action blocks in SAP MII to connect to the FTP server.

FTP Input: This action block is used to fetch and view the content of a file available at a specified remote location. Provide the connection and credential alias as configured and the remote file and folder, as shown in Figure 6-94.

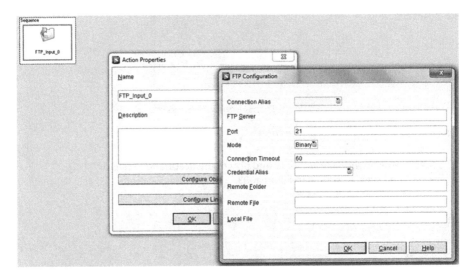

Figure 6-94. *FTP Input action block*

FTP Output: This action block is used to create file to a specified remote folder path. It also allows you to append content of a file available at a specific location. See Figure 6-95.

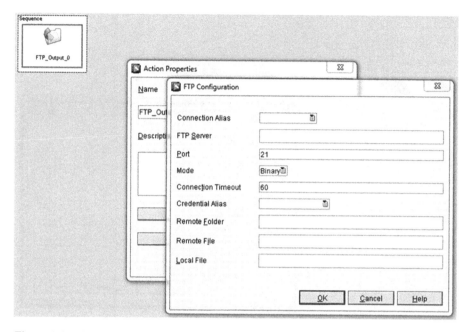

Figure 6-95. *FTP Output action block*

FTP Get File List: This action block fetches the list of all files available in a specified remote location. The list can be filtered depending on mask (file format) and date time format. See Figure 6-96.

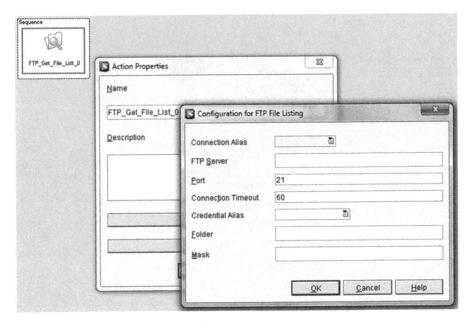

Figure 6-96. *FTP Get File List action block*

FTP Delete File: This action block deletes all the available files from a specified remote folder path. See Figure 6-97.

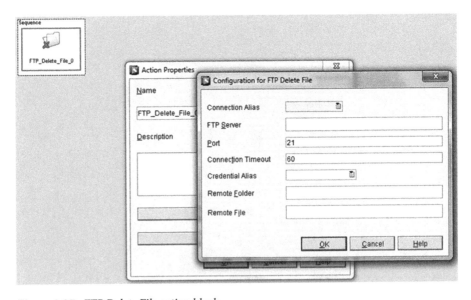

Figure 6-97. *FTP Delete File action block*

FTP Create Directory: This action block creates a new folder at a specified remote location. See Figure 6-98.

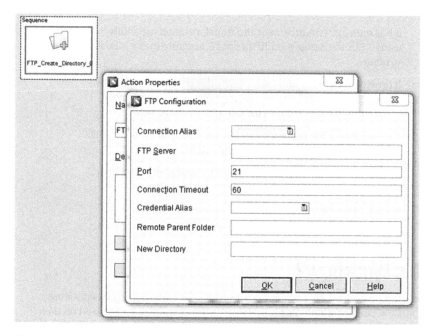

Figure 6-98. *FTP Create directory action block*

Integrating SAP MII with Other Manufacturing Products

SAP has few other manufacturing products to help process executions. Two major manufacturing products of SAP are SAP ME and SAP OEE. SAP ME is mainly for discrete industries and intended users of SAP OEE product are process industries. Both products consist of two segments of the product—process handling with multiple functional screens and integration.

Process handling with multiple screens is developed by SAP on top of SAP MII and that is standard as those are products of SAP. For the integration, both products have their own components—MEINT and OEEINT. As the architecture of both products are the same, so the processing steps are the same for both products. MEINT and OEEINT are dedicated to connect to SAP ECC. To install MEINT and OEEINT, you need to execute one CTC wizard file specific to MEINT or OEEINT on NetWeaver. When you execute this file, all the standard configurations for MEINT and OEEINT are configured automatically (including the Scheduler, Message Service, Listener, etc.). The only customizable parts of MEINT and OEEINT are the workflow, supported plants, and global configuration.

SAP OEEINT and MEINT using SAP MII provides the following features:

- It provides a standard interface to integrate with SAP ERP and SAP ME/OEE for all message types.

- It has message enhancement and transformation capability using XSLT to change the ERP message structure into a MES level structure.

- It provides flexibility and extensibility through the interface by allowing users to define their own specific customized logic configured in the workflows for different message types.

- Extensibility of the interface can also be provided using ME-SDK Java based customization or by using MII BLS.

- Bi-directional data processing is possible and plant specific or message type specific data handling is also possible.

- Robust message monitoring functionalities is available with proper execution results for each step of the workflow.

What Is Workflow?

Workflow is the predefined dependent execution of steps where users can either use the standard available components for that step or can customize steps based on their requirements. Workflow involves multiple steps that make the integration steps more flexible so that one message can be manipulated and validated multiple times during processing and the final manipulated message can be passed to the shopfloor through MES, which can be executed directly. Workflow works bi-directionally, so workflow customization is possible for message flow from ECC to ME/OEE and vice versa.

There are three types of workflows available:

- *Standard workflow*: This helps transform the inbound message and can transfer it to destination system. This is the only workflow that can send the data to other systems. This workflow can work bi-directionally from ECC to ME/OEE or vice versa.

- *Split workflow*: This is based on certain conditions on which it can split the inbound messages into multiple messages with different message types. This workflow is dependent on standard workflow, i.e., split workflow provides the data on the standard workflow, which finally pushes the data into the destination system. Generally split workflow is used for ECC to ME/OEE single directional flow. For example, if MATMAS 02 comes from ECC and there is multiple plant scenario for SAP ME/OEE, split workflow will split the MATMAS02 into multiple messages based on plant IDs to send the messages to ME/OEE using the plant-specific web services.

- *Co-relational workflow*: This has the opposite functionality of split workflow. This workflow merges different message types into one message and passes them to the standard workflow.

Configuring Workflow

The major customizations are handled through workflow in MEINT and OEEINT. There are seven steps involved in workflow configuration. The following are the steps needed to configure the workflow:

1. Pre-XSLT transaction

2. Request XSLT

3. Post-XSLT transaction

4. Service transaction

5. Response XSLT

6. Pass handler

7. Fail handler

Apart from this, for each segment there are three sections as per their execution priority:

- *Customer*: This is defined as part of customization as required by the client organization's IT team.

- *Partner*: This is defined by the SAP partners providing the solution to the customer client.

- *Standard*: This is defined by SAP to provide a standardized solution.

At the time of customization, it is always best for the partner to check first if any standard transactions or XSLT are defined in the standard section. If there are, the partner should copy the standard content and then the customization should be done on that. Similarly, the customer should first see if the partner solution is available. If it is, it will customize on the partner solution; otherwise, it will go for the standard solution if it's available.

In both integration components, SAP provides a standard workflow for most of the messages available in ECC, but sometimes it's necessary to do co-customizations on the standard messages. For example, BOMMAT03 is a standard IDoc in ECC, so ECC directly sends BOMMAT03 to be transferred to ME/OEE. In MEINT and OEEINT, standard workflow for BOMMAT03 is available. But sometimes due to customer requirements, you must customize BOMMAT03 and then renamed to Z_BOMMAT03. To handle these customizations, you also must customize the standard workflow in MEINT/OEEINT.

It is up to the developer to decide into which step of the workflow the changes need to be incorporated in order to handle the customized IDoc based on the required changes. It is possible to handle this in two ways—by enhancing the standard BOMMAT03 workflow or by copying the standard workflow and creating a new workflow with the changes.

If workflow customizations are completed using MII transactions, then the following transaction properties for the BLS are always fixed:

- Variable Name: InputXML, Datatype: XML, Variable Type: Input

- Variable Name: OutputXML, Datatype: XML, Variable Type: Output

- Variable Name: Error, Datatype: String, Variable Type: Output

At the time of workflow execution, the output of the first step acts as the output of the second step and so on until the execution is complete. For example, the IDoc message will be the input for Pre-XSLT Transaction step and the output of Pre-XSLT transaction will be the input for Request XSLT and so on. Figure 6-99 shows the workflow steps: how they execute and how customization is possible.

Message Type:	BOMMAT03 🔳
Workflow:	Standard Workflow
Workflow Handler:	java.com.sap.me.integration.frame.workflow.StandardWorkflow

Workflow Handler Parameters:	plant=/BOMMAT03/IDOC/E1STZUM/E1MASTM/WERKS;identifier=concat(/BOMMAT0:
Retry Limit:	3

Pre XSLT Transaction:	
Pre XSLT Transaction Parameters:	
Partner Pre XSLT Transaction:	
Partner Pre XSLT Transaction Parameters:	
Customer Pre XSLT Transaction:	
Customer Pre XSLT Transaction Parameters:	

Request XSLT Address:	WEB://Visiprise/XSLT/Inbound/BOM/BOMRequest.xslt
Partner Request XSLT Address:	
Customer Request XSLT Address:	

Post XSLT Transaction:	
Post XSLT Transaction Parameters:	
Partner Post XSLT Transaction:	
Partner Post XSLT Transaction Parameters:	
Customer Post XSLT Transaction:	
Customer Post XSLT Transaction Parameters:	

Service Transaction:	Visiprise/ERPShopFloorIntegration/frame/workflow/MEWebService
Service Transaction Parameters:	serviceUrl=manufacturing-erpservices/ErpBOMService;timeOutInSec=60
Partner Service Transaction:	
Partner Service Transaction Parameters:	
Customer Service Transaction:	
Customer Service Transaction Parameters:	

Response XSLT Address:	WEB://Visiprise/XSLT/Inbound/GenericResponse.xslt
Partner Response XSLT Address:	
Customer Response XSLT Address:	

Pass Handler Transaction:	
Pass Handler Transaction Parameters:	
Partner Pass Handler Transaction:	
Partner Pass Handler Transaction Parameters:	
Customer Pass Handler Transaction:	
Customer Pass Handler Transaction Parameters:	

Fail Handler Transaction:	
Fail Handler Transaction Parameters:	
Partner Fail Handler Transaction:	
Partner Fail Handler Transaction Parameters:	
Customer Fail Handler Transaction:	
Customer Fail Handler Transaction Parameters:	

Save Request XML:	true ▼
Save Response XML:	true ▼

Figure 6-99. *The Workflow Configuration screen*

- *Pre-XSLT Transaction*: Supports SAP MII Transactions and Java classes (from ME 6.0 and OEE 1.0). If validation and customization are required in the received IDoc message, this step is ideal for this scenario.

185

- *Request XSLT*: Supports XSLT only. In this step, IDoc message structure is transformed into the shopfloor level message structure. If required, customization is also possible in this step by making changes to the XSLT file.

- *Post-XSLT Transaction*: Supports MII Transactions and Java classes (from ME 6.0 and OEE 1.0). After the transformation of the XML into the shopfloor message structure, if more validations or customization are required, this is where to do them.

- *Service Transaction*: It supports MII Transactions and Java classes(from ME 6.0 and OEE 1.0).In this step standard web services are by default configured to push the messages into the destination systems through web services.

- *Response XSLT*: Supports XSLT only. In this step the response of the web service execution is transformed to readable XML format from the web service output.

- *Pass Handler and Fail Handler*: Supports MII Transactions and Java classes (from ME 6.0 and OEE 1.0). Based on the response XSLT step, if the service transaction execution is successful, the pass handler will be called where some activities, such as notification or acknowledgement trigger etc. are possible. If the execution fails, the fail handler will be called to take further action, such as logging the exact error message.

Summary

In this chapter, you learned about the different integrations possible through SAP MII and their respective configuration steps. You also learned about the basics of SAP MII query templates, transactions, and action blocks that, as a new developer, you need to know in SAP MII. The concept of SAP MII integrations with other SAP manufacturing product integration modules, i.e., MEINT and OEEINT, was also discussed.

In the next chapter, you will learn about newly added features in SAP MII.

CHAPTER 7

■ ■ ■

New Features of SAP MII

With the advancement in the technology, SAP MII has evolved with new patches and upgraded versions. It started with SAP MII version 11.5 and the latest version is 15.1.

This chapter explains the new features available in SAP MII. The following features of SAP MII are covered in this chapter:

- MDO

- Visualization services

- UI5 and SSCE

- KPI and alerts

- PIC

- PCo

- Session handling in queries and JRA

- New action blocks from SAP 15.X

What Are MDOs?

MDOs are the manufacturing data objects that can store data in the SAP MII backend application DB, which is received from different data sources and configured and integrated with SAP MII. It is used to define the data object model's structure and to persist the data. This feature was added in the 12.2 version of SAP MII and was further enhanced in later versions.

When you need to refer to a set of data that's not being updated too frequently, it is best to use an MDO as storage. Though SAP MII can integrate with external storage systems, many times, due to an external database server crash, connectivity issues, and security access issues, SAP MII will not be able to fetch data from an external database. Apart from that, external databases require additional cost and maintenance. They need additional expert resources to handle them. SAP has designed the MDO in such a way that if SAP MII uses the MDO, it will be stored in the backend application. MDO storage will happen in standard DB; otherwise, if SAP MII is installed on top of the HANA platform, the MDO storage will be in HANA DB. HANA in-memory processing is faster so MDO data processing will also be faster if it's stored in HANA DB. No additional cost is required to keep the data in MDO, and developers with SAP MII expertise can also handle the MDO and its design.

© Suman Mukherjee and Saptaparna Mukherjee (Das) 2017
S. Mukherjee and S. Mukherjee (Das), *SAP MII*, DOI 10.1007/978-1-4842-2814-2_7

How MDOs Work

As the name suggests, MDOs are instances of manufacturing data objects. Developers can create MDOs from the Object tab in Workbench, just like any other object type.

As soon as an MDO object is created in the MII Workbench, a data object is created in the SAP MII database. Object creation involves creating a table with column definitions. That newly created data object points to a newly created database table specific to that MDO. Any data operation done to that MDO will in turn be stored in the corresponding database table.

SAP MII provides three types of MDOs:

- Persistent MDOs

- On-demand MDOs

- Joined MDOs

Persistent MDOs

These are like physical database tables. Internally, SAP MII creates a data table for any persistent MDO that is available in the same database where SAP MII is installed and uses the same underlying application database schema. Persistent MDOs can retain the data stored in the MDO until it is manually deleted.

On-Demand MDOs

No physical data tables are created for on-demand MDOs. There is no option to store data in the database. Data is populated on demand. When data from an on-demand MDO is queried, the Data Provider runs in the backend to provide datasets at runtime and the data exists until runtime. Data instances cannot be retrieved once the MDO is executed.

Joined MDOs

These are joins of two or more persistent MDOs to get a combined view of multiple MDO tables. Joined MDOs support INNER joins and LEFT OUTER joins between the MDOs.

Creating MDOs

The following sections describe how to create the MDO types in SAP MII.

Creating a Persistent MDO

Follow these steps to create a persistent MDO:

1. Open SAP MII Workbench.

2. Open the Object tab.

3. Right-click on the folder where the MDO object needs to be created.

4. Select New File ➤ Persistent MDO, as shown in Figure 7-1.

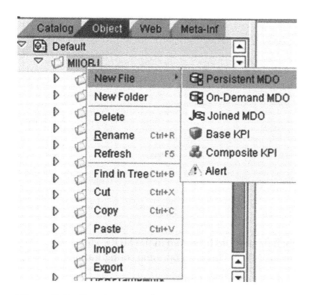

Figure 7-1. *Creating a persistent MDO*

5. The list of available screens for an MDO can be found at the bottom-left corner of the page under the Template Categories tab (see Figure 7-2). The available configurations are as follows:

- Data Provider

- Attributes

- Properties

- Lifecycle

- Visualization

- Security

189

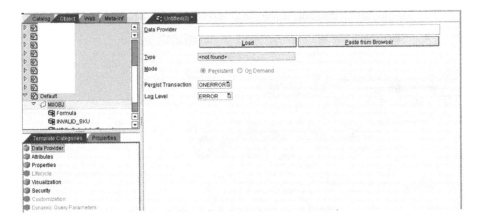

Figure 7-2. The MDO Data Provider Screen

Data Provider

Data Provider is the object from which data would be stored in the MDO. This configuration provides initial data to the MDO. This is an optional configuration.

1. To define the Data Provider, click on the Load button, as shown in Figure 7-3.

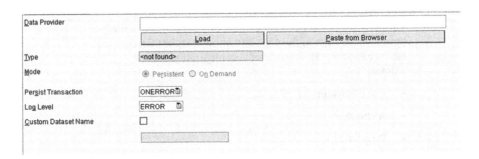

Figure 7-3. Defining a Data Provider

2. Select the object (BLS or Query template) from the available tree, as shown in Figure 7-4.

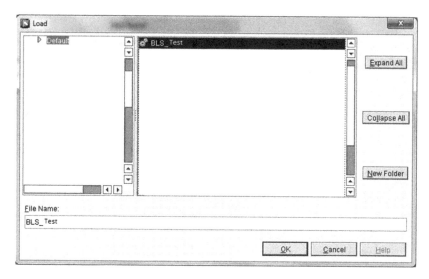

Figure 7-4. *Loading the object*

3. Click on OK to confirm the object for Data Provider and then select the Attributes configuration from the left template panel.

Attributes

This configuration defines the data structure and design for the data model. Attributes are mandatory.

1. When you select the Attributes configuration, the screen in Figure 7-5 appears.

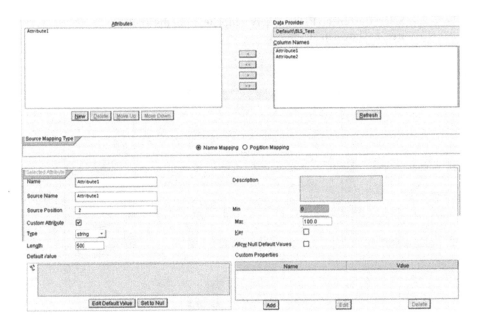

Figure 7-5. *MDO Attribute Configuration screen*

Column Names lists all columns as per the Data Provider. The required columns can be dragged and dropped under the Attribute list. If no Data Provider is mentioned initially, then it is mandatory to define the attributes by clicking the New button and assigning the properties of the attributes.

The Source Mapping Type radio buttons specify whether you want to map the attributes by name or position. You can modify the attribute values. Two different types of attributes are:

- Data attribute (directly mapped to the columns of the Data Provider)

- Custom attribute (not mapped to the columns of the Data Provider and newly created by the developer)

Source Name: In the case of the Data Attribute type, the source name links the MDO attribute name to the Data Provider attribute name and must exactly match the Data Provider attribute name.

Source Position: When the Data Provider is used then the source position can be provided and the attribute takes in the output as returned in the dataset by the Data Provider.

Custom Attribute: This feature is bound to the attribute whenever any new attribute is created without reference to a Data Provider (source name and position).

Key: If this checkbox is selected, the attribute behaves like a primary key of the MDO table structure.

Allow Null default Values: If this is checked then the column will allow a default null value into the MDO table; otherwise, the column has to be inserted with a value.

A default value can be defined for that column, so in case no value is passed to MDO table, it can take the default value defined against the attribute column.

Lifecycle

Lifecycle can be used to define the duration the data will persist in the MDO. This is applicable only to persistent MDOs. This is visible only when the Data Provider is selected. See Figure 7-6.

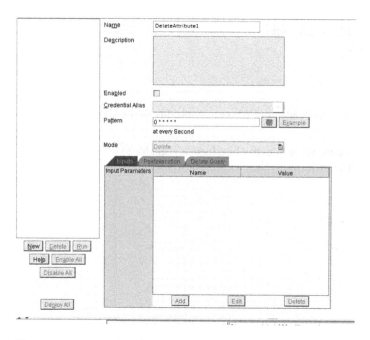

Figure 7-6. *MDO Lifecycle configuration*

Any Task can be scheduled based on the pattern defined. You need to provide a credential alias to execute it from the scheduler. The following types of modes are available:

- *Replace*: When the MDO Data Provider is executed, the persisted data is deleted and replaced with the resulting dataset.

- *Update*: When the MDO Data Provider is executed, the persisted data is updated with the resulting dataset, which is based on the key attributes for the MDO.

- *Delete*: When the MDO Data Provider is executed, the persisted data stored in the MDO will be completely deleted.

- *Inputs*: The Data Provider Transactional or Query Input parameters can be provided by default values for runtime execution.

- *Post-execution*: This defines any transaction found to be necessary as part of the dependent logic in the process, after the MDO is executed with Replace, Update, Delete mode.

- *Delete Query*: This defines the Query template to be executed to delete the MDO data. This tab is enabled only if the Delete mode is selected.

Security

This configuration defines the Reader and Writer role sections for the MDO object to be executed.

1. The Reader and Writer roles can be added as available in NetWeaver from the available roles drop-down, as shown in Figure 7-7.

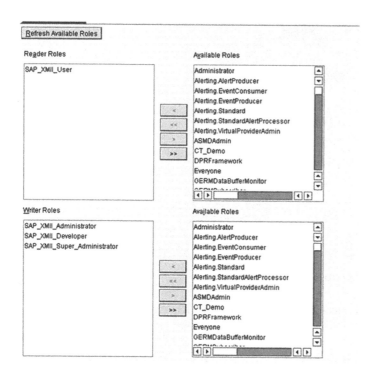

Figure 7-7. *The MDO Security configuration*

The persistent MDO is created and executed now.

Creating an On-Demand MDO

On-demand mode MDOs refer to data that is retrieved from the defined Data Provider when a query request is issued to the object. This data can be all of the object data or a filtered subset of the Data Provider content, depending on your reporting needs. It does not persist the data, so no INSERT/UPDATE/DELETE MDO queries can be used here. Step-wise creation is the same as with a persistent MDO.

Creating a Joined MDO

Follow these steps to join two or more MDOs:

1. Open the SAP MII Workbench.

2. Open the Object tab.

3. Right-click on the folder where the MDO object needs to be created.

4. Select New File ➤ Joined MDO, as shown in Figure 7-8.

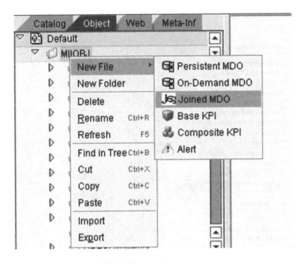

Figure 7-8. Joined MDO creation

5. When you select the joined MDO, the screen in Figure 7-9 appears.

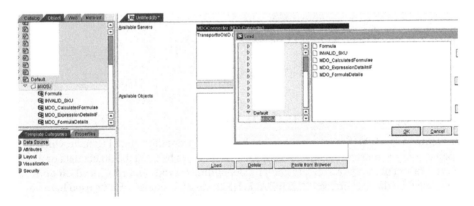

Figure 7-9. The joined MDO object selection

The following configurations are possible:

*   Data Source

*   Attributes

*   Layout

*   Visualization

*   Security

Data Source

Data Source provides the configurations for selecting server and MDO objects to apply to the join. The available servers option lists the MDO connectors configured on the MII server, among which only one MDO connector needs to be selected.

The available objects option enables you to browse through all the project's MDOs available on the server. You can load multiple MDOs from multiple projects from the available list.

Attributes

You can select attributes from the respective available MDO objects. At least one condition needs to be defined for the INNER or LEFT OUTER INNER join (see Figure 7-10). Further, a WHERE clause could be specified with the help of filter expressions. The following options are available:

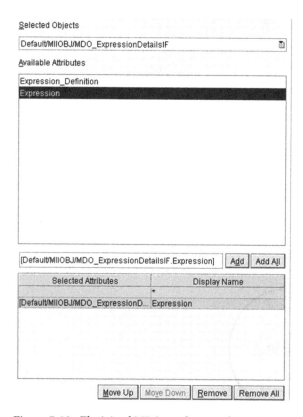

Figure 7-10. *The joined MDO attribute configuration screen*

- *Selected Objects*: This lists all the MDOs selected in the previous step for JOIN operation.

- *Available Attributes*: This lists the attributes for the selected MDOs from Selected Objects list.

- *Selected Attributes*: Whatever attributes are selected and added for the JOIN operation will be listed under this section table.

- *Display Name*: You can change the JOIN output name of the column as desired.

Figure 7-11 shows how join types can be selected.

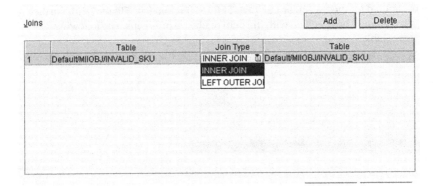

Figure 7-11. *Available joins in a joined MDO*

■ **Note** An INNER join is the same as a JOIN. They are also referred to as EQUIJOINs. The SQL INNER join returns the records where `table1` and `table2` intersect an INNER join. See Figure 7-12.

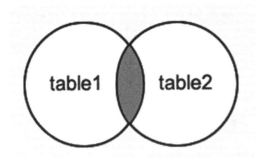

Figure 7-12. *Example of an INNER join*

LEFT OUTER join: The LEFT OUTER join returns all rows from the left-side table specified in the ON condition and only those rows from the other table where the joined fields are equal (where the join condition is met). See Figure 7-13.

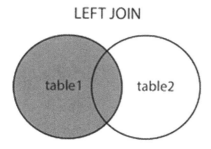

Figure 7-13. Example of a LEFT OUTER join

1. At least one condition needs to be defined between the MDOs to apply the join to the available operators, as shown in Figure 7-14.

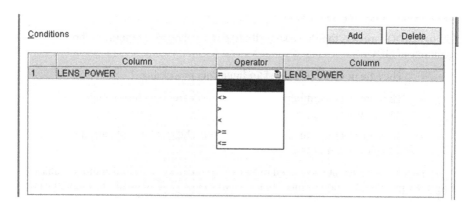

Figure 7-14. Condition available in a joined MDO

2. Further, you can filter the attributes selected for the join output, as shown in Figure 7-15.

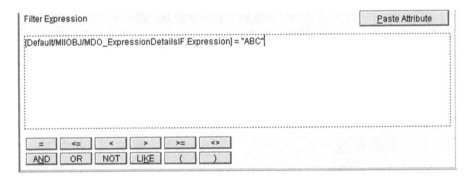

Figure 7-15. *Filter expression in a joined MDO*

Layout

Displays the graphical view of the joins between the MDO objects. This screen reflects any changes made on the Attribute tab.

Security

The same as for persistent and on-demand MDOs.

Limitations of MDOs

Although MDOs are free, they have some limitations. Following are some of the limitations of MDOs:

- They are not recommended for huge data processing.

- They are not recommended when there are frequent hits of high data volume.

- They are not recommended for querying a high volume of data at a single execution call.

Details of the MDO tables created in MII are stored in the backend standard tables using a unique identification number (such as MDO3567) and not with the name the user provided while creating the MDO. That makes it very difficult to identify specific MDOs from the backend MII standard table through Illuminator services. SAP will likely change the design of MDOs in the next release so that it will be easier to call MDOs when fetching the different details dynamically.

Visualization Services

Data visualization is the practice of visual communication (descriptive statistics) that involves study and visual representation of data. Data visualization services visualize data interactively. They begin with data analysis and end with final designed and developed product. A final product can be interactive reports, dashboards, interactive presentation apps (mobile or web), etc.

Like many other platforms, SAP MII let users create dashboard objects and web pages that can be used in various kinds of applications. SAP MII visualization services are divided into two parts:

- Dynamic page generators
- Animated objects

Dynamic Page Generator

This creates an SAP MII based HTML page content or chart servlet URL. This can be accomplished by selecting the appropriate display template and query template and various other properties related to dimensions and other configurations.

Follow these steps to create display templates:

1. On the SAP MII administration menu, choose Content Development ➤ Workbench.

The SAP MII Workbench screen appears. Do one of the following:

2. Choose File ➤ New to display the template types you can create.

There are display templates that are applet based and there are some newly added ones that are UI5 based. See Figure 7-16.

The different display templates available are as follows:

- iGrid
- iTicker
- iChart
- iSPC Chart
- iBrowser
- iCommand
- iCalendar
- i5Chart
- i5Grid
- i5SPC Chart
- i5ValueHelp

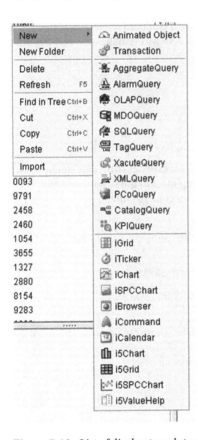

Figure 7-16. *List of display templates in SAP MII*

Apart from these display templates, the Animated Objects option is also available and SVG images can be altered using it (Animated Objects are covered later in this chapter). The following sections cover some frequently used display templates.

iGrid

Data can be viewed using the Grid display template using SAP MII connectors. You can define color context-sensitive highlighting to accentuate data elements based on data values or ranges. A grid can be used to present a single or multiple selection listbox to the users. Here are the iGrid properties that can be configured from the SAP MII Workbench (see Figure 7-17):

- Grid Area
- Layout
- Header
- UI Behavior

- Row Heading

- Color Context

- Context Menu Behaviors

- Refresh Page

- Security

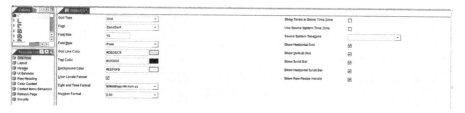

Figure 7-17. *iGrid configuration*

iTicker

Enables a scrolling stock ticker that can display data returned from any SAP MII connector. The iTicker uses the applet height and width tags to automatically size the applet window. Ticker text is automatically centered vertically. Data values can be highlighted in different colors in the ticker.

Configurable iTicker properties include the following (see Figure 7-18):

- Ticker Area

- Data Mapping

- Color Context

- Refresh Page

- Security

Text Color	#00FF00		Scroll Delay	30
Background Color	#000000		Font	Arial
Include Column Names	☐		Font Size	16
Color by Column	☐		Font Style	Plain
User Locale Format	☑		Border Color	#FFFFFF
Date and Time Format	MM/dd/yyyy HH:mm:ss		Border Width	4
Number Format	0.00		Use Source System Time Zone	☐
Show Times in Server Time Zone	☐		Source System Timezone	
Number of Cell Padding Spaces	3			

Figure 7-18. *iTicker configuration*

iChart

Processes and displays datasets with up to 32 tags and thousands of observations per tag in a variety of chart types. SAP MII uses the iChart applet, which supports the SelectionEvent applet parameter and allows JavaScript functions to be linked to items in the chart legend.

iChart properties can be configured on the following screens of the SAP MII Workbench (see Figure 7-19):

- Chart Area
- Title
- Data Mapping
- Legend
- X-Axis
- Y-Axis
- Server Scaling
- Data Series Details
- Context Menu Behaviors
- Refresh Page
- Security

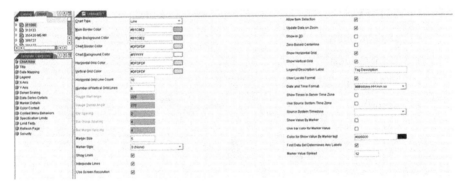

Figure 7-19. iChart configuration

iSPC Chart

Processes and displays datasets with thousands of observations per tag in a variety of statistical process control (SPC) chart formats. Each SPC chart includes the following (see Figure 7-20):

- A set of summary statistics appropriate for the analysis type

- Raw data views and full statistical calculation result views

- SPC rule violations with drill-down capability on a point-by-point basis

- Additional attribute information for each point

- Collaborative point documentation capabilities

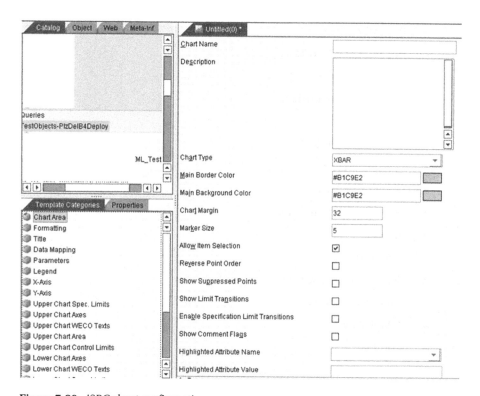

Figure 7-20. *iSPC chart configuration*

Figure 7-20 shows different views or multi-dimensions of the data that can be displayed while interacting with the SPC charts of the application. When the user clicks on a data point in the SPC chart, the screens are updated to show information specific to that point. If additional data of any dimension is returned from the data query linked to the SPC chart, that can be displayed as added context to the view.

Here are the iSPC chart configurable properties in SAP MII Workbench:

- Chart Area

- Formatting

- Title

- Data Mapping

- Parameters

- Legend

- X-Axis

- Y-Axis

- Upper Chart Spec. Limits

- Upper Chart Axes

- Upper Chart WECO Texts

- Upper Chart Area

- Upper Chart Control Limits

- Lower Chart Axes

- Lower Chart WECO Texts

- Lower Chart Spec. Limits

- Lower Chart Area

- Lower Chart Control Limits

- Alarms

- Limit Texts

- Context Menu Behaviors

- Context Menu Security

- Refresh Page

- Security

iBrowser

Using iBrowser, you can map data from a range of sources to the SAP MII tree, list, or drop-down list views, which provide selection, drill-down, and other functions.

When a query is created to map to a browser, the following applies:

- When a single column is returned from the query, the browser is configured as a listbox or a drop-down listbox.

- When two columns are returned and the Data Link Mode is selected, the second column shows the data link value for the item and the column is hidden. The browser is configured as a listbox or a drop-down listbox.

- When two columns are returned and the Data Link Mode checkbox is not selected, the browser is configured as a tree. The query must return the name of the item in the first column and the name of its parent item in the second column.

- When three or more columns are returned, the browser is configured as a tree. The query must return the name of the item in the first column and the name of its parent item in the second column.

- When four columns are returned and the Data Link Mode checkbox is selected, the system assumes the first column includes an item, the second column includes the parent node, the third column includes the data link value for the item, and the fourth column includes the data link value for the parent node.

- When the browser is configured as a tree, a selected node can be deselected by pressing Ctrl and clicking the node or by pressing the spacebar when the tree has focus.

Here are the configurable iBrowser properties in the SAP MII Workbench (see Figure 7-21):

- General

- Data Mapping

- Security

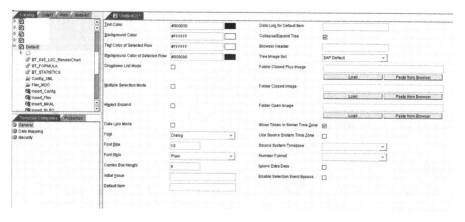

Figure 7-21. *iBrowser configuration*

iCommand

iCommand allows the execution of SQL command queries without performing an HTTP POST. Because it can hold the dataset, a data query template can be loaded into a hidden object on the screen and that data can be used in DHTML, HTML tables, other applets, etc. iCommand does not necessarily require display elements to be defined and the applet does not require any pre-execution of the template query request. That makes it more efficient than a grid.

Electronic signature and audit logging is supported by SAP MII through the iCommand applet. This functionality enables end users to implement 21 CFR Part 11-compliant solutions. There are special settings in an iCommand applet display template for these functions. See Figure 7-22.

The following configurations are available:

- General

- Security

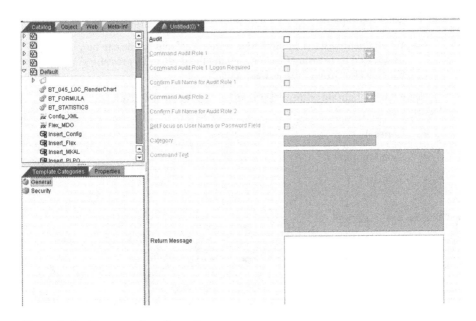

Figure 7-22. *iCommand configuration*

iCalendar

A calendar on an applet can be included and linked to other applets or web page form elements. SAP MII supports the Gregorian calendar only. It is recommended to set the applet dimensions to 200 pixels wide by 188 pixels high. See Figure 7-23.

The following configuration options are available:

- General
- Security

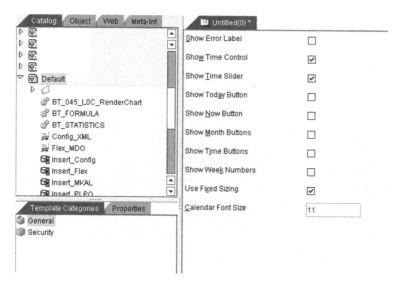

Figure 7-23. *iCalendar configuration*

i5Grid

In the latest versions of SAP MII (from MII 14.0 SP04), some UI5 based display templates have been added along with applet based display templates web page or browser-based scripting. JavaScript can be used to dynamically control the behavior and appearance of an i5Grid or similar display templates, including methods and events. These are basically grids where data from queries are being loaded. They have faster execution times than applets. See Figure 7-24.

Figure 7-24. i5Grid creation

Figure 7-25 shows the example of an i5Grid marked with all the available properties.

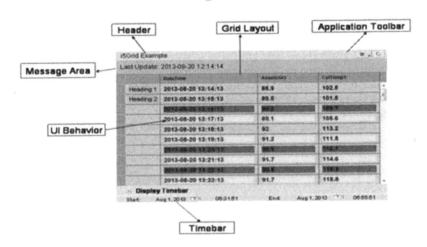

Figure 7-25. Graphical representation of an i5Grid

Here is a list of the configurations available in i5Grid. Grid area is one of main configurations to populate the grid. See Figure 7-26.

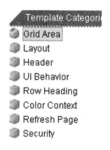

Figure 7-26. i5Grid configuration options

- *i5Grid Area*: Grid Area configuration configures the general properties of the display template. In Grid Area, grid type can be specified. See Figure 7-27.

Figure 7-27. Various configurations of i5Grid

- *i5Grid Layout*: Layout configuration configures the data source and the column properties of the i5Grid. See Figure 7-28.

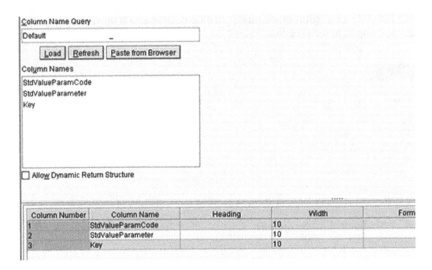

Figure 7-28. *i5Grid layout configuration*

- *i5Grid Header:* This configures the header property. See Figure 7-29.

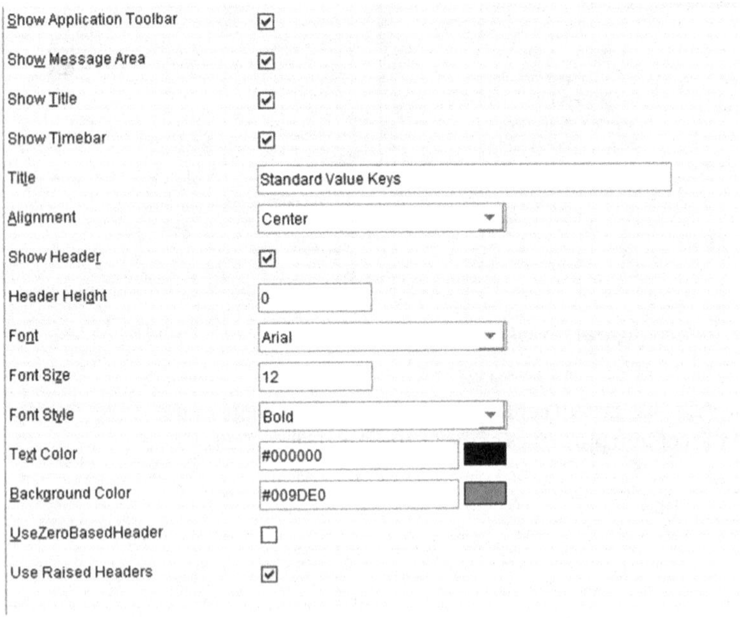

Show Application Toolbar	☑
Show Message Area	☑
Show Title	☑
Show Timebar	☑
Title	Standard Value Keys
Alignment	Center ▼
Show Header	☑
Header Height	0
Font	Arial ▼
Font Size	12
Font Style	Bold ▼
Text Color	#000000 ⬛
Background Color	#009DE0 ⬛
UseZeroBasedHeader	☐
Use Raised Headers	☑

Figure 7-29. *i5Grid header configuration*

- *i5Grid UI Behavior*: User interface behavior of the i5Grid can be defined. See Figure 7-30.

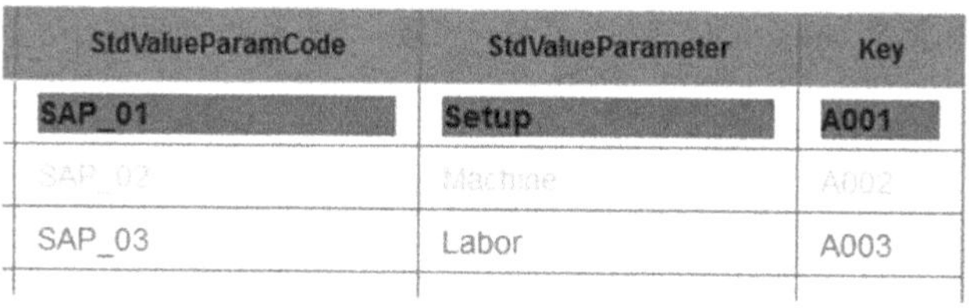

StdValueParamCode	StdValueParameter	Key
SAP_01	Setup	A001
SAP_02	Machine	A002
SAP_03	Labor	A003

Figure 7-30. *i5Grid UI behavior sample*

The UI behavior can be configured in i5Grid display, as shown in Figure 7-31.

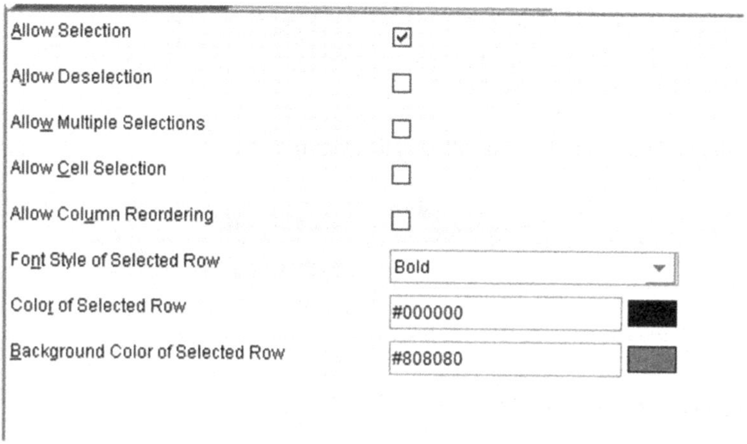

Allow Selection	☑
Allow Deselection	☐
Allow Multiple Selections	☐
Allow Cell Selection	☐
Allow Column Reordering	☐
Font Style of Selected Row	Bold ▼
Color of Selected Row	#000000
Background Color of Selected Row	#808080

Figure 7-31. *i5Grid UI behavior configuration*

- *i5Grid Row Heading*: Row headings of SAP MII grids can be set. See Figure 7-32.

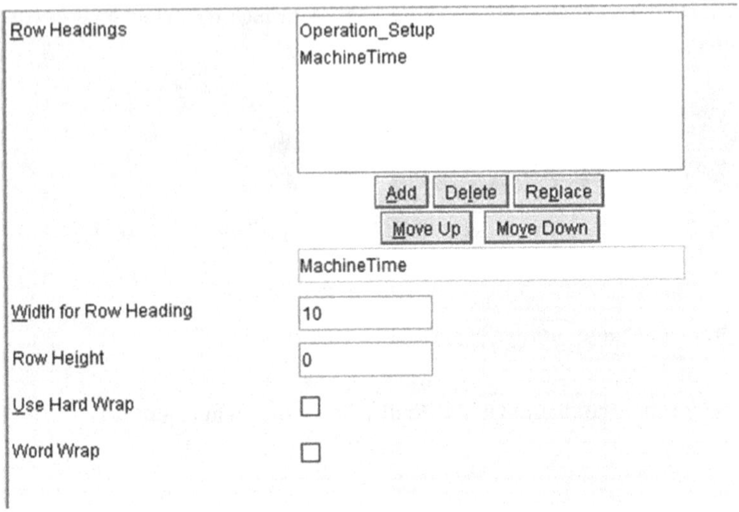

Row Headings
Operation_Setup
MachineTime
Add
Delete
Replace
Move Up
Move Down
MachineTime
Width for Row Heading
10
Row Height
0
Use Hard Wrap
Word Wrap

Figure 7-32. *i5Grid row heading configuration*

Once the row heading is set, the grid will look like Figure 7-33.

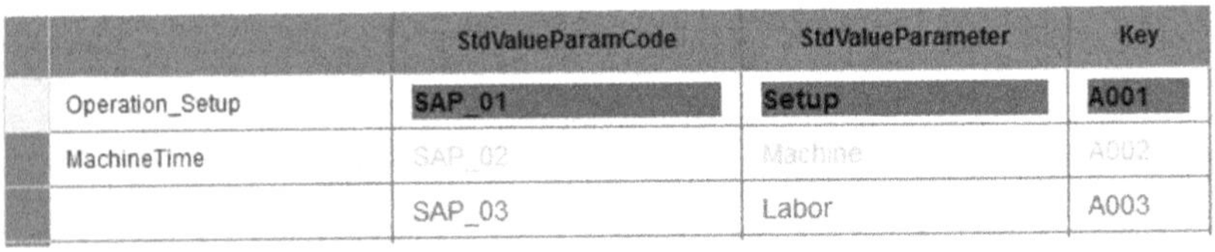

StdValueParamCode
StdValueParameter
Key
Operation_Setup
SAP_01
Setup
A001
MachineTime
SAP_02
Machine
A002
SAP_03
Labor
A003

Figure 7-33. *i5Grid row heading sample*

- *i5Grid Color Context*: The color context of the grid can be set. See Figure 7-34.

Query Template
Default/
Load
Refresh
Paste from Browser
Column Names
StdValueParamCode
StdValueParameter
Key
Dynamic Background
Thre
Col...
Icon
StdValueParamCode
Choose Icon
String:EXACT_MATCH:SAP_01
Choose Icon
String:EXACT_MATCH:SAP_02

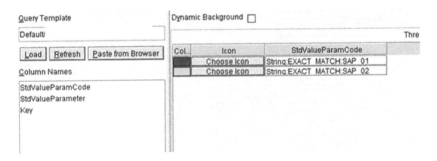

Figure 7-34. *i5Grid Color Context*

Once the Color context is configured as shown in Figure 7-34, the text of the row is displayed in the color against the conditions defined. See Figure 7-35.

StdValueParamCode	StdValueParameter	Key
SAP_01	Setup	A001
SAP_02	Machine	A002

Figure 7-35. *i5Grid color context sample*

- *i5Grid Refresh Page*: Used to configure the Refresh option, as shown in Figure 7-36.

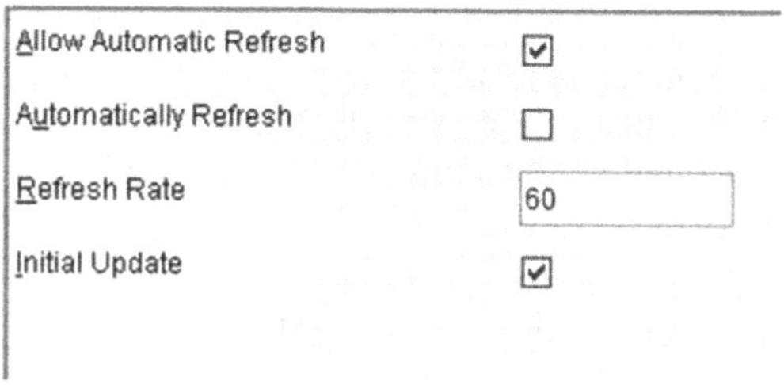

Allow Automatic Refresh	☑
Automatically Refresh	☐
Refresh Rate	60
Initial Update	☑

Figure 7-36. *i5Grid refresh page configuration*

i5Grid Output

Web page or browser-based scripting can be used to dynamically control the behavior and appearance of an i5Chart in SAP Manufacturing Integration and Intelligence (SAP MII). Scripting can to do the following:

- Change i5Chart properties

- Call i5Chart methods

- Use i5Chart events, such as user selections, to link i5Chart for drill-down or data correlation applications

Figure 7-37 shows the final output sample. The code to include the i5Chart in the HTML page is as follows:

```
var i5Grid = new com.sap.xmii.grid.init.i5Grid("Default/Saptaparna/i5Grid_
Exercise", "Default/Saptaparna/MDO_ReadSVKs");
i5Grid.setGridWidth("1240px");
i5Grid.setGridHeight("500px"); i5Chart.draw("GridDiv");
```

	StdValueParamCode	StdValueParameter	Key
Operation_Setup	SAP_01	Setup	A001
MachineTime	SAP_02	Machine	A002
	SAP_03	Labor	A003

Figure 7-37. *i5Grid final output sample with all features*

i5Grid Features

i5Grid has the following features:

- *Application Toolbar*: Located at the top-right corner of each grid and contains some icons by default.

  - *Data*: Data can be exported from the grid in three formats: HTML, CSV, and XML.

  - *Current Value*: Displays current values for all the tags available in the query. The values are displayed in HTML format in a new window for queries, which supports the Tag, PCo, and Catalog modes.

  - *Statistics*: Displays the statistical values for all the tags available in the query. The values are displayed in HTML format in a new window.

  - *Refresh Rate*: Frequency in seconds at which the grid is refreshed.

  - *Refresh Automatically*: Refreshes the grid as per the specified frequency.

  - *Print*: Prints the grid preview.

  - *Help*: Provides SAP MII Standard application help documents of the version being used.

- *Timebar*: Used to configure the hide/unhide feature of the timebar.

  The grid area displays a timebar for all query-based data. The grids are refreshed accordingly based on the selected date-time ranges. The arrows on the timebar display the charts in full screen, quarter screen, or for the current data. Date Range, Start Date, and End Date can be configured in the template or using the Date/Time Picker. The main properties are Slider, Picker, Duration, and Date/Time Picker. These new features add to the versatility of the visualization.

There are various scripting methods to return information from SAP MII i5Grid, such as getGridObject(), doPrint(), update(Boolean ReloadData), and many more.

i5Chart

A new MII HTML5 based display template called i5Chart was introduced in the MII 14.0 SP04 release. i5Chart uses HTML5–based SAP UI5 technology to render charts. It provides a variety of configurable charts to display and analyze data. It is one of the most important and powerful visualization components of SAP MII. i5Chart's display template supports the SelectionEvent parameter and allows JavaScript functions to be linked to items in the chart. A variety of i5Chart types—such as Line, Bar, GroupBar, Pie, StackedBar, Scatter, Gauge, HorizontalBar, HorizontalGroupBar, Bubble, Donut, and Custom—are supported. See Figure 7-38.

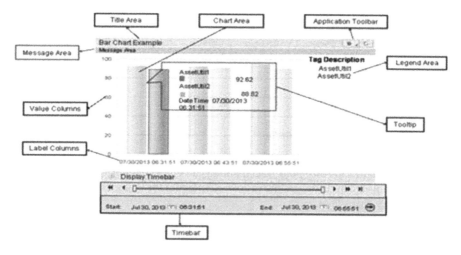

Figure 7-38. *Graphical representation of i5Chart*

- *i5Chart Chart Area*: *The* Chart Area tab configures chart type, colors, fonts, general chart parameters, and behaviors while elements are displayed in a chart. See Figure 7-39.

Figure 7-39. *i5Chart chart area configuration with available chart types*

- *i5Chart Title*: This sets the title, color, font, and other properties for i5Charts. See Figure 7-40.

Figure 7-40. *i5Chart title configuration*

- *i5Chart Data Mapping*: Data mapping tab maps columns returned by a query to the various elements of the i5Chart object. See Figure 7-41.

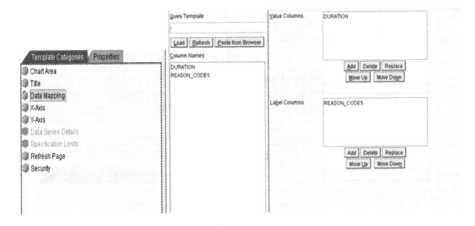

Figure 7-41. *i5Chart data mapping configuration*

- *i5Chart X-axis*: The X-axis tab configures parameters associated with the X-Axis (horizontal axis). See Figure 7-42.

Figure 7-42. i5Chart X-axis configuration

- *i5Chart Y- Axis*: The Y-axis tab configures parameters associated with the Y-axis (the vertical axis). See Figure 7-43.

Figure 7-43. i5Chart Y axis configuration

- *i5Chart Data Series Details*: Data Series Details configure data series colors of the chart.

- *i5Chart Specification Limits*: The Specification Limits tab configures the specification limits for your query output by defining the upper and lower limits in the chart. See Figure 7-44.

Allow Specification Limit Alarm	☐
Upper Limit Column	▼
Center Line Column	▼
Lower Limit Column	▼
Upper Limit	0
Center Line	0
Lower Limit	0
Color of Upper Limit Line	#FF0000
Center Line Color	#00FF00
Lower Limit Line Color	#FF0000

Figure 7-44. i5Chart specifications limit

- *i5Chart Refresh Rate*: The Refresh Page tab sets the refresh rate and the refresh mode (automatic/manual) for the chart. See Figure 7-45.

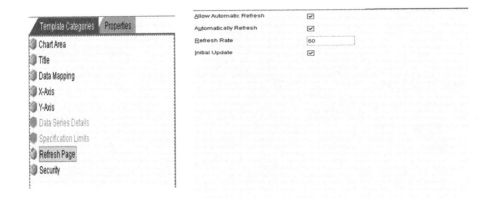

Figure 7-45. i5Chart refresh rate configuration

i5Chart Output

Web page or browser-based scripting, using JavaScript, can dynamically control the behavior and appearance of an i5Chart in SAP MII. Scripting can be used to:

- Change i5Chart properties

- Call i5Chart methods

- Use i5Chart events, such as user selections, to link i5Chart to drill-down or data correlation applications

Figure 7-46 shows the i5Chart final output. Here's the code to include the i5Chart in an HTML page:

```
var i5Chart = new com.sap.xmii.chart.hchart.i5Chart("Default/Chart/CHA_
I5Chart", "Default/Query/MDOQuery_GetData);
i5Chart.setChartWidth("400px");
i5Chart.setChartHeight("400px");
i5Chart.draw("chartDiv");
```

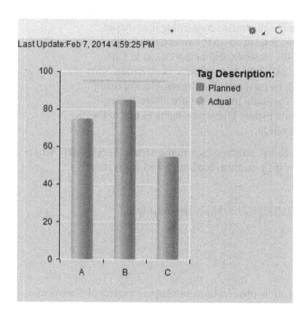

Figure 7-46. *i5Chart final output*

i5Chart Features

i5Chart has the following features:

- *Access Toolbar*: Located at the top-right corner of each chart and contains some icons by default.

  - *Data*: Data can be exported from a grid in three possible formats: HTML, CSV, and XML.

  - *Current Value*: Displays current values for all the tags available in the query. The values are displayed in HTML format in a new window for queries that support the Tag, PCo, and Catalog modes.

  - *Statistics*: Displays the statistical values for all the tags available in the query. The values are displayed in HTML format in a new window.

221

- *Refresh Rate*: Frequency in seconds at which the grid is refreshed.

- *Refresh Automatically*: Refreshes the grid as specified.

- *Print*: Prints the grid preview.

- *Glossy Effect*: Displays the chart with glossy effect and can be enabled or disabled in the chart area section.

- *Timebar*: Display Timebar hides/unhides the timebar. The chart area displays a timebar for all queries containing time-based data. The grids are refreshed based on the selected date-time ranges. The arrows on the timebar display the charts in full screen, quarter screen, or for the current data. Date Range, Start Date, and End Date can be configured in the template or using the Date/Time Picker. The main properties are Slider, Picker, Duration, and Date/Time Picker. These new features add to the versatility of the visualization.

There are various scripting methods to return information from the SAP MII i5Chart, including getChartObject(), Refresh(), update(Boolean), and many more.

```
JavaDocs Source:
https://<server>:<port>/XMII/JSDOC/i5ChartAllClasses.html.
```

i5SPC Chart

The chart displays datasets with multiple observations per tag in a variety of Statistical Process Control (SPC) chart formats. Each SPC chart includes:

- A variety of i5SPC Chart types such as XBAR, XBAR-MR, XBAR-RANGE, XBAR-SDEV, INDIVIDUALS, INDIVIDUALS-MR, MR, EWMA, EWMA-RANGE, EWMA-SDEV, MEDIAN, MEDIAN –RANGE, HISTOGRAM, INDIVIDUALS-SHORT-RUN, INDIVIDUALS-MR-SHORT-RUN, XBAR-RANGE-SHORT-RUN, MR-SHORT-RUN, P, NP, C, U, and so on for different types of process control and statistical quality analysis.

- Data point highlighting and suppression capabilities for ad hoc analysis by users

- Auto-calculated standard statistical and quality indexes

- Visual alarms in the chart for SPC rule violation conditions and comment text addition for each data point

i5SPC chart configuration options are very similar to the iSPC chart's options. The major difference is that i5SPC is dedicated to the UI5 extension. The following template configurations are available in the i5SPC chart (see Figure 7-47):

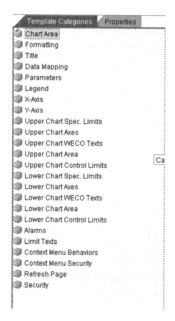

Figure 7-47. i5SPC chart configuration options

When the i5SPC chart is configured, the chart is displayed as shown in Figure 7-48.

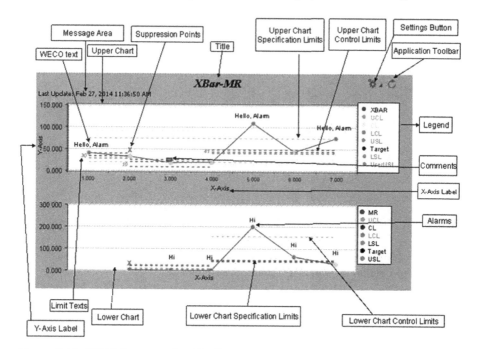

Figure 7-48. i5SPC chart sample with all properties

- *i5SPC chart area*: The Chart Area tab configures chart type, colors, fonts, general chart parameters, and behaviors while elements are displayed in a chart. Different possible chart types are as follows (see Figure 7-49):

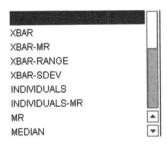

Figure 7-49. *i5SPC chart available chart types*

- *i5SPC chart formatting*: This function is available to configure the formatting properties for SAP MII SPC charts. See Figure 7-50.

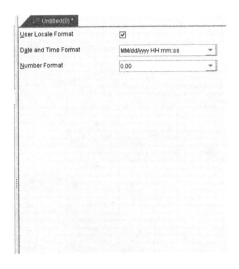

Figure 7-50. *i5spc chart formatting*

- *i5SPC chart title*: This tab sets the title, color, font, and other properties for your i5SPC charts. See Figure 7-51.

Show Application Toolbar	☐
Show Message Area	☑
Show Title	☑
Show Timebar	☑
Title	
Color	#000000
Font	Arial ▾
Font Size	12
Font Style	Bold Italic ▾
Alignment	Center ▾

Figure 7-51. *i5SPC chart title configuration*

- *i5SPC chart Data Mapping*: The Data Mapping tab maps columns returned by a query to the various elements of the i5SPC chart object. See Figure 7-52.

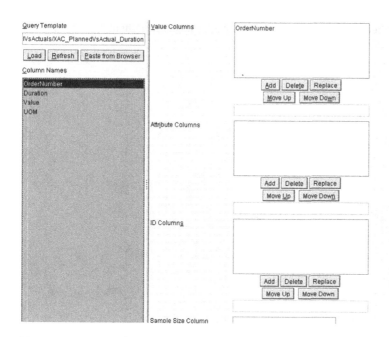

Figure 7-52. *i5SPC chart data mapping configuration*

- *i5SPC chart parameters*: The Parameter tab configures the parameters that are specific to individual chart types. See Figure 7-53.

Subgroup Size	1
Sample Size	100
Lambda	0.2
Use Average of all Subgroups for 1st Point Calculation	☑
Upper Chart Sigma Coefficient	3
Lower Chart Sigma Coefficient	3
Lower Limit of Box	25
Upper Limit of Box	75
Whisker Lower Limit	0
Whisker Upper Limit	100
Histogram Cell Count	10
Tolerance Type	0

Figure 7-53. i5SPC chart parameter configuration

- *i5SPC chart legend*: The Legend tab configures the appearance and behavior of the chart legend that appears on the right of the SPC chart. See Figure 7-54.

Show Legend	☑	
Background Color	#FFFFFF	
Border Color	#FFFFFF	
Font	Arial	▼
Font Size	10	
Font Style	Plain	▼

Figure 7-54. i5SPC chart legend configuration

- *i5SPC chart X-axis*: The X-axis tab configures parameters associated with the X-axis (the horizontal axis). See Figure 7-55.

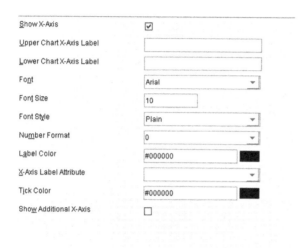

Figure 7-55. *i5SPC Chart X-Axis Configuration*

- *Y-axis tab*: Used to configure parameters associated with the y-axis (the vertical axis). See Figure 7-56.

Figure 7-56. *i5SPC chart y-axis configuration*

- *Upper chart limit:* The i5SPC chart can be configured with upper spec limits as described here (see Figure 7-57):

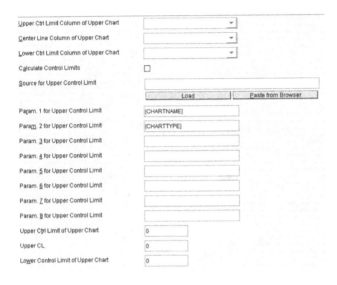

***Figure 7-57.** i5SPC chart upper chart control limit configuration*

- The Upper Chart Spec Limits tab configures the specification limits of the upper chart for the statistical process control (SPC) chart.

- The Upper Chart Axes tab configures the upper chart axes of the statistical process control (SPC) chart.

- The Upper Chart Area tab configures the upper chart area of the Statistical Process Control (SPC) chart.

- The Upper Chart Control Limits configuration configures the upper chart control limits of the Statistical Process Control (SPC) chart. See Figure 7-58.

Show Upper Tick Marks	☑	Upper Chart Background Color	#ffffff	☐	Warning Limit Color for Upper Chart	#C3C3C3	▦
Show Upper Labels	☑	Upper Chart Border Color	#F1C8C2	▦	Color of Upper Control Limit	#AUSUSC	▦
Use Scaling	☐	Color of Upper Chart Line	#0000FF	■	Show Upper Control Limits	☑
Min. Range of Upper Chart	0	Color of Upper Centerline	#00FFFF	☐	Show Upper Warning Limits	☐
Max. Range of Upper Chart	100	Upper Bar Color	#00FF00	☐	Show Upper Inner Limits	☐
Automatically Scale	☑	Color of Upper Chart Marker	#00FF00	☐	Show Normal Dist. Curve for Histogram	☐
Show Violation Border	☑	Selected Marker Color of Upper Chart	#0000FF	■	Line Thickness	1
Upper Violation Border Color	#FF0000	Upper Warning Color	#FF0000	▦	Line Style	Solid	▾
Violation Border Line Thickness	2	Color of Upper Inner Limit	#C3C3C3	▦		
Limit Line Thickness	1					

Show Upper Tick Marks	☑
Show Upper Labels	☑
Use Scaling	☐
Min. Range of Upper Chart	0
Max. Range of Upper Chart	100
Automatically Scale	☑
Show Violation Border	☑
Upper Violation Border Color	#FF0000 ▦
Violation Border Line Thickness	2
Limit Line Thickness	1

Figure 7-58. i5SPC Chart's various control limit configuration properties

The lower spec limits are similar, as you can see in Figure 7-59.

Show Upper Specification Limits	☑
Show Upper User Specification Limits	☐
Show Upper User Target	☐
Spec. Limit Color of Upper Chart	#FF00FF ▦
Color of Upper Chart Target	#000000 ■
Spec. Limit Color of Upper Chart User	#FF8C00 ▦
Target Color of Upper Chart User	#DC143C ▦

Figure 7-59. i5SPC chart's lower spec limit

- *I5SPC chart alarms*: The Alarms tab configures the alarms of an SPC chart when data values violate certain rules. See Figure 7-60.

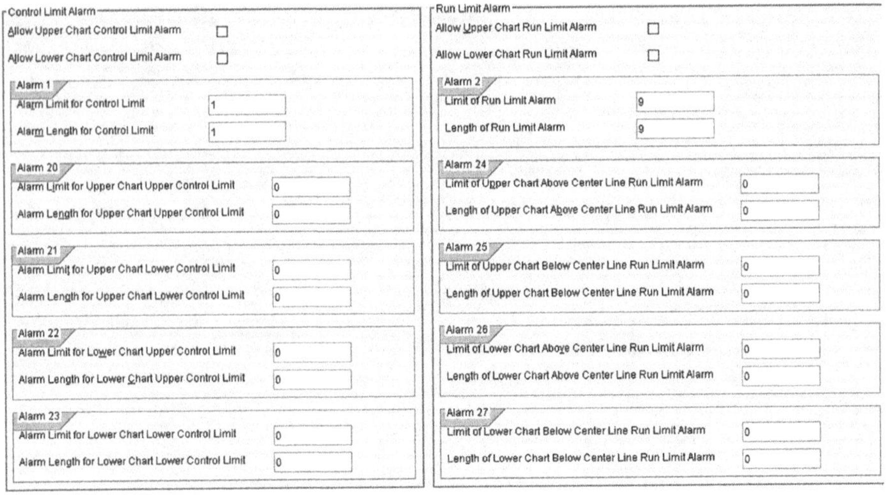

Control Limit Alarm

Allow Upper Chart Control Limit Alarm ☐

Allow Lower Chart Control Limit Alarm ☐

Alarm 1
Alarm Limit for Control Limit | 1
Alarm Length for Control Limit | 1

Alarm 20
Alarm Limit for Upper Chart Upper Control Limit | 0
Alarm Length for Upper Chart Upper Control Limit | 0

Alarm 21
Alarm Limit for Upper Chart Lower Control Limit | 0
Alarm Length for Upper Chart Lower Control Limit | 0

Alarm 22
Alarm Limit for Lower Chart Upper Control Limit | 0
Alarm Length for Lower Chart Upper Control Limit | 0

Alarm 23
Alarm Limit for Lower Chart Lower Control Limit | 0
Alarm Length for Lower Chart Lower Control Limit | 0

Run Limit Alarm

Allow Upper Chart Run Limit Alarm ☐

Allow Lower Chart Run Limit Alarm ☐

Alarm 2
Limit of Run Limit Alarm | 9
Length of Run Limit Alarm | 9

Alarm 24
Limit of Upper Chart Above Center Line Run Limit Alarm | 0
Length of Upper Chart Above Center Line Run Limit Alarm | 0

Alarm 25
Limit of Upper Chart Below Center Line Run Limit Alarm | 0
Length of Upper Chart Below Center Line Run Limit Alarm | 0

Alarm 26
Limit of Lower Chart Above Center Line Run Limit Alarm | 0
Length of Lower Chart Above Center Line Run Limit Alarm | 0

Alarm 27
Limit of Lower Chart Below Center Line Run Limit Alarm | 0
Length of Lower Chart Below Center Line Run Limit Alarm | 0

Figure 7-60. *i5SPC chart alarm configuration*

I5SPC Chart Output

Figure 7-61 shows the output for the i5SPC chart display.

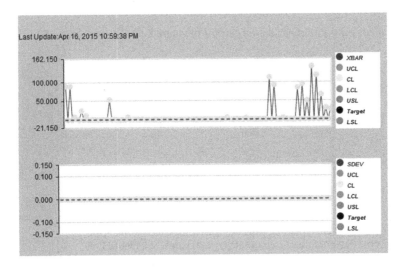

Figure 7-61. *i5SPC chart sample output*

It is possible to create different kinds of i5SPC charts like XBAR, Histogram, etc., as shown in Figure 7-62.

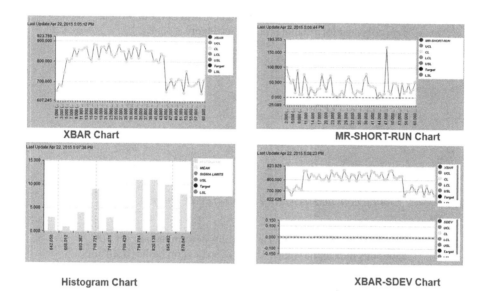

XBAR Chart

MR-SHORT-RUN Chart

Histogram Chart

XBAR-SDEV Chart

Figure 7-62. *i5SPC chart samples with various chart types*

i5SPC Chart: Rendering Options of i5SPC Charts in UI

The code to include the i5SPC chart in an HTML page is as follows:

```
var i5SPCChart = new com.sap.xmii.chart.hchart.i5Chart("Default/Saptaparna/
i5SPCChart", "Default/Saptaparna/TagQuery);
i5SPCChart.setChartWidth("400px");
i5SPCChart.setChartHeight("400px");
i5SPCChart.draw("SPCchartDiv");
```

i5SPC Chart Features

The following are some features of the i5SPC chart:

- *Control limits and specifications limits*: Specification limits are external tolerance values set by the user/customer and apply to individual units. Control limits are horizontal lines on a control chart that represent borderlines for a process.

- *Control limits*: Control limits indicate the behavior of the process and whether the process is in control. The upper control limit (UCL) and lower control limit (LCL) are calculated statistically from the data available in the queries. UCL and LCL are set by calculating the mean, standard deviation, and range of process data collected for a stable process. See Figure 7-63.

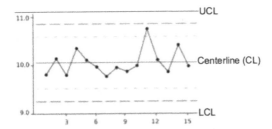

Figure 7-63. *Control limit and specification limit of i5SPC chart*

- *Specification Limits*: Specification limits determine process capability and sigma values. Upper specification limits (USL) and lower specification limits (LSL) for each chart can be defined. Control limits are limits or averages that are calculated based on previous history.

    a) *Subgroup*: An important aspect of SPC chart is organizing the data collection into subgroups. Each subgroup must be in control. Data points are either averages of subgroup measurements or individual measurements plotted on the Label and Value columns.

    b) *Warning Limits*: Warning limits on control charts are limits that are inside the control limits. Upper warning limits and lower warning limits can be defined. When warning limits are used, control limits are referred to as action limits. By default, warning limits are set at 2-sigma. Advantages of using warning limits are that they signal process changes more quickly than the 3-sigma action limits. WECO rule is considered for a process when two of the three data points are between 2-sigma and 3-sigma of the chart centerline.

In control charts:

- If the mean lies within warning limits, no action is taken.

- If the mean lies between warning and action limits, take another sample.

- If the mean lies outside action limits, take action.

    c) *Inner Limits*: Inner limits are set at +/- 1 sigma distance from the centerline. You can set inner limits for upper and lower charts.

i5ValueHelp

i5ValueHelp provides the feature of filtering the correct input data from any table. If value help is used in any table, when the user starts typing the words or part of a word in the text field of Value help, the table is filtered instantly and returns any matches. To use Value help, a query template is mandatory.

In the i5Value help configurations, four properties can be configured:

- General

- Search Results

- Search Criteria

- Template Security

Animated Objects

Animated objects are the customized User Interface (UI) widgets for applications such as digital cockpits or dashboards, label generation, specialized UI, and report components, which you can use without applets or other controls.

These objects are created in the SAP MII Workbench and are based on Scalable Vector Graphics (SVG), an XML-based format for representing vector drawings.

SVG files and animated objects are transformed into image files using SVG Renderer and Animation Renderer actions under Business Logic Transactions in the SAP MII Workbench.

Configuring an Animated Object

Follow these steps to create an animated object:

1. An animated object can be created using the File ➤ New ➤ Animated Object menu option in the SAP MII Workbench.

2. Once an animated object has been created, the various options for configuring it become available in the bottom-left panel of the Workbench, as shown in Figure 7-64.

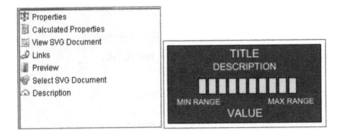

Figure 7-64. Configuration options and an example of an animated object

Selecting a SVG Document

You can select an SVG document, which provides the animated object definition to render the image. See Figure 7-65.

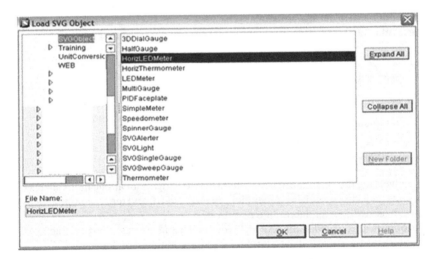

Figure 7-65. Various types of animated objects that support SAP MII

Properties of Animated Objects

You can view a list of all the public properties of the animated object. Public properties are object properties of the animated object that can be accessed and manipulated from a BLS transaction, as shown in Figure 7-66.

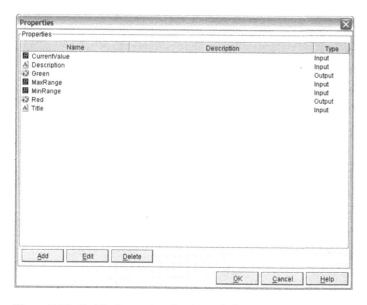

Figure 7-66. *Public Properties of animated objects*

From the public property configurations, a user can create or update any public property. Other than that, User also can define some condition or calculations under calculated properties for that same animated object. If user wants, they can check the XML beneath the object. User also can manipulate Internal and external properties of Object to manipulate the animation and once done user can preview the final animated object.

Action Blocks for Animated Objects

In MII Workbench, MII provides this set of action blocks used to render an animated object as an image in a web page:

- *SVG Renderer*: Used to take a SVG document and generate an image that represents the rendered drawing in a supported image format.

- *Animation Renderer*: Used to generate a SVG document with animation applied to the image.

- *Image Combiner*: Used to combine two generated images.

- *Image Creator*: Used to create an image with specified properties.

- *Image Scaler*: Used to scale an image to a certain height and width.

235

Figure 7-67. *Action block to handle animated objects in SAP MII*

Figure 7-68 shows the code sample needed to view animated objects on a web page.

```
<html>
<head>
<title>Dynamic Graphics</title>
<script language="javascript">
var Time;
function doit(){
imagename = "/XMII/Runner?Transaction=                              Dynamic
Graphics/SpeedoMeterTransaction&OutputParameter=ImageOut&content-type=image/png";
tmp = new Date();
tmp = "?"+tmp.getTime()
document.images["refresh"].src = imagename+tmp;
Time = setTimeout("doit()", 1000);
}
</script>
</head>
<body onload="doit()">

<img src="/XMII/Runner?Transaction=                               'Dynamic
Graphics/SpeedoMeterTransaction&OutputParameter=ImageOut&content-type=image/png"
name="refresh">
</body>
</html>
```

Figure 7-68. *Code sample to view animated objects in a web page*

SAP UI5

In SAP MII (14.0 and above), it's best to use the SAP UI5 frontend technology. It can be used in earlier versions as well, but the complete UI5 library must be loaded separately in the Workbench. SAP UI5 (SAP user interface library needs to be or HTML 5) is a collection of libraries that developers can use to build desktop and mobile applications that run in a browser.

SAP UI5 provides rich Internet applications, as it based on a cross-browser JavaScript library. SAP UI5 is a lightweight programming model consisting of standard and extension controls. Additionally, you can create new custom controls or extend the existing ones.

i5Charts, i5Grids, and i5SPC charts use SAP UI5's library to represent data that is obtained from the data sources graphically. The SAP UI5 application for the SAP MII environment can be developed following the MVC (Model View Controller) pattern. See Figure 7-69.

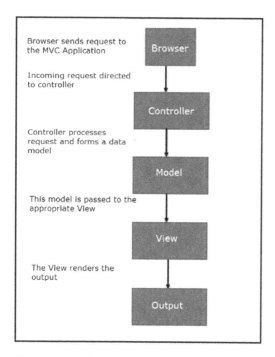

Figure 7-69. *The SAP UI5 execution model*

■ **Note**   Model View Controller (MVC) is an architectural pattern that separates an application into three main logical components: the model, the view, and the controller. Each of these components is built to handle specific development aspects of an application. MVC is one of the most frequently used industry-standard web development framework to create scalable and extensible projects.

MVC consists of three concepts. Views can be defined using different languages like JavaScript or HTML. Controller binds the views and models used with views.

Views can be defined using XML with HTML, mixed, or standalone:

- *XML*: sap.ui.core.mvc.xmlview

- *JavaScript*: sap.ui.core.mvc.JSView

- *JSON*: sap.ui.core.mvc.JSONView

- *HTML*: sap.ui.core.mvc.HTMLView

Controllers are bound to a view. They can also be used with multiple views. In the Model part, data binding can be used on the views. See Figure 7-70.

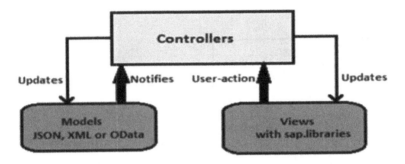

Figure 7-70. SAP UI5 data binding

The SAP UI5 application can be developed using different views:

- JS View

- XML View

- JSON View

- HTML View

XML view is newly introduced and is mainly used for Fiori like the Frontend using SAP UI5 and can be deployed in the Fiori Launchpad. SAP Fiori is a new user experience (UX) for SAP software and applications. It provides a set of applications that are used in regular business functions, like work approvals, financial apps, calculation apps, and various self-service apps. SAP Fiori enables multiple device applications that allow users to start a process on their desktop/laptops and to continue that process on a smartphone or tablet. SAP has developed Fiori apps based on the UI5 user interface.

SAP UI5 (SAP user interface for HTML 5) is a collection of libraries that developers can use to build desktop and mobile applications that run in a browser. With SAP's SAP UI5 JavaScript toolkit, developers can build SAP web applications using HTML5 web development standards.

SAP UI5 supports all the key web browsers and latest versions like IE, Mozilla Firefox, Google Chrome, and Safari.

SAP UI5 Data Binding

Data binding is used by the UI5 controls to hold the application data. It allows you to change the controls automatically whenever there is a change to the application data. When two-way data binding is used, application data is updated whenever the value of a bound control changes.

Data Binding Model Types

SAP UI5 supports three types of model implementation:

- *JSON Model*: Supports data in JavaScript Object Notation format. It supports two-way data binding.

- *XML Model*: Supports XML data. It supports two-way data binding.

- *OData Model*: Creates OData requests and handles responses accordingly. It only supports OData-compliant data. It supports experimental two-way data binding.

SSCE

SAP MII has launched the Self-Service Composition Dashboard, which is integrated within the SAP MII package. Using SSCE, you can develop frontend screens easily by dragging and dropping UI components and binding corresponding data to them. Moreover, in the backend, the UI code is generated and can be modified at any place for the required output.

It creates, designs, configures, and displays complete dashboards as per the requirements. It is a role based application. To access the SSCE components, the XMII_SSCE_ALL role must be assigned to the user. Main SSCE features and functionalities are available::

- *Dashboard creation*: Using any SAP MII content (Query Templates, Display Templates, MDO/KPI Objects, and Resource Files), UI elements, and tags from Plant Information Catalog, dashboards can be created.

- *Configuration of selected objects*: The selected tags from Plant Information Catalog (PIC) can be positioned on images. Colors, graphics, and icons can be configured as per the required conditions for the selected tags. A tag trend (line chart) is displayed when a tag is moved to an empty cell on SSCE.

- *Flexible layouts*: This displays data from any query template and user specific UI controls using different layouts of SSCE.

- *Flexible dashboards*: This saves the created dashboard for later use and so if required it can be modified easily as needed.

- *Customization*: This customizes the created dashboard by adding the saved content to the navigation tree.

- *Preview of dashboards*: This previews the created dashboard with either static or live images.

- *Security*: This secures your dashboards by assigning roles.

239

The three main components are Design, Preview, and Source Code. Figure 7-71 shows the design dashboard.

Figure 7-71. *SSCE design dashboard*

- *Design*: This is mainly used to create a dashboard using standard layouts while selecting respectable content, such as the following:

  - *MII Content*: Display Templates, Query Templates, MDO/KPI Objects, and Resource Files are the predefined objects for this section. See Figure 7-72.

Figure 7-72. *SSCE MII content menu*

  - *UI Elements*: SSCE provides features to create more interactive pages by adding UI elements such as labels, text input fields, buttons, images, and drop-down boxes. These elements can be directly dropped and dragged in the Design dashboard. See Figure 7-73.

» **UI Elements**

UI Controls | Properties

🔲 TextView
🔲 TextField
🔲 TextArea
▓▓ Button
⊙ Radio Button
☐ CheckBox
🔲 DropdownBox
🔲 Image

Figure 7-73. *SSCE UI elements menu*

✓ A reference grid is created in the background of the layout and the first UI element is always placed at the top-left cell of the grid. The consecutive elements are placed at the cursor position of the grid.

✓ Once the selected UI element is chosen, the Properties tab displaying all the properties associated with that UI element appears on the right pane, as shown in Figure 7-74.

Figure 7-74. *UI element properties in SSCE*

Properties of the UI elements like ID, text value, visibility, event handlers, and so on can be configured.

✓ Upon adding an EventHandler, a JavaScript method is created in the custom code area in the Source Code tab. The UI elements along with the configurations in the Preview tab can be seen. See Figure 7-75.

241

Figure 7-75. Setting events of an UI element

Once the Source code tab is clicked, the auto-generated code of the event handler is shown, as in Figure 7-76.

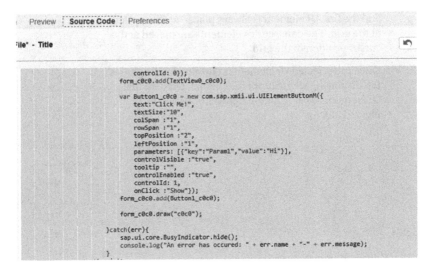

Figure 7-76. Event handler auto-generated code in SSCE

- *Plant Information catalog*: A tag from the Plant Information Catalog can be moved to an empty cell, on to an image, or on a tag trend. It can be repositioned to the desired location. The selected tag can be viewed in trends and current views in live and design modes. The changes/configurations to the tag are automatically captured in the Preview mode.

Customized dashboard layouts can be searched and opened from the Open Dashboard command. Moreover, content that you create can be configured and previewed in the Preview tab.

Merging, Unmerging, and deleting the dashboard are also possible. A live mode of dashboard can also be viewed as per requirement. Navigation links to the dashboards can also be created. Security is an added advantage.

The UI Dashboard can be seen in the Preview tab, as shown in Figure 7-77.

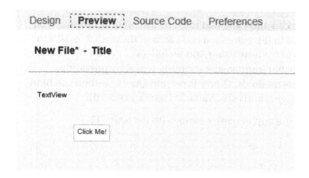

Figure 7-77. Preview window in SSCE

The Source Code tab can be used to view the generated HTML source code for the created dashboard. External code can be appended to the existing source code with additional CSS or JavaScript from the SAP MII Workbench. JavaScript is added to the generated source code in the section that is marked for a user-entered script.

When you choose Edit, the entire source code area is split into two parts, as shown in Figure 7-78.

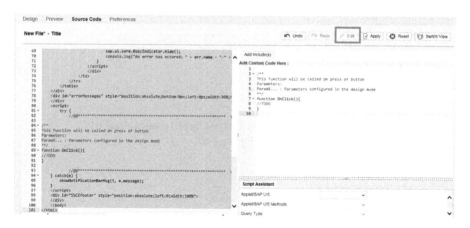

Figure 7-78. Source Code editor in SSCE

- The left part represents the generated HTML source code, which is not editable.

- The right part represents the hook points that can be edited. This section is further split into two areas: Custom Code and Script Assistant.

In the Custom Code area, you can add code that must be available at runtime. You can use any objects that are created in the generated code area or the available APIs to modify the behavior of the objects at runtime using Add Include(s).

In Script Assistant, you can further improve the scripting syntax by providing available options with the applet, its methods, Query Type, and Query methods, to bind with the applet. The following configurations are available (see Figure 7-79):

- *Applet/SAP UI5*: Lists the applet names along with the SAP UI5 objects.

Figure 7-79. *Available UI5 applets in SSCE*

- *Applet/SAP UI5 Methods*: Lists the base applet names along with SAP UI5 object methods. See Figure 7-80.

```
12   This function will be called on press of button
13   Parameters:
14   ParamX... : Parameters confi    deregisterCreationEventHandler()
15   **/                              deregisterFirstUpdateEventHandler()
16 ▾ function Show(Param1){          deregisterLowerChartSelectionEventHandler()
17   //TODO                          deregisterUpdateEventHandler()
18   }                               deregisterUpperChartSelectionEventHandler()
19                                   draw(id)
                                     exportCurrent()
Script Assistant                    exportStatistics()
                                     getChartObject()
Applet/SAP UI5                       getDisplayTemplate()

Applet/SAP UI5 Methods              deregisterCreationE  ⌄

Query Type                    ⌄

Object Methods                ⌄
```

Figure 7-80. *Available UI5 methods in SSCE*

- *Query Type*: Lists the query type if any associated with the Applet method being selected. See Figure 7-81.

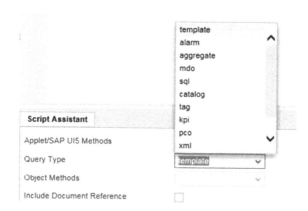

```
                              template
                              alarm            ⌃
                              aggregate
                              mdo
                              sql
                              catalog
                              tag
Script Assistant              kpi
                              pco
Applet/SAP UI5 Methods        xml              ⌄
Query Type                    template   ⌄
Object Methods                        ⌄
Include Document Reference    ☐
```

Figure 7-81. *Available query types in SSCE*

- *Object Methods*: Lists the object method names that apply to the selected applet/SAP UI5 object. See Figure 7-82.

245

Figure 7-82. Available object methods in SSCE

- *Include Document Object Reference*: If the checkbox is selected, the system adds the document object as a prefix to the applet name to reference an applet or a control on the web page. It is recommended to use a prefix. For example, when the checkbox is checked, a document prefix reference is added (see Figure 7-83).

```
Add Custom Code Here :
1
i 2   document.iGrid.getQueryObject().buildPostData()
3  |
```

Script Assistant		
Query Type	mdo	⌄
Object Methods	buildPostData()	⌄
Include Document Reference	✓	

Insert   Reset

Figure 7-83. Including a document reference in SSCE

If the checkbox is not selected, no reference to the document prefix is created, as shown in Figure 7-84.

Figure 7-84. Excluding a document reference in SSCE

Key Performance Indicators (KPIs)

Key Performance Indicators (KPI) are numerical index measures that monitor critical operational areas and let the business know how well the area or the organization is performing. KPIs are critical for performance evaluation. KPIs are generally configured for specific business scenarios and to let the associated management know whether areas are performing well, need monitoring, or need immediate attention and improvement.

KPIs can be created and configured in SAP MII and can also be monitored using the built-in KPI monitoring screen.

The KPI Framework

The KPI framework is a built-in feature of SAP MII that allows you to define KPIs and create logic to calculate and monitor. This framework also allows you to create custom UIs and consume the KPI data from SAP MII. It can fetch required data for KPI calculation from any shopfloor system or historians using data connectors. Custom logic creation is also possible for KPI calculation.

Here are the major steps of the KPI framework:

- KPI definition
- Data acquisition
- Data consumption

KPI Definition

KPI definition is where KPIs are created and configured. It needs the XMII_DEVELOPER role assigned to create KPI.

Type of KPIs

SAP MII has two types of KPIs:

- *Base KPIs*: Not dependent on any other KPI

- *Composite KPIs*: Dependent on different other KPIs to get data

Base KPIs

Base KPIs are independent, self-sufficient performance indicators that can collect and calculate values by themselves without the help of an external system. These base KPIs can be part of other KPIs to gather required data.

To configure base KPIs, follow these steps:

1. Open the SAP MII menu and choose Workbench ➤ Launch Workbench.

2. Open the Object tab.

3. Right-click on the Project folder.

4. Select New File ➤ Base KPI, as shown in Figure 7-85.

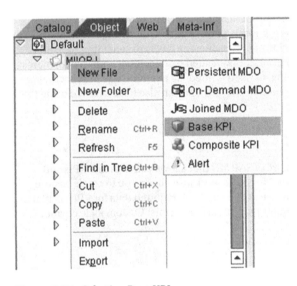

Figure 7-85. *Selecting Base KPI*

5. There are links to different configuration pages found in the bottom-left corner of the page. See Figure 7-86.

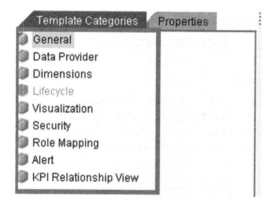

Figure 7-86. Template categories for Base KPIs

The General page contains the header information of the KPI. Available fields in this page are shown in Figure 7-87.

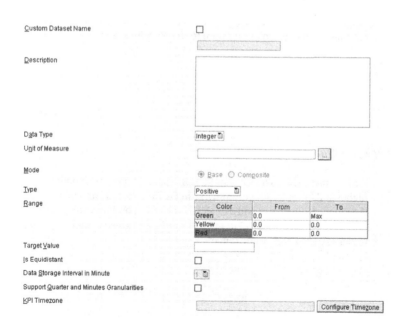

Figure 7-87. General screen in Base KPI

- *Description*: This specifies the description of the KPI.

- *Data Type*: This field specifies the data type of the generated KPI values. Available types are integer, double, float, and long.

- *Unit of Measure*: This specifies the measuring unit of the KPI.

- *Mode*: This is a read-only field that specifies the type of the KPI (base/composite).

- *Type*: Three available types are:

  – *Positive*: The higher value KPI indicates better performance. As shown in Figure 7-88, when the type is selected as positive, green is defined for +10 to Max KPI value, yellow is defined for +5 to +10 KPI values, and red is defined for 0 to +5 KPI values.

Type	Positive		
Range			

Color	From	To
Green	10.0	Max
Yellow	5	10.0
Red	0.0	5.0

Figure 7-88. Sample for positive type Base KPI

  – *Negative*: The opposite of the positive indicator. Red falls within the range of -10 to max negative KPI value, yellow comes within -5 to -10 KPI values, and green comes for 0 to -5 KPI values. See Figure 7-89.

Type	Negative		
Range			

Color	From	To
Red	10.0	Max
Yellow	5	10.0
Green	0.0	5.0

Figure 7-89. Sample for negative type Base KPI

  – *Bidirectional*: This means it should be in a specific range with both higher and lower limits. For this type, in Figure 7-90, red falls within the range of +20 to max and 0 to +5 KPI values, yellow falls within the range of _+15 to +20 and +5 to +10 KPI values, and green comes under +10 to +15 KPI value range.

Type	Bi-directional		
Range			

Color	From	To
Red	20.0	Max
Yellow	15.0	20.0
Green	10.0	15.0
Yellow	5	10.0
Red	0.0	5.0

Figure 7-90. Sample for bidirectional type Base KPI

Range: Depends on the type. For a positive KPI, green is at the top followed by yellow and red. It's the opposite for a negative KPI.

Aggregation Logic: This field specifies the logic to be used for aggregation of values while querying the KPIs. Available options are:

- *Min*: Returns the minimum value of the retrieved result.

- *Max*: Returns the maximum value of the retrieved result.

- *Avg*: Returns the average value of the retrieved result.

- *Sum*: Returns the Summation of all values of the retrieved result.

- *Range*: Returns the difference between maximum and minimum values.

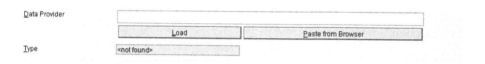

Figure 7-91. *Data provider in Base KPI*

The Data Provider page configures the data source of the KPI (see Figure 7-91). It can be a query template, a transaction, or another KPI. Click on the Load button and select the required object. Then click the OK button. Figure 7-92 shows the loading process.

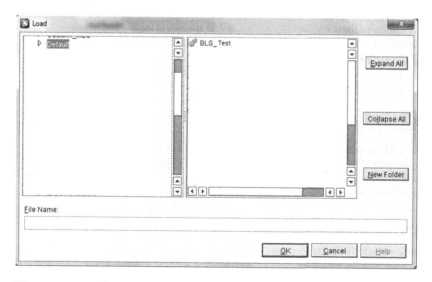

Figure 7-92. *Loading an object in the Data Provider*

Dimensions are the KPI attributes to which data coming from the Data Provider as columns can be mapped. Dimension and timestamp are two standard available attributes. Additional attributes may also be available through the Data Provider. Configure those attributes on the Dimensions page, as shown in Figure 7-93.

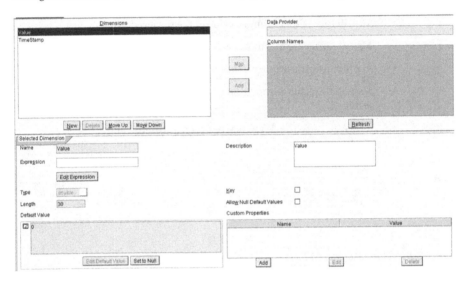

Figure 7-93. *Dimension screen in a base KPI*

Lifecycle configuration schedules the KPI to gather data at a given time. For that, a scheduler needs to be configured. Without a scheduler, KPI cannot store data. Click the Create New button and provide the mandatory information. Select the Enabled checkbox. Select a time pattern for the scheduler to run. Select the mode for the scheduler—Append, Insert, Update, or Delete. Click the Deploy All button to deploy the scheduler. It will create the scheduler itself and it will start running.

Assign the roles to the KPI to ensure that only the authorized users will be able to consume the KPI. Then save and deploy the KPI.

Composite KPIs

A composite KPI is calculated depending on the values of each of its dependent KPIs or systems. Composite KPIs may be dependent on base KPIs, composite KPIs, or both. They can be configured to collect data from multiple data sources, such as transactions, query templates, or other KPIs.

Configuring a Composite KPI

Follow these steps to configure a composite KPI:

1. Open the SAP MII menu and choose Workbench ➤ Launch Workbench.

2. Open the Object tab.

3. Right-click on the Project folder.

4. Select New File ➤ Composite KPI, as shown in Figure 7-94.

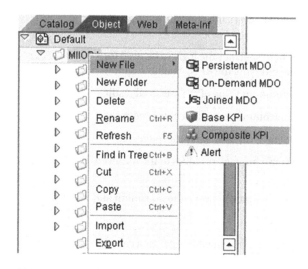

Figure 7-94. *Selecting a composite KPI*

5. There are links to different configuration pages found in the bottom-left corner of the page.

6. The General page contains the header information of the KPI. Available fields on this page are:

    • *Description*: This specifies the description of the KPI.

    • *Data Type*: This field specifies the data type of the generated KPI values. Available types are integer, double, float. and long.

    • *Unit of Measure*: This specifies the measuring unit of the KPI.

    • *Mode*: This read-only field specifies the type of the KPI (base/composite).

    • *Type*: The three available types are:

        – Positive

        – Negative

        – Bidirectional

A KPI type that's positive means a higher value KPI indicates better performance. A negative type is the opposite. A bidirectional type means it should be in a specific range with both higher and lower limits.

- *Range*: Depends on the type. For a positive KPI, Green is at the top followed by Yellow and Red. It's the opposite in the case of a negative KPI.

- *Aggregation Logic*: This field specifies the logic to be used for aggregating values while querying the KPIs. Available options are:

  - *Min*: Returns the minimum value of the retrieved result.

  - *Max*: Returns the maximum value of the retrieved result.

  - *Avg*: Returns the average value of the retrieved result.

  - *Sum*: Returns the summation of all values of the retrieved result.

  - *Range*: Returns the difference between the maximum and minimum values.

7. On the Data Provider page, there is an additional area called KPI Data Provider (see Figure 7-95). This field allows you to add the KPIs on which composite KPI is dependent. To add dependent KPIs, click the Load button and then select the KPIs from the popup box. Click OK.

8. If the values for the composite KPI are coming from an external system, the Data Provider needs to be selected at that time.

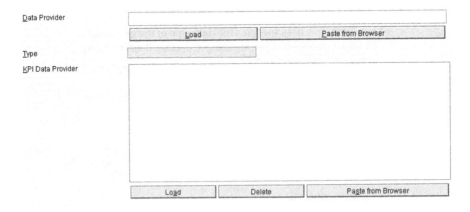

Figure 7-95. Data Provider screen in a composite KPI

9. The Dimension page of a composite KPI is quite similar to that of the base KPI until you try to map a value of multiple KPIs to the composite KPI. To set a value for a composite KPI, click on the Edit Expression button. Choose to edit the expression, then click OK.

10. The Lifecycle configuration schedules the KPI to gather data at a given time. For that, a scheduler needs to be configured. Without a scheduler, KPI cannot store data. Click the Create New button and add the mandatory information. Select the Enabled checkbox. Select a time pattern for the scheduler to run. Select mode for the scheduler—Append, Insert, Update, or Delete. Click the Deploy All button to deploy the scheduler. It will create the scheduler and will start running.

11. Assign roles to the KPI to ensure that only authorized users can consume the KPI.

12. Save and deploy the KPI.

Data Consumption and Monitoring

In the manufacturing industry, various parameters must be measured to monitor performance from multiple perspectives. These are called key performance indicators (KPIs). You must also monitor the data used for calculating the KPIs and the final KPI results on a regular basis. These are crucial industry requirements, as ISO certifications and quality clearance is dependent on the KPI results. SAP MII has built-in features to calculate KPI using standard KPI formulas and, if required, certain levels of custom KPI formulation can be created. This section describes how to configure and use KPIs and query data using KPI queries, as well as how to visualize that data.

KPI Query

A KPI query is a new type of query template that allows you to query KPI data.
Follow these steps to configure a KPI query:

1. Launch Workbench.

2. Go to the Catalog tab

3. Right-click on any project and select New ➤ KPI Query. See Figure 7-96.

4. The KPI Query screen has different configuration pages available at the bottom-left corner of the screen. The pages are:

   • Data Source

   • General

- Date Range
- Select Query
- Delete Query
- Insert Query
- Parameters
  - Transformation
  - Security

5. On the General page, you specify a Data Server and a connector. SAP MII provides a default data server named KPIConnector. This data server can be used to query the KPI values created on that server.

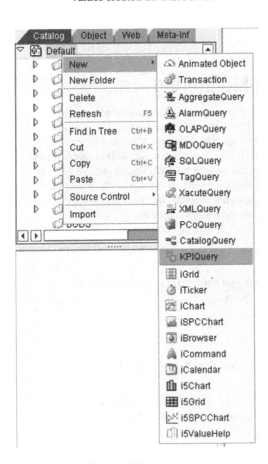

Figure 7-96. *Selecting KPI query*

6. This data server can be enabled or disabled depending on the requirements of using the server and can be maintained in the SAP MII Admin menu.

7. Click on the Load button and then select the KPI to be queried from the popup. Click OK.

8. Select the mode from the drop-down list. The available mode options are:

    • *Attribute List*: This shows the list of all KPI dimensions.

    • *Delete*: This deletes the data of the selected KPI.

    • *Info*: This shows the list of all the KPI's metadata.

    • *Insert*: This inserts data into the KPI.

    • *KPI List*: This shows the list of KPIs created and configured on the selected data server.

    • *Mode List*: This shows different modes that a KPI query can run.

    • *Select*: This retrieves data from the selected KPI.

9. Open the Dimensions page and select a dimension from the available dimensions. Choose Add. See Figure 7-97.

10. Filter expressions also can be configured from the Dimensions page.

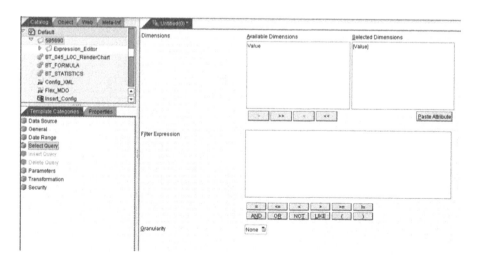

Figure 7-97. *Defining dimensions in KPI*

11. Granularity in the Dimension screen determines how the data is represented when the KPI is queried. The available granularity types are:

- *Hour*: Data will be aggregated hourly according to the aggregation logic.

- *Day*: Data will be aggregated daily according to the aggregation logic.

- *Month*: Data will be aggregated monthly according to the aggregation logic.

- *None*: Aggregation logic will be applied to the whole dataset.

- *Raw*: It will display all the KPI data available.

- *Week*: Data will be aggregated weekly according to the aggregation logic.

12. Save the query with a suitable name.

13. Create a display template.

14. Add the display template to the visualization page of the KPI query.

15. Execute the KPI query.

KPI Monitor Page

The KPI you just created needs to be monitored. SAP MII provides the facility to create a personalized dashboard to monitor using display templates or the KPI Monitor screen. See Figure 7-98.

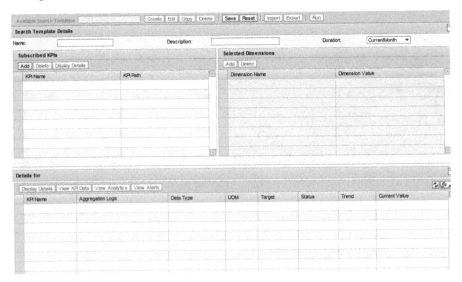

Figure 7-98. *KPI Monitor screen*

Open the KPI Monitor page from the SAP MII Admin menu by choosing the KPI & Alert category. Click on the Create button –and then choose Create Search Template with Name, Description, and Duration. Add the KPI to monitor and then click OK. Configure the dimensions of the KPI further, if needed.

Using Alerts in KPIs

KPIs can be configured to raise alerts whenever the KPI value crosses a specific limit. Multiple alerts can be configured for a single KPI.

Follow these steps to create and configure an alert:

1. Select the Object tab of the Workbench.

2. Right-click on any project folder and then choose New File ➤ Alert. See Figure 7-99.

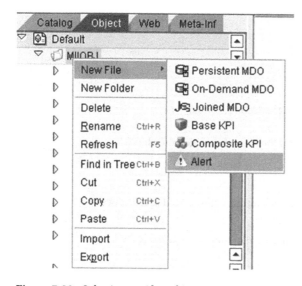

Figure 7-99. *Selecting an Alert object*

3. Add short and long text. See Figure 7-100.

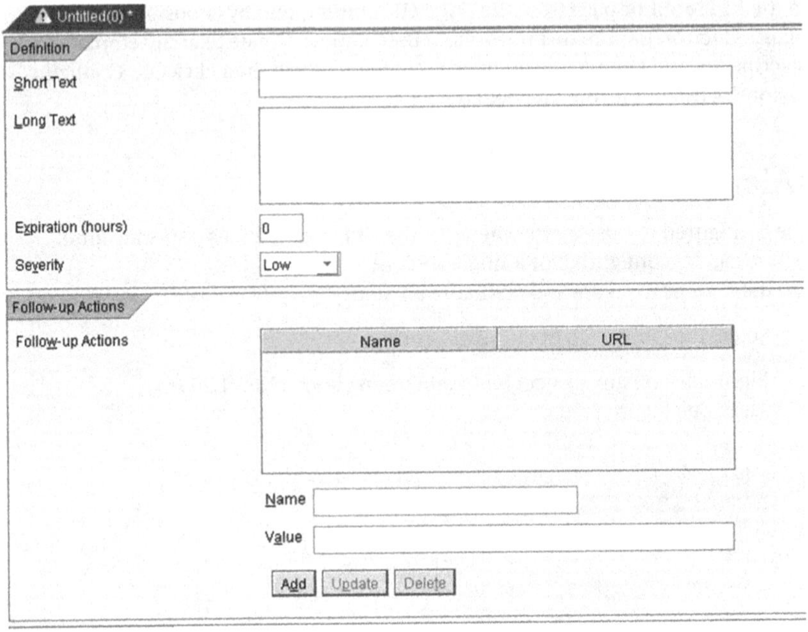

Figure 7-100. Adding short and long text to the Alert object

4.   Add expiration hours for the alert after which the alert will automatically expire.

5.   Enter an alert severity.

6.   Add follow-up actions, such as the steps needed to take once the alert is raised.

7.   Add any container properties that may be required to complete the alert.

8.   Choose a delivery transaction that will be triggered once the alert is raised to inform the concerned users about the alert. See Figure 7-101.

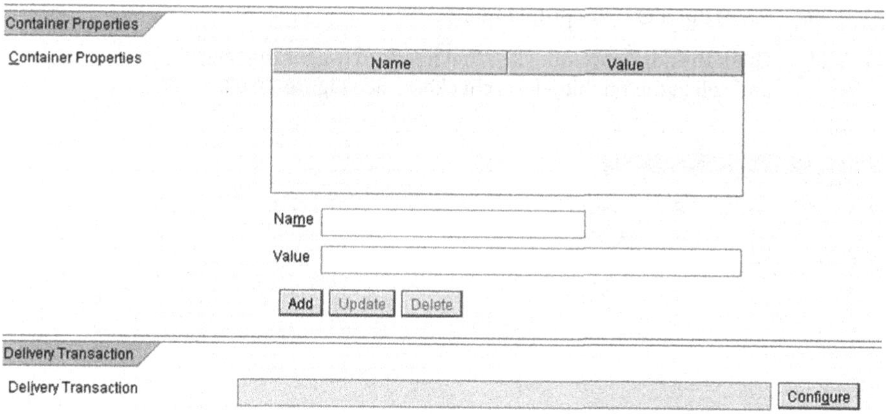

Figure 7-101. *Delivery Transaction configuration*

9. Add roles. See Figure 7-102.

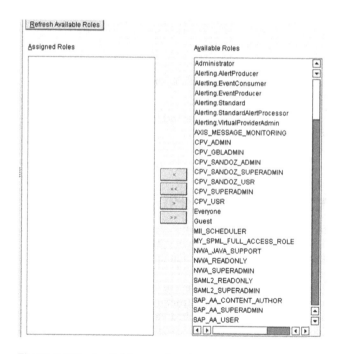

Figure 7-102. *Available security roles*

10. Save your alert with proper name.

11. Open the corresponding KPI that needs to trigger that alert and select the Enable Alerts checkbox. See Figure 7-103.

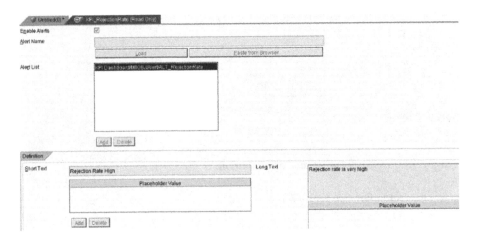

Figure 7-103. *Enabling alerts in KPI*

12. Click on the Load button in the Alert Name area and select the specific alert. Click OK.

13. Select the alert from the list and click on the Add button to add the alert to the object list.

14. Save and run.

The Plant Information Catalog (PIC)

Every manufacturing industry has data in their shopfloor systems that's stored in an unorganized manner and without any business consistency. The Plant Information Catalog (PIC) is a framework available in SAP MII for maintaining and defining the relationship of that data in an organized manner.

On the shopfloor, many systems store or capture data for different data points, such as temperature, pressure, etc., which is stored in a flat structure without any relationship to other datasets or associated business objects. The pain area for the business is that they have all the data available, but no business context associated with it. As a result, it is difficult for the business to search for specific data and analyze or use it.

Advantages of PIC

The Plant Information Catalog (PIC) has the following advantages:

- PIC provides the framework to create hierarchical, plant-specific catalogs of data points or tags from different shopfloor systems.

- PIC provides the business context to this hierarchy from ERP.

- Through PIC, shopfloor assets can be grouped logically and by business rules defined in SAP ERP systems.

- Business friendly naming conventions can be followed for the objects and data points or tags to make it easily usable to business users and developers.

PIC comes between shopfloor and enterprise systems (see Figure 7-104). It gets data from the shopfloor system and gets business context from the ERP systems and combines those into a hierarchical format to increase usability.

PIC hierarchy contains two types of objects:

- *Group*: These are logical groups containing logical tags

- *Tag*: These are data points of shopfloor systems

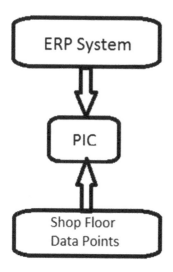

Figure 7-104. *Placement of PIC in middleware solutioning*

Creating a PIC Hierarchy in SAP MII

Creating a PIC hierarchy in SAP MII involves multiple steps, all of which are covered sequentially in the following sections.

Creating a Property Set

Property set is collection of properties that allows you to add specific values of these properties to the PIC object with which the property set is associated. Adding, updating, and deleting properties from that property set is possible from the Property Set Admin screen of SAP MII, by choosing the menu option Catalog Services ➤ Property Set. See Figure 7-105.

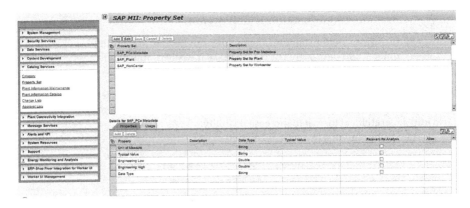

Figure 7-105. *Property Set screen in catalog services*

SAP MII includes predefined property sets that start with SAP_. These property sets contain some standard properties and cannot be updated or deleted.

The Usage tab (see Figure 7-106) gives the list of PIC objects where the selected property set is mapped. As soon as the property set is edited and saved, the system displays the list of PIC objects where the property set is mapped and asks for the choice to push the changes. If the changes are pushed, they will be reflected in the PIC hierarchy. Even if the changes are not pushed, they can be pulled from the PIC hierarchy of the Plant Information Maintenance screen.

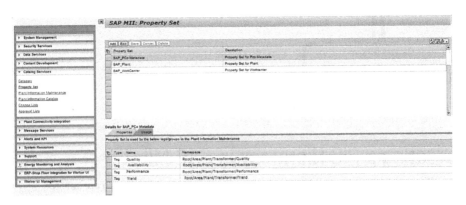

Figure 7-106. *Usage tab in Property Set*

The property set cannot be deleted if it is being used in the Plant Information Catalog.

The nodes that are not selected for updating identify themselves with an Out of Sync status and can be checked from the PIC screen for their sync status, as shown in Figure 7-107.

Figure 7-107. *Sync status in PIC*

Creating a Category

Categories define the types of PIC objects. As soon as a category is added to a PIC object, the property set associated with that category will also be added to that PIC object. Categories can be created, edited, or deleted from the Category Admin screen, which you can reach from the SAP MII menu path Catalog Services ➤ Category.

SAP MII includes predefined categories that start with SAP_ for property sets of functionally valid properties. These categories cannot be deleted or associated to a property set and cannot be removed. But they can be edited. Any changes to a category can be pushed to the PIC hierarchy, as per the user selection (similar to a property set). See Figure 7-108.

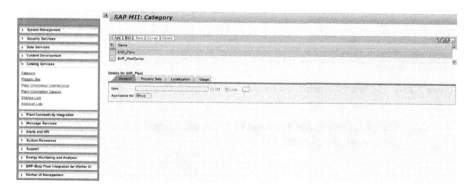

Figure 7-108. *General Category screen*

1. From the Property Sets tab, you can add a property to the Category while adding a new category or editing an existing category. See Figure 7-109.

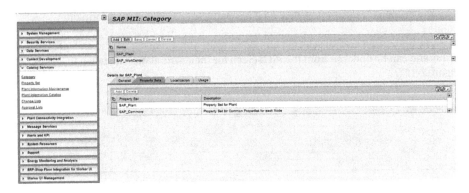

Figure 7-109. *Category screen: Property Sets*

2. In the Localization tab, different languages can be specified and, depending on the user Locale, the category description can be changed. See Figure 7-110.

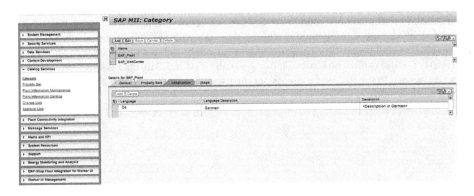

Figure 7-110. *Category Localization screen*

3. The Usage tab shows the usage of the saved categories in to the system. See Figure 7-111.

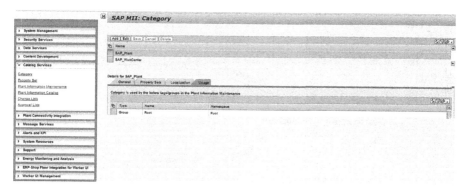

Figure 7-111. *Category Usage screen*

The category cannot be deleted if it is being used in the plant information catalog.

Creating a Change List and Marking it as the Default

Under the Catalog Services group on the SAP MII menu, there are the following two screens:

- *Plant Information Maintenance*: Plant asset hierarchy and mapping PIC objects to the actual shopfloor objects is done here. All changes are done, approved, and applied. Then the changes move to the PIC.

- *Plant Information Catalog*: This is a read-only screen for viewing the PIC hierarchy already created on the Plant Information Maintenance screen and approved.

There can be multiple change lists created by a particular user and they can remain open at the same time. Only one of them can be the current change list. Changes to the PIC hierarchy are maintained in the current change list until those changes are approved and applied to the PIC. Once all the changes to the PIC hierarchy are complete, the change list is submitted for approval. Authorized groups of users are allowed to approve or reject the change list. If it is approved, choose Approved State ➤ Apply Changes. If it is rejected, the changes are assigned back to the user for reset (the changes are reverted and the change list is closed). Figure 7-112 shows the lifecycle of a change list.

The Catalog Services ➤ Change List screen has different functionalities to work on change lists, including Create, View, Set as Current, Reset, Submit for Approval, and Delete. There is a Display Details button that gets the list of the changes made to that particular change list in a popup.

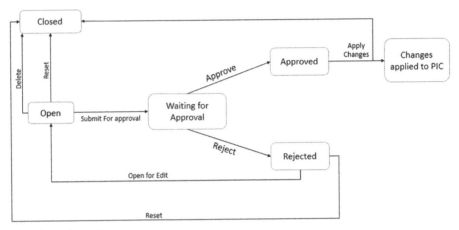

Life Cycle of a Change List

Figure 7-112. *Lifecycle of a change list*

The popup has five tabs:

- *New*: Consists of the new object changes.

- *Edit*: Consists of the edited object changes.

- *Log*: Shows the list of phases the change list has passed through.

- *Delete*: Consists of the list of deleted objects.

- *Notes to Approver*: All the extra information that an approver should know are mentioned here.

Figure 7-113 shows a created change list with a status of open.

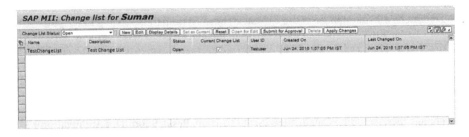

Figure 7-113. *Existing change list*

If users create a multiple change list and want to specify one of the specific change lists as the current one, they must select the change list and click on the Set as Current button to mark it. The current marked change list will appear on top of the Waiting for Approval list.

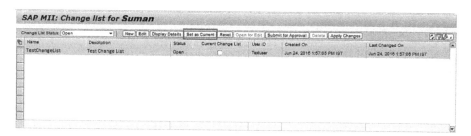

Figure 7-114. *Setting a change list as the current one*

Selecting a change list and clicking on Display Details will show the details of the particular change list. See Figure 7-115.

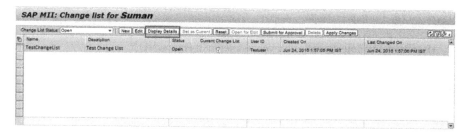

Figure 7-115. *Displaying details of a change list*

When you click Display Details, a popup will open with the new change list details. Users can either click on Submit or Reset from that screen to proceed to the next step. See Figure 7-116.

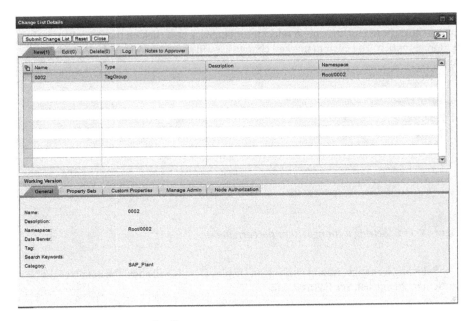

Figure 7-116. *Change List details screen*

Users can add notes to the approver, as shown in Figure 7-117.

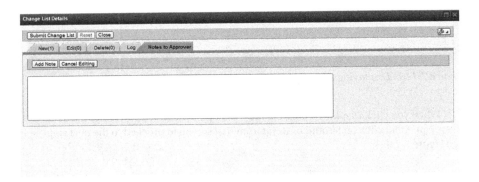

Figure 7-117. *Notes to Approver feature*

The change list is closed once it's approved and changes are applied or they are rejected and reset.

Creating a PIC Hierarchy in Plant Information Maintenance

Open Plant Information Maintenance by choosing Catalog Services ➤ Plant Information Maintenance from the SAP MII menu. The screen is divided into two parts—Plant Information Sources on the left side and Plant Information Catalog on the right side. See Figure 7-118.

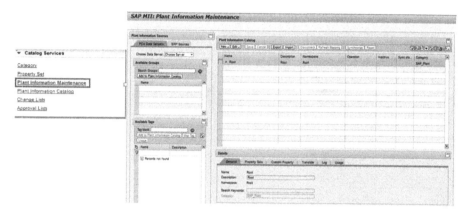

Figure 7-118. *Plant Information Maintenance screen*

At the right side of the screen, the PIC hierarchy can be created. As discussed earlier, PIC hierarchy can have two object types: Tag, which is the leaf node representing the measurement point, and Group, which are tag containers grouped logically. See Figure 7-119.

Plant Information Catalog

Name	Description	Namespace	Operation	Inactive	Sync st...	Category
▼ Root	Root	Root				SAP_Plant
▼ DemoPlant	DemoPlant	Root/DemoPlant				SAP_Plant
▶ L3PinChainEast	L3 Pin C...	Root/DemoPlant/L3Pin...				SAP_Equipment
▼ L3PinChainWest	L3 Pin C...	Root/DemoPlant/L3Pin...				SAP_Equipment
▶ L3SauceApplicator		Root/DemoPlant/L3Pin...				SAP_Equipment
▼ Palletizer	Pallet M...	Root/DemoPlant/L3Pin...				SAP_Equipment
▼ L3RapidPakEast	L3 Rapid...	Root/DemoPlant/L3Pin...				SAP_Equipment
▶ PackingMachine	Packing ...	Root/DemoPlant/L3Pin...				SAP_Equipment
· Tag2		Root/DemoPlant/L3Pin...				
· Tag2		Root/DemoPlant/L3Pin...				
· Rate	Rate	Root/DemoPlant/L3Pin...				

Figure 7-119. *Plant Information Catalog hierarchy*

271

PIC hierarchy has a default node called Root and all the created objects are located under this Root node (group). The following buttons are available at the top of the Plant Information Catalog screen:

- *New*: The options of creating a group or tag are available here (see Figure 7-120). Upon selecting the desired option, it will ask you for the Name, Description, and Category in a popup window. when you click OK, it will create the object under the selected node. *A new group or tag can be created under any group, but objects cannot be created under any tag.*

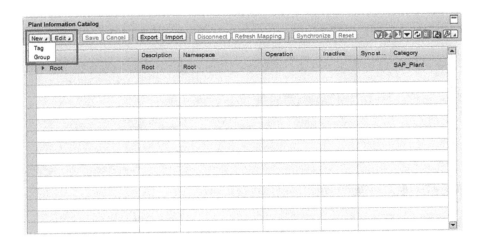

Figure 7-120. Selecting a new PIC

The New Group screen appears, as shown in Figure 7-121.

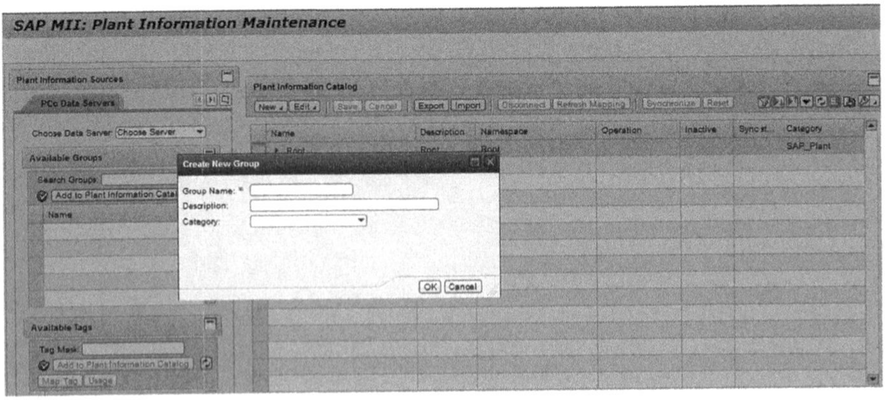

Figure 7-121. Creating New Group PIC

Once the object is created, there are five tabs available just below the screen with the details of that particular object:

- *General*: Specifies the general properties like name, description, namespace, and category.

- *Property Set*: Specifies the associated property sets to which values can be assigned.

- *Custom Property*: Specifies the custom properties added to that object with corresponding values.

- *Log*: Specifies the list of activities taken on that particular object.

- *Translate*: Specifies the language dependent description text for the selected object.

- *Edit*: Upon clicking this button, all edit functionalities like Edit, Cut, Copy, Paste, and Delete will be available (see Figure 7-122).

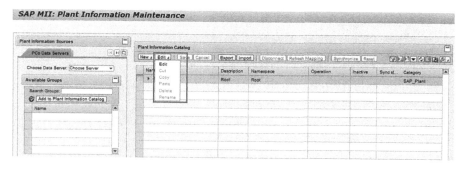

Figure 7-122. *Editing the PIC*

- *Save*: This button will be enabled when the Edit button is clicked. It allows you to save the changes made to the object.

- *Cancel*: This button will be enabled when the Edit button is clicked. It allows you to discard all the changes made after clicking on the Edit button.

- *Export*: Upon clicking this button, it exports the whole hierarchy of the selected node with all its child objects in XML format.

- *Import*: Upon clicking this button, it imports the whole hierarchy available in the XML format file with all its child nodes available in that XML file.

Adding Groups and Tags

Now we are looking at the left side of the screen, i.e., the Plant Information Sources section. This section includes the PCo Data Server tab, which lists all the shopfloor systems connected to SAP MII through PCo connectors of SAP MII. The desired data server can be selected and the proper tags can be searched and mapped or added. See Figure 7-123.

Figure 7-123. *Adding already added PCo tags to PIC from PCo data server*

There are two ways to map/add shopfloor tags to a PIC hierarchy. They can be added to the hierarchy under a group by clicking the Add to Plant Information button. Another way is to create a tag in the hierarchy and then map it to a tag from the list of shopfloor tags using the Map Tag button. The Usage button of this section shows the PIC tags mapped to that shopfloor tag in a popup.

Once a tag from the PIC hierarchy is mapped to a shopfloor tag, all the properties can be mapped to the metadata of the shopfloor tags. In that case, property values cannot be assigned manually. Values will be fetched from the shopfloor and stored. The Refresh button can be used to fetch the tag value from the shopfloor again. See Figure 7-124.

Figure 7-124. Adding PCo tags created from the PIC and mapping them to the PIC

Only one user can work on an object at a time. If a user is working on any object, that object is locked by his/her name shown in the Operations column of the PIC hierarchy and cannot be edited by any other user.

Adding Business Context

To add business context, ERP system data needs to be fetched. SAP MII has five configurable resource adapters to serve this purpose. These adapters allow you to bring all five resources to one point and fetch the data from there.

You configure ERP systems in the resource adapters using the following steps:

1. Log in to SAP NetWeaver Administrator.

2. Navigate to Configuration ➤ Infrastructure ➤ Application Resources.

3. Search the Plant Information Catalog. The list of all five adapters will be shown.

4. Go to the Properties tab.

5. Enter the required fields: Name, Type, Value, and Description.

6. Click Save.

Once the configuration is complete, ERP objects can be mapped to the PIC objects from the ERP Resources tab available in the Plant Information Sources section.

Approving the Change List

The hierarchy is ready now and needs to be approved. Unless the change in hierarchy is approved by an authorized person, it will not move to the PIC from the Plant Information Maintenance section. Users should have the SAP_XMII_Approver role assigned to their UME profiles to have the authorization to approve or reject the changes to the PIC hierarchy. The Catalog Services ➤ Approval List menu path will show the list of change lists submitted for approval with an option to display the details of that change list, and approve or reject them. See Figure 7-125.

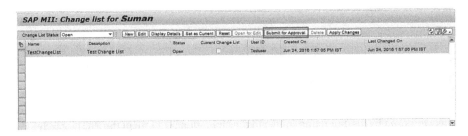

Figure 7-125. *Submitting the change list for approval*

Applying Changes to the Change List

Once the change list is approved, it comes to the same list again with the status approved and waiting for the changes to be applied. The Apply Changes button will be enabled for the change lists with approved status. Once Apply Changes is clicked, the locks acquired on the objects of that change list are released and the changes are reflected in the Plant Information Catalog screen. See Figure 7-126.

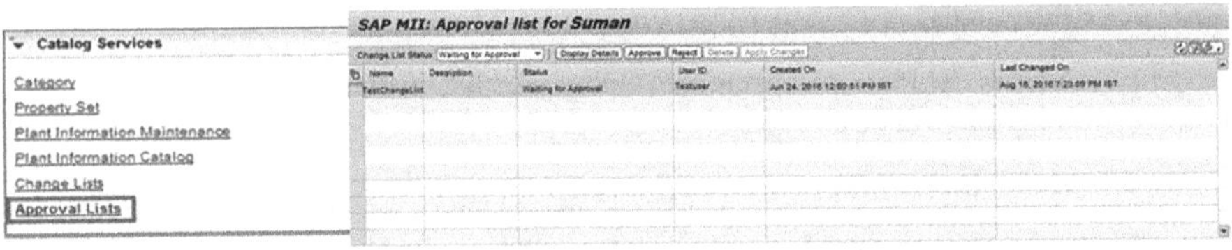

Figure 7-126. *Approval list screen*

Consuming the PIC Hierarchy

In the Query template, there is the Catalog query. This is specifically used to consume the PIC hierarchy. When a PIC is created, PIC tags are mapped to the PCo data server's tags or to the shopfloor tags. PIC saves the mapping, not the data. When a PIC tag is queried, live data is fetched from the shopfloor or PCo Data Server at that moment.

But ERP object mapping works differently. As soon as the mapping is done, all business contexts are saved to the corresponding properties in the local SAP MII system.

Follow these steps to create and configure the Catalog query:

1.   Launch Workbench.

2.   Go to the Catalog tab.

3.   Right-click on any folder and select New ➤ Catalog Query, as shown in Figure 7-127.

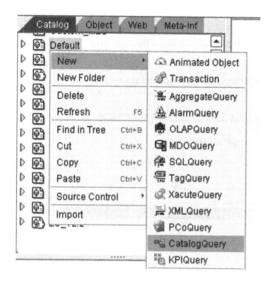

Figure 7-127. *Selecting a Catalog query*

The Template Categories options shown in Figure 7-128 are available to configure the Catalog query.

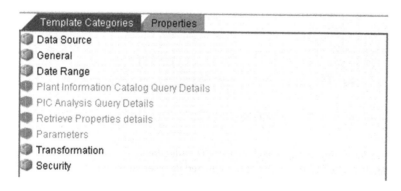

Figure 7-128. *Template Categories configuration in Catalog query*

4. From the Data Source screen, select the source data server and mode of the query (see Figure 7-129). Available modes are:

- *ModeList*: Shows the list of modes.

- *GroupList*: Shows the list of all groups available in the PIC hierarchy.

- *TagList*: Shows the list of all tags available in the PIC hierarchy.

- *Current*: Shows the current value for the tags and property values.

- *History*: Shows interpolated historical value of the tags and the property values.

- *HistoryEvents*: Shows the historical value of the tags and the property values.

- *Statistics*: Shows the statistical data as per shopfloor records.

- *RetrieveProprties*: Shows the property values.

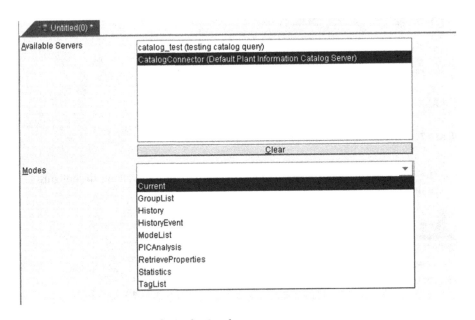

Figure 7-129. Available modes in the Catalog query

5. In the Plant Information Catalog Query Details screen, navigate to the PIC hierarchy of the selected data server in the PIC tree. See Figure 7-130.

6. Move the tag objects to the selected tags section either by dragging and dropping or using the available buttons.

7. Select Tag from the selected tags list and select the corresponding properties.

8. From Extended tab, SELECT the catalog server and the PCo Server used for mapping.

9. Select metadata for all the PCo servers.

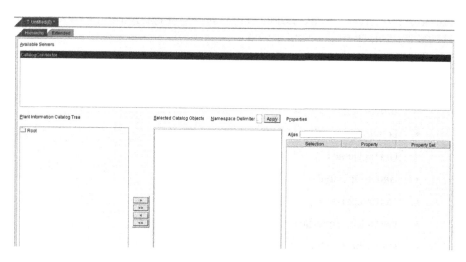

Figure 7-130. *Configuring hierarchy Catalog query*

10. The Retrieve Properties Details screen is quite similar to the Plant Information Catalog Query Details screen and is used for the Retrieve Properties mode. There is an option on this screen to choose groups as well as tags.

Catalog queries can also be used in illuminator services as shown:

```
<Protocol>://<Server IP>:<Port>/XMII/Illuminator?QueryTemplate=<Query
Path>&content-type=text/xml&Group=<Group Name>
```

PIC Web Services

PIC provides four web services. All the operations on PIC can be done using any of those web services.

The web services are as follows:

- Catalog Service

- Catalog Admin Service

- Change List Service
- Property Set Service

Catalog Service

Using Catalog Service, you can perform all the operations available using the Plant Information Catalog Screen as methods within the service. The WSDL URL for this web service is:

```
<Protocol>://<Server IP>:<Port>/PlantInformationCatalogService/PlantInformation
CatalogServiceBean?wsdl&mode=ws-policy
```

Available methods are:

- BrowseGroups
- BrowseTags
- FetchAllCustomProperties
- GetTagDetails
- GetGroupDetails
- GetCategories
- GetObjectProperties
- GetPropertyValue
- SearchGroups
- SearchTags

Catalog Admin Service

Using Catalog Admin Service, you can perform all the operations that can be performed using Plant Information Maintenance screen available as methods within the service. The WSDL URL for this web service is:

```
<Protocol>://<Server IP>:<Port>/PlantInformationMaintenanceService/Plant
InformationMaintenanceServiceBean?wsdl&mode=ws-policy
```

Available methods are:

- AddProperties
- BrowseGroups
- BrowseTags
- CreateGroup

- CreateTag

- DeleteGroup

- DeleteTag

- DeleteProperties

- GetGroupDetails

- GetTagDetails

- GetPropertyValue

- MaintainGroup

- MaintainTag

- SearchGroups

- SearchTags

Change List Service

Using Change List Service, you can perform all the operations that can be performed in Change List Screen available as methods within the service. The WSDL URL for this web service is:

```
<Protocol>://<Server IP>:<Port>/ChangeListServices/ChangeListServicesBean?
wsdl&mode=ws-policy
```

Available methods are:

- CreateChangeList

- SearchChangeLists

- ManageChangeListStatus

- ResetObjects

- ApplyChanges

Property Set Service

Using Property Set Service, you can perform all the operations that can be performed in the Property Set screen available as methods within the service. The WSDL URL for this web service is:

```
<Protocol>://<Server IP>:<Port>/PropertySetServices/PropertySetServicesBean?
wsdl&mode=ws-policy
```

Available methods are:

- AddProperties

- DeleteProperties

- CreatePropertySet

- EditPropertySet

- DeletePropertySet

- SearchPropertySets

What Is SAP Plant Connectivity (PCo)?

SAP Plant Connectivity (PCo) is a framework and set of services and management tools that provides bidirectional communication paths among control systems, control devices, files, historians, TCP sockets, and SAP. It is developed on Microsoft.Net.

Why PCo?

In any manufacturing industry, there are numerous machines and devices that continuously generate huge amounts of process data. It's critical to ensure that that data is analyzed properly and acted upon in real-time to ensure smooth operations and quick decisions in the case of deviations.

With SAP MII and PCo, real-time integration with manufacturing automation system can be easily achieved, even when the underlying systems provides different types of connection protocols. To drive real-time intelligence, PCo acts as a connection adapter and SAP MII provides the business logic to manage data and incorporate business rules.

History of PCo

PCo is the second generation of the SAP manufacturing connector technology. It replaces the xMII UDS (Universal Data Server) product that was originally developed by Lighthammer Corp. and brought into SAP with the acquisition of Lighthammer by SAP in July, 2005.

The original release of PCo, version 2.0, was in December 2008. That release only supported the real-time event-based notifications, and provided the following agents and destinations.

Agents:

- *OPC DA Agent: Supports OPC DA 2.05a and 3.0 specifications*

- OPC A&E Agent

- *OPC UA Agent:* Supports subscribing to OPC UA variable data, change events, and OPC UA v1.0 build 224 [and later] builds

- Socket Agent: Enables receiving streams and oriented socket messages

Destinations:

- *MII Destination*: Supports delivering notification messages to MII 11.5, 12.0, and 12.1

- *RFC Destination*: Used for enabling bi-directional communication between EWM and the socket agent and only used with the socket agent for the EWM scenario

- Does not provide general RFC usage

Integrating PCo with Automation Systems

PCo provides the following connectors as source systems:

- OPC Data Access (OPC DA)

- OPC Historical Data Access (OPC HDA)

- OPC Alarms and Events (OPC A&E)

- OPC Unified Architecture (OCP UA)

- Object Linking and Embedding Database (OLEDB)

- Open Database Connectivity (ODBC)

- iHistorian

- OSISoft PI

- TCP/IP Sockets

- File Monitor

It provides a Query mechanism using tag queries, PCo queries, and SQL queries from SAP MII and retrieves data from the underlying system on an on-demand basis.

PCo also provides Notification mechanisms. Subscription to one or more tags of the source system is possible to receive PCo notification to the target system for tag value changes and when a particular condition is satisfied.

PCo can send notifications to the following destination systems:

- SAP MII

- SAP ME (Manufacturing Execution)

- SAP HANA Database

- SQL Server

- Business Enterprise System (SAP ERP/EWM)

It is possible for PCo to send unprocessed tag information to the destination systems. But to make it more meaningful, SAP MII is used as middleware to easily develop the logic to attach corresponding machine or process parameters to the data received from PCo and consolidate it to the actual destination system for further processing.

Machine Data Connection

PCo connects directly to the automation control systems with SAP MII. First a source system in PCo needs to be configured to the automation control system. PCo can connect to SCADA or the Plant Historian System through an OPC server or directly to the source system through connectors. Certain parameter values of a machine signifies the machine downtime and are commonly known as tags. These tags are available in the Plant Data Historian. OPC simulators are generally used as automation system simulators.

Being a Microsoft Windows executable program, it is recommended to install PCo and source systems in the same Windows server to avoid complex firewall and DCOM security configurations.

What Is OPC?

OPC stands for OLE for Process Control. OPC is a software interface standard that allows Windows programs to communicate with industrial hardware devices (such as the PLC device).

OPC implementation is done in client/server pairs where the OPC server is a software program to convert hardware communication protocol used by PLC into OPC. See Figure 7-131.

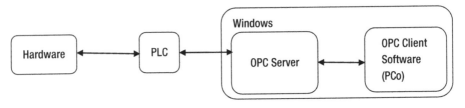

Figure 7-131. Data flow diagram and placement of OPC

Protocol and OPC client software is any program that needs to connect to the hardware, such as PCo. The OPC client uses the OPC server to get data from or to send commands to the hardware.

OPC is an open standard and results in lower cost for the manufacturer and more options for users. Hardware manufacturers need to provide only a single OPC server for their devices to communicate with any OPC client. Software vendors simply include OPC client capabilities in their products and they become instantly compatible with thousands of hardware devices. Users can choose any OPC client software they need, resting assured that it will communicate seamlessly with their OPC-enabled hardware and vice versa.

Configuration in PCo Management Console

Follow these steps for source system configuration:

1. Open the PCo Management console.

2. Click on New Source System icon.

3. Select Type of Source System from the drop-down (Suppose OPC DA Source System). Select the Source System Type depending on the source system connector type.

4. Specify the name of the source system.

5. Specify the description of the source system.

6. Click OK. the Source system is created now.

7. Select the newly created source system. It shows the corresponding connectivity details in the right pane.

8. Select the server details of the source system. See Figure 7-132.

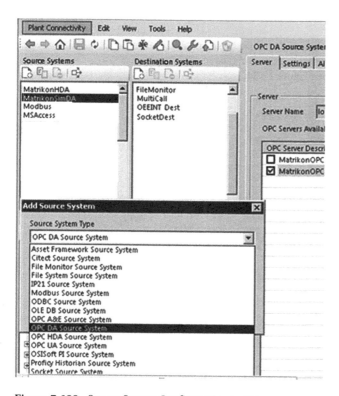

Figure 7-132. Source System Configuration in PCo

9. Add the server name. If the source system and PCo is installed on the same server, then the server name can be given as localhost. Otherwise, the hostname or the IP of the source system server needs to be mentioned.

10. PCo now will automatically determine the OPC DA server available in that particular host. See Figure 7-133.

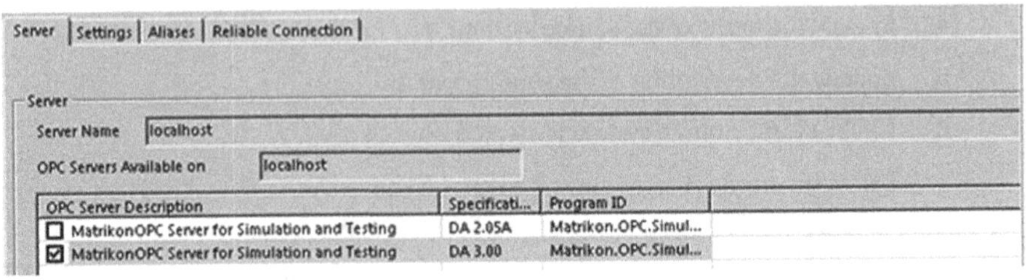

Figure 7-133. OPC server selection in PCo

11. Certain other properties can also be selected in the Settings, Aliases, and Reliable Connection tabs of OPC agent configuration. See Figure 7-134.

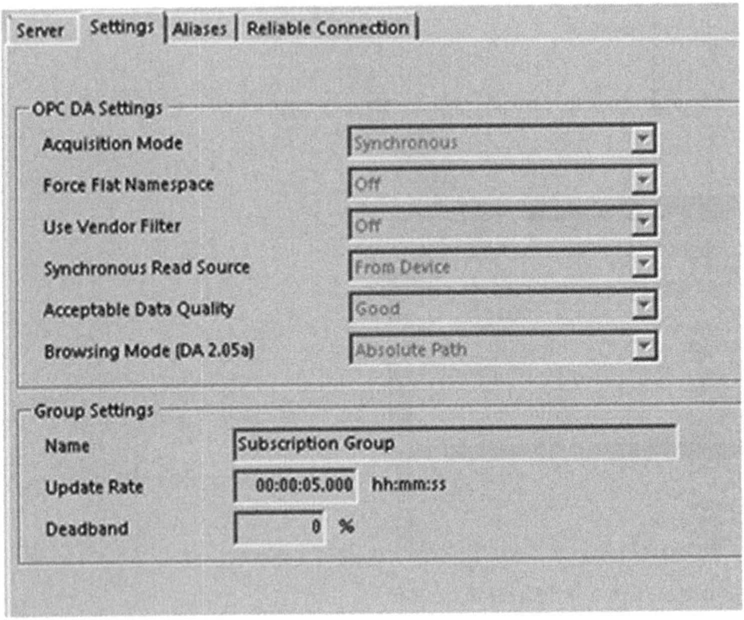

Figure 7-134. The OPC DA setting in PCo

The max number of retries and the retry interval can be set from the Reliable Connection window, as shown in Figure 7-135.

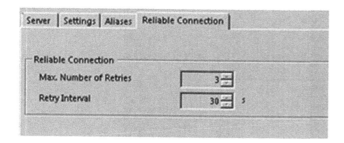

Figure 7-135. *OPC connection retention configuration in PCo*

PCo Agent Configuration

The next step is to configure the agents, the destination system, and the notification to capture real-time data. You process the data using process intelligence.

1. Click on the new icon in the agent instances from the PCo menu.

2. Select the source system for which the agent needs to be configured.

3. Specify a name.

4. Enter a description. The agent is created now.

5. Select general parameters like log level (error, fatal, information, or warning).

6. Specify a service mode and authentication if required.

7. Specify notification message queue and dispatch settings to enable queuing of notification messages sent from the PCo.

8. Create a new agent. See Figure 7-136.

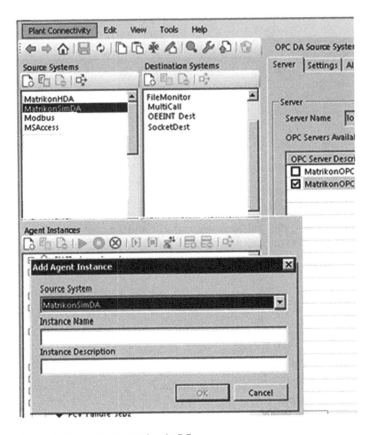

Figure 7-136. *Agent creation in PCo*

Once the new agent is created, multiple agent specific configuration needs to be done. See from Figure 7-137 to Figure 7-142.

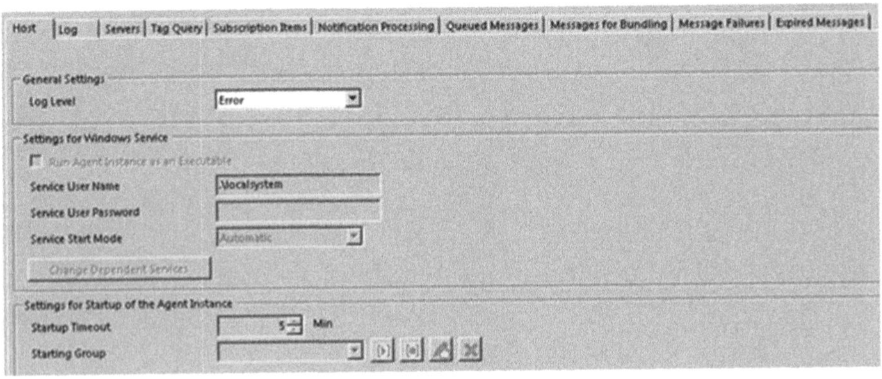

Figure 7-137. *Host configuration of created agent in PCo*

The Log tab shows all the info and error logs while reading the tag and triggering the notification. See Figure 7-138.

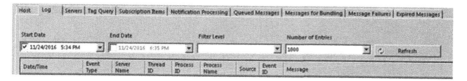

Figure 7-138. *The log of the agent in PCo*

The Servers tab is where you configure the port and the server type for an agent, as shown in Figure 7-139.

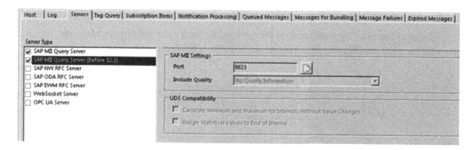

Figure 7-139. *The server type and port configuration for an agent in PCo*

The Tag Query tab is where you configure a tag query that can help to cache the data from data source, as shown in Figure 7-140.

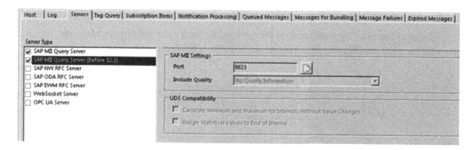

Figure 7-140. *Tag Query configuration for an agent*

The Subscription Items tab is where you add all the tags required to club together for the particular agent, as shown in Figure 7-141.

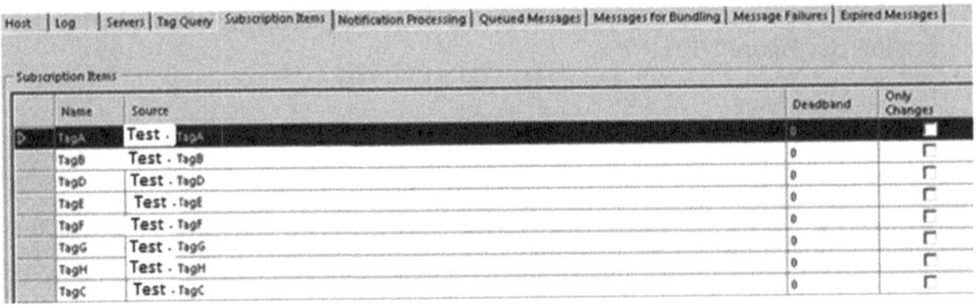

| | Host | Log | Servers | Tag Query | Subscription Items | Notification Processing | Queued Messages | Messages for Bundling | Message Failures | Expired Messages | |

Subscription Items

Name	Source	Deadband	Only Changes
TagA	Test . TagA	0	☑
TagB	Test . TagB	0	☐
TagD	Test . TagD	0	☐
TagE	Test . TagE	0	☐
TagF	Test . TagF	0	☐
TagG	Test . TagG	0	☐
TagH	Test . TagH	0	☐
TagC	Test . TagC	0	☐

Figure 7-141. *Subscription items configuration for an agent*

9. If the application needs a notification scenario to be enabled, the corresponding tags for which the value needs to be monitored and notification needs to be triggered should be specified in the Subscription Items tab.

The Notification Processing tab is where you configure the automatic Message queuing method and dispatching rule to handle the notification, as shown in Figure 7-142.

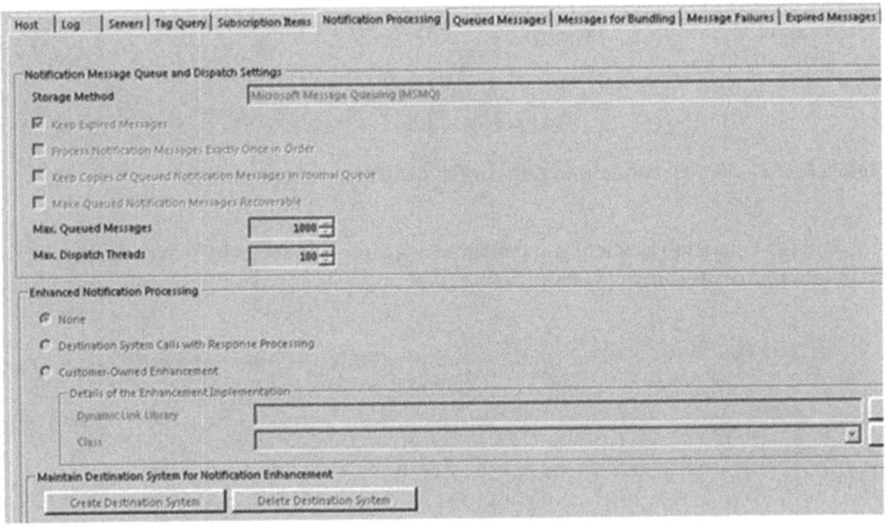

| Host | Log | Servers | Tag Query | Subscription Items | Notification Processing | Queued Messages | Messages for Bundling | Message Failures | Expired Messages |

Notification Message Queue and Dispatch Settings

Storage Method   [Microsoft Message Queuing (MSMQ)]

☑ Keep Expired Messages
☐ Process Notification Messages Exactly Once in Order
☐ Keep Copies of Queued Notification Messages in Journal Queue
☐ Make Queued Notification Messages Recoverable

Max. Queued Messages   [1000]
Max. Dispatch Threads   [100]

Enhanced Notification Processing

⦿ None
○ Destination System Calls with Response Processing
○ Customer-Owned Enhancement
    Details of the Enhancement Implementation
    Dynamic Link Library   [   ]
    Class   [   ]

Maintain Destination System for Notification Enhancement
    [Create Destination System]   [Delete Destination System]

Figure 7-142. *Notification processing configuration for an agent*

Destination System Configuration

You must configure a destination system only when there is a notification scenario and PCo needs to send a notification message to the destination system for a particular change in tag values.

Destination systems are not required when tag values are queried from SAP MII on an ad-hoc basis.

Different types of destination systems can be configured in PCo to send notification messages, and one of those is SAP MII.

Once SAP MII receives notification messages from PCo, it processes the messages through business logic to add business context, as it is not possible for PCo to add all the business context. PCo messages only contain tag information.

Notification Processing Event Configuration

When a tag value in an automation system changes due to some change in a physical parameter in the machine, some action must be triggered. If a tag is maintained in the historian, a plant maintenance notification will be triggered.

For an OPC DA source system, the source system itself evaluates the condition specified in PCo for sending the signal to PCo to trigger the notification.

For any other source system, PCo evaluates the triggering condition continuously based on the tag value update rate or the event interval in the source system settings configuration to trigger the notification.

1. Select the agent created earlier.

2. Click on the Create Notification icon. See Figure 7-143.

3. Specify a name.

4. Specify a description.

5. Click OK. A notification is created.

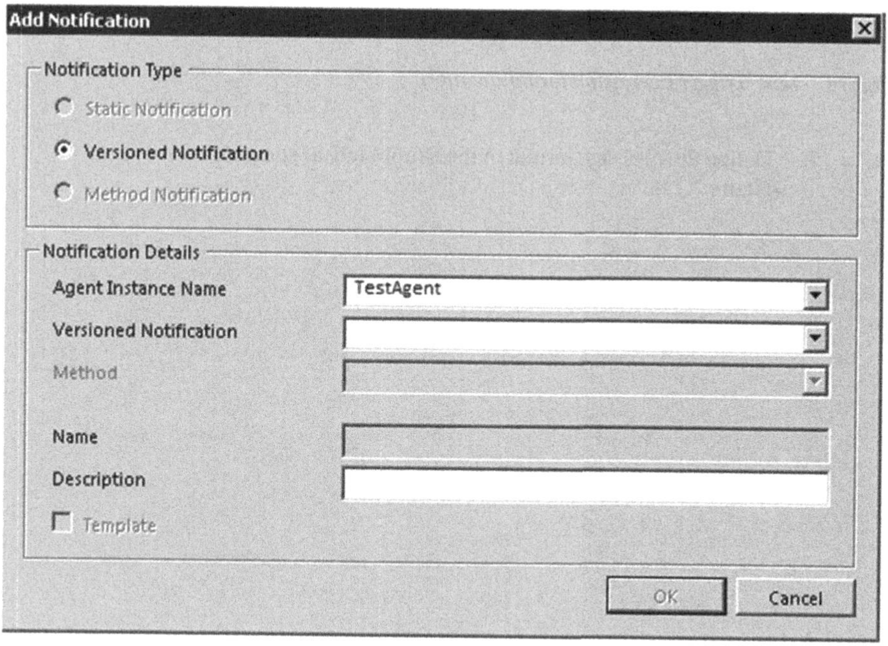

Figure 7-143. Notification for an agent instance

Once the notifications are added to the agent instance name, all the notification names with status and details are shown under the agent instance name, as shown in Figure 7-144.

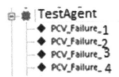

Figure 7-144. *Created notification with status*

6. Specify the trigger condition in the Notification tab. Specify any condition using the subscribed tags. , as shown in Figure 7-145.

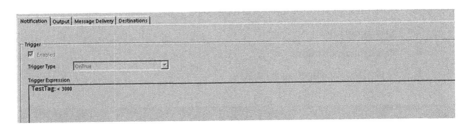

Figure 7-145. *Trigger expression for notification*

7. Define the message format in the Output tab, as shown in Figure 7-146.

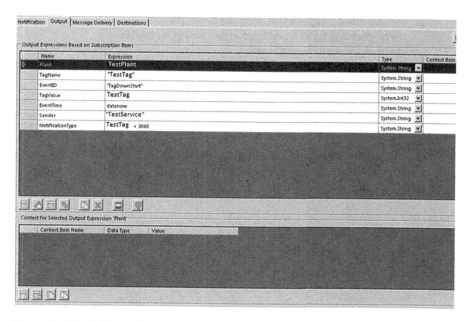

Figure 7-146. *Defining the output structure of notification*

    8.   Specify the conditions for message delivery in the Message
            Delivery tab, as shown in Figure 7-147.

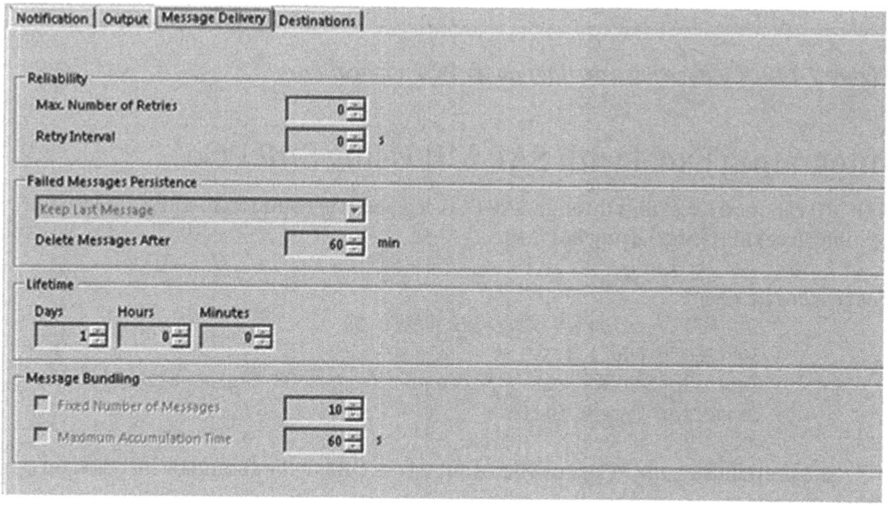

Figure 7-147. *Message delivery time configuration*

9. Specify the destination system in the Destination tab. The BLS to be executed for PCo notification processing is mentioned here, as shown in Figure 7-148.

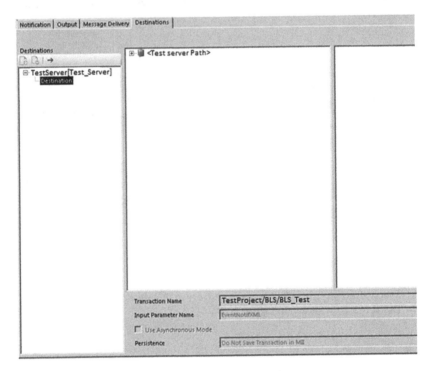

Figure 7-148. Configuring a destination for PCo notification

Integrating Excel with SAP MII Using SAP PCo

SAP MII can read Excel files through SAP PCo. It's become common to integrate PCo for reading Excel files (.xlsx) using SAP MII.

```
Tested Environment :
        SAP MII Version :  12.2 SP6 Patch 15
        SAP PCO : PCo 2.1.5.1
        Installation Package : Microsoft Access DB Engine X32-bit
        Connector Type : OLEDB
```

As a prerequisite, the PCo and Microsoft Access DB Engine should be installed on the same server.

■ **Note** The SAP MII version and PCo version are independent and should be configurable if the required provider exists. Reading Excel files (.xlsx) through PCo into MII requires the SAP recommended provider, called "Microsoft Office 12.0 Access Database Engine OLE DB Provider."

To read the Excel files, you need to set up some configurations in the PCo Management Console and in the SAP MII connection details. For step-by-step details, refer to this blog: https://blogs.sap.com/2015/10/26/procedure-to-integrate-pco-with-sap-mii-to-read-excelxlsx-files/.

Managing Notifications from the MII Menu Page

You can now directly manage notifications of SAP PCo from SAP 15.0 from the SAP MII menu options. You don't have to log in to the plant management console to create, configure, and manage PCo notifications. See Figure 7-149.

The benefits of having notifications managed directly in SAP MII are as follows:

- Users can manage and maintain multiple PCo installations centrally, from the same screen.

- User can directly modify, pause, and resume the notification in SAP MII.

- Enriched with the business context available in SAP MII PIC.

- Modified even when an agent instance is running, which was not possible through the Plant management console.

Figure 7-149. PCo notification management from the SAP MII menu page

As shown, when the Notification Management under Plant Connectivity Integration option is check, the Plant Connectivity Management screen opens and has the following window tabs further available:

- Manage Notifications by SAP Plant Connectivity

- Manage Notification by PIC

- Browse Notifications

Manage Notifications by SAP Plant Connectivity Screen

Once you choose Manage Notifications by SAP Plant Connectivity, you'll see the screen shown in Figure 7-150.

Figure 7-150. *Manage notifications by plant connectivity from the SAP MII menu page*

Once the PCo server is selected, all the notifications will be displayed in a list with descriptions and other details, as shown in Figure 7-151.

Plant Connectivity Data Servers	
Name	**Description**
Test_PCo	
Test1_PCo	
Test1_Source	Source for Test1 from PCO
PIC_Excel_Pco	Making a different instance for doing query via pco to read excel file
PNWPCo	
Action_Source	Action source system
SAM_PCo	
Test_MSAccessCon	
test2instances	
TestAG_DataS	testing pco access (ag)
TestAG_HDA	test HDA
	Cancel

Figure 7-151. *List of notifications from the manage notification*

The PCo Servers list contains all the notifications configured for the corresponding PCo data servers configured in that SAP MII server. Users can view, monitor, and analyze against the name of the PCo data server selected by the created date, Modified On date, Modified by, and the status of the data server (running, stopped, or pending).

Once a data server is selected, the configured notifications will be displayed and if no notifications are available, then no data is displayed. In the bottom-right corner there is a button to create notifications directly in SAP MII against the data server, as shown in Figure 7-152.

Figure 7-152. The Create Notification button

Manage Notification by PIC Screen

From this screen, you can view the Plant Information Catalog hierarchy and manage the notifications against the tags. If required, you can also create new notifications. See Figure 7-153.

Figure 7-153. Manage Notification By PIC screen

Browse Notifications Screen

From this screen, all the notifications associated with the PCo data servers can be monitored for status and versioning using filter options, as shown in Figure 7-154.

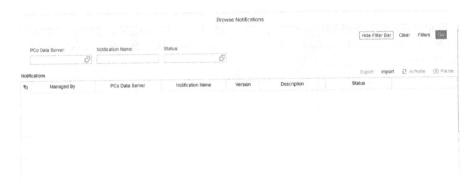

Figure 7-154. Browse Notifications from the manage notification

On the selected notification, you can do the following actions:

- View the notification
- Import the notification details in XML format to the SAP MII system
- Export the notification in XML format
- Activate
- Pause
- Resume

Sessioning in Queries and JRA

A *session* is a series of interactions between two communication endpoints that occur during the span of a single connection. SAP introduced some new features in MII that enable users to query SQL database logically. This ensures users can query in sessions along with using commit and rollback for appropriate transactions. The constraint is that data servers of IDBC and DataSource can use this functionality. These are the action blocks included in SAP MII Transaction for calling these specific databases in session. See Figure 7-155.

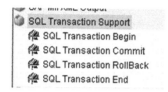

Figure 7-155. *SQL Session Support in SAP MII*

SQL Transaction Begin

This action is used mainly to begin the session for a logical database transaction. While executing, the data server is connected to the connection pool. This action block has inputs like Server Details and Connection Timeout. See Figure 7-156.

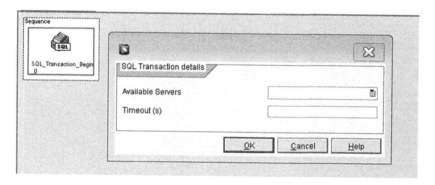

Figure 7-156. *SQL Transaction Begin action block and configuration*

SQL Transaction Commit

This action block performs commit actions on the database transaction. This action commits all the action made by the SAP MII SQL query template after beginning the transaction. The main input parameter is the SQL Transaction action block name for commit. Committing a transaction means making permanent the changes performed by the SQL statements within the transaction. See Figure 7-157.

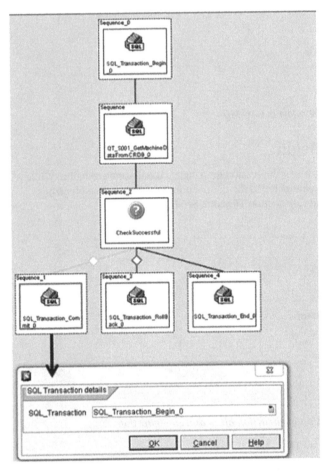

Figure 7-157. SQL Transaction Commit action block and configuration

SQL Transaction Rollback

This action rolls back a transaction. This option is provided to choose the transaction to roll back all the changes made in the SAP MII Transaction by the MII SQL Query Template after beginning a transaction. The main input is the SQL Transaction begin action block name. Rollback restores the state of the transaction until the last commit was performed. See Figure 7-158.

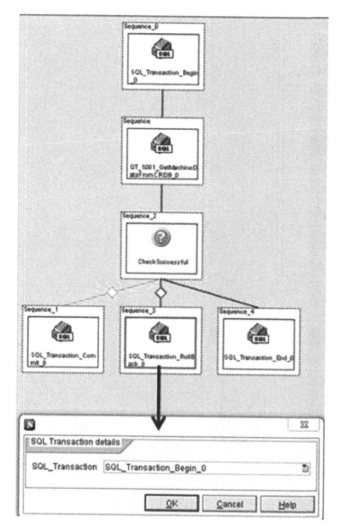

Figure 7-158. *SQL Transaction Rollback action block and configuration*

SQL Transaction End

This action ends the current database logical transaction. The input here is again the SQL Transaction begin action block name. This disconnects the data server configured in the SQL Transaction Begin action block. It is always best to end the transaction to disconnect the server when a process is completed. See Figure 7-159.

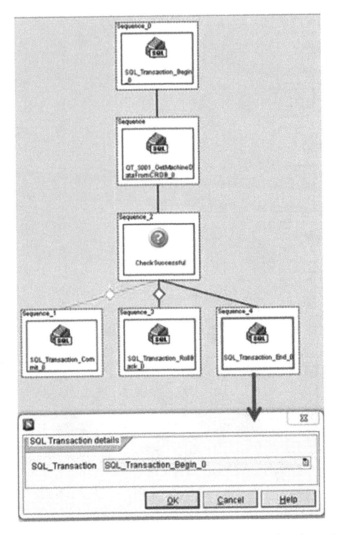

Figure 7-159. SQL Transaction End action block and configuration

Apart from sessions in the SAP MII SQL Query Transaction, SAP maintains SAP ECC (SAP ERP Central Component) calls from SAP MII in sessions as well. This is done for both SAP JCo (SAP Java Connector) and SAP JRA (Java Resource Adapter) connectivity.

Using SAP JRA (Java Resource Adapter)

The Java Resource Adapter (JRA) allows for both synchronous and asynchronous communication with the SAP ERP system. In SAP MII, it is used for both types of communication with SAP ERP. In this section, only the synchronous communication through action blocks is covered.

To use JRA, users need to configure the JCA connection factory in NetWeaver administrator (NWA).

Follow these steps to configure a JRA adapter:

1. Log in to the NetWeaver Administrator page
    (http://<server>:<port>/nwa).

2. Select Configuration Management ➤ Infrastructure ➤
    Application Resources.

3. Select JCA Resources.

4. Select SAPJavaResourceAdapter15 from the resource list.

5. In the Resource Details section, select the Dependent JCA
    Connection Factories tab.

6. Choose Copy and Add New JCA Connection Factory to define
    the JRA connection. See Figure 7-160.

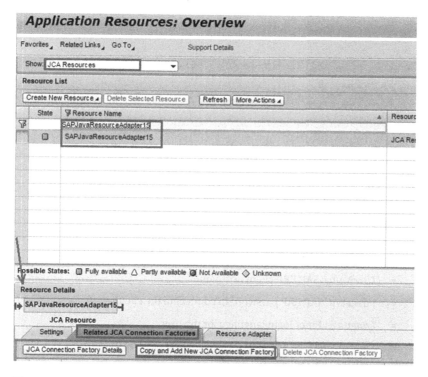

Figure 7-160. JCA Connection factory configuration creation

7. Enter a relevant resource name for the JNDI (Java Naming Directory Interface) name (see Figure 7-161):

- *NonGlobal*: SAP ERP specific connections. This setting will not be enlisted into distributed (Java Transaction API or JTA) transactions.

- *Shareable*: This default JRA operation and, as it's sharable, only one physical connection is created even if an application wants to acquire multiple connections.

- *Unsharable*: Each connection for the application will use separate physical connections from the connection pool.

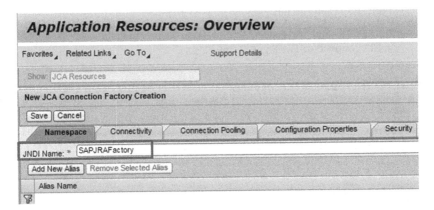

Figure 7-161. JNDI configuration for JRA factory

8. Go to the Configuration Properties tab.

9. Enter the following values for the JRA communication configuration (see Figure 7-162):

- *SAPClient*: SAP ERP client number

- *UserName*: SAP ERP client username

- *Password*: SAP ERP password to connect to the client

- *Language*: Enter login language for the user

- *ServerName*: The SAP ERP server URL as it resolves on your network (fully qualified)

- *PortNumber*: ERP defined system number you are connecting to

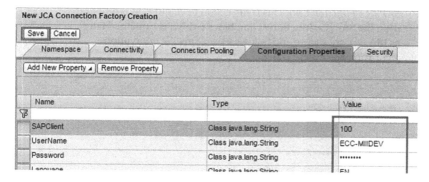

Figure 7-162. JCA Adapter properties configuration

    10.   Save the configuration now.

Now, as the JRA adapter has been configured and saved, the JRA action blocks can be used for development in SAP MII.

For SAP JRA the different action blocks in SAP MII are described here:

- *SAP JRA Start Session*: This action is to open a session between SAP MII and the SAP ERP Central Component (SAP ECC) using the SAP Java Resource Adapter (SAP JRA). Users have to select the configured JCA factory connection from the JRA Connector Name list, as shown in Figure 7-163.

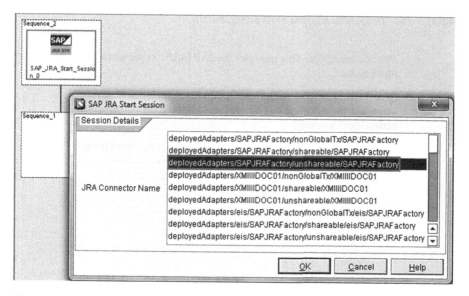

Figure 7-163. JRA factory connector list for start session action block

- *SAP JRA Function Call*: This is the action to call RFC. It is different from the SAP JCo function action block (which is explained later), as JRA is more secure and follows a user-specific encryption algorithm. See Figure 7-164.

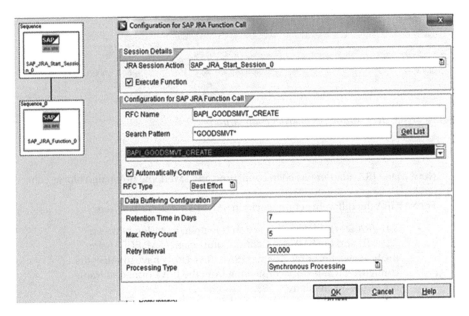

Figure 7-164. *JRA function action block configuration*

- *JRA Session Action*: This provides the SAP JRA Start session action block name.

  (Other configuration options in the JRA function block have the same functionality and will be explained later in the JCo function action block section).

- *SAP JRA Commit*: This action performs a commit function during a session between SAP MII and SAP ERP Central Component (SAP ECC) using the SAP Java Resource Adapter (SAP JRA). See Figure 7-165.

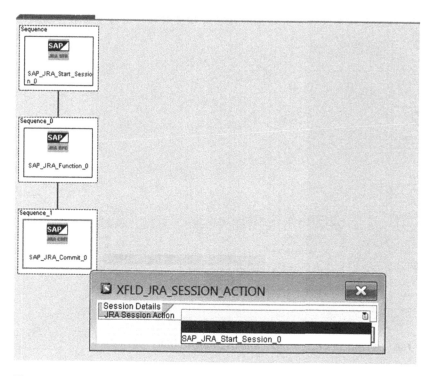

Figure 7-165. JRA commit action block and its configuration

- *SAP JRA Rollback*: This action can be used to roll back a function call during a session between SAP MII and SAP ERP Central Component (SAP ECC) using SAP Java Resource Adapter (SAP JRA). See Figure 7-166.

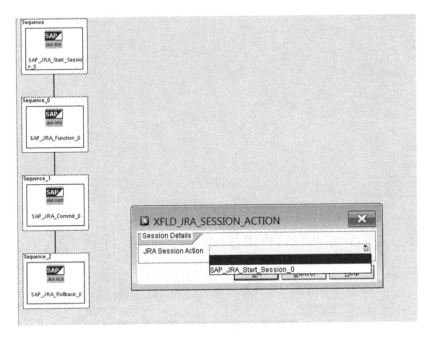

Figure 7-166. *JRA rollback action block and its configuration*

- *SAP JRA End Session*: This action can be used to close a session between SAP MII and SAP ERP Central Component (SAP ECC) using the SAP Java Resource Adapter (SAP JRA). See Figure 7-167.

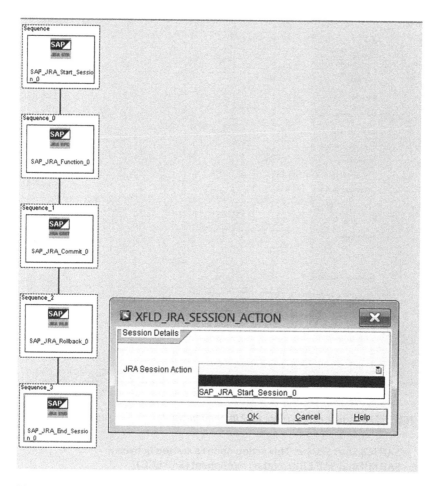

Figure 7-167. *JRA end session action and its configuration*

Using SAP JCo (SAP Java Connector)

SAP JCo action blocks call a Business Application Programming Interface (BAPI) using the SAP Java Connector (SAP JCo). They also control sessions between SAP MII and SAP ERP Central Component (SAP ECC).

The components are described here:

- *SAP JCo Interface*: This action creates a connection to the SAP Java Connector (JCo) interface from the ERP server and creates a Remote Function Call (RFC) request. The SAP JCo Interface action is used to send XML messages to and from the ERP system. This does not require session handling. See Figure 7-168.

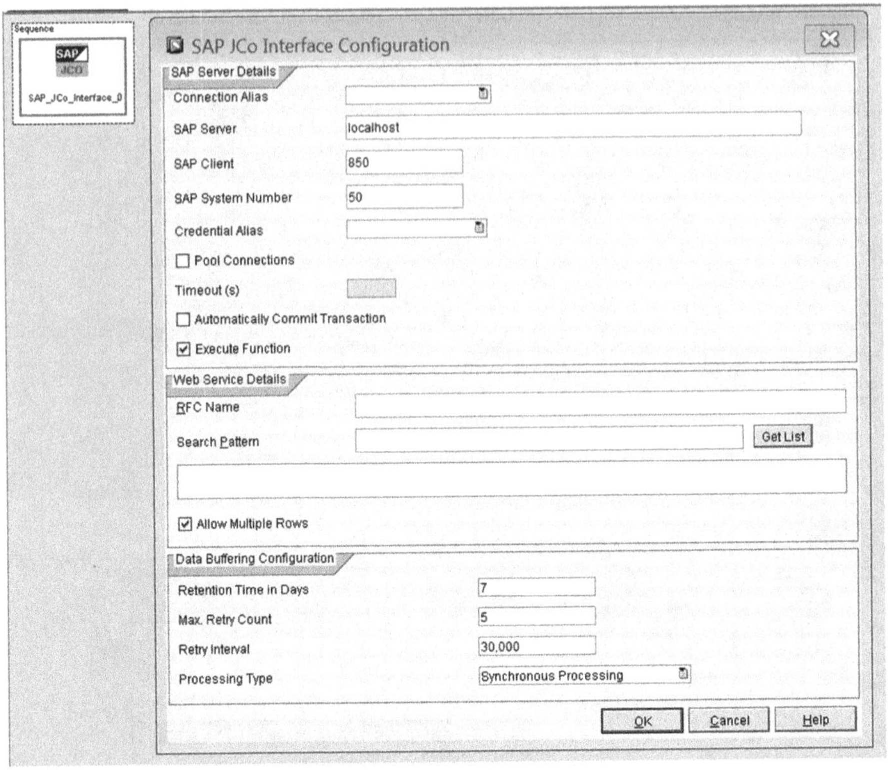

Figure 7-168. JCo interface action block and its configuration

- *SAP JCo Start Session*: This action opens a session between
  SAP MII and SAP ERP Central Component (SAP ECC).
  See Figure 7-169.

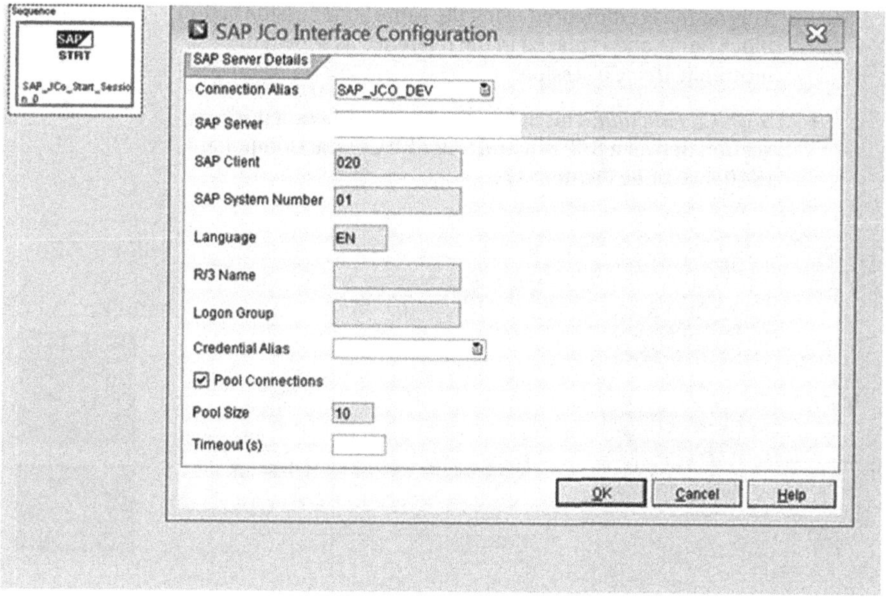

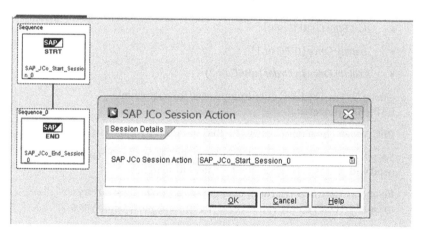

Figure 7-169. *JCo Start Session action block and its configuration*

- *SAP JCo End Session*: This action closes a session between
  SAP MII and SAP ERP Central Component (SAP ECC).
  See Figure 7-170.

Figure 7-170. *SAP JCo End Session action block and its configuration*

This action is configured using the same Start Session action block name and is placed in the reference as shown to terminate the JCo session.

- *SAP JCo Function*: This action performs a function during a session between SAP MII and SAP ERP Central Component (SAP ECC). See Figure 7-171.

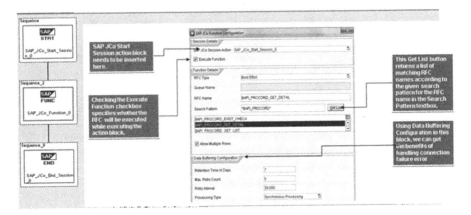

Figure 7-171. *SAP JCo function action block and its configuration*

The following often used options are there to configure the JCo function: The following RFC types are available:

- *Best Effort* (sRFC or 0)

- *Exactly Once* (tRFC or 1)

- *Exactly Once in Order* (qRFC or 2)

- *Queue Name*: The tRFC queue name used for sequential BAPI/RFC processing.

- *RFC Name*: The name of the BAPI/RFC to call.

- *Search Pattern*: Used to search for a BAPI/RFC by name. It can be used with the asterisk character for wildcard searches.

- *Retention Time in Days*: Number of days to asynchronously retry to call SAP ECC. It only applies to asynchronous processing types.

- *Max. Retry Count*: Maximum number of times to retry the call to SAP ECC. It only applies to asynchronous processing types.

- *Retry Interval*: Amount of time in seconds between SAP ECC communication retries.

- *Processing Type*: One of the following strategies used to communicate with SAP ECC:

  1. *Synchronous processing*: The BAPI/RFC is executed only once, even if it fails.

  2. *Asynchronous processing on error*: The BAPI/RFC is executed once. The transaction waits until the initial call succeeds or fails and then continues. If communication to SAP ECC is down, it retries in the background.

  3. *Asynchronous processing*: The BAPI/RFC is always executed in the background. The transaction continues without waiting for a response.

- *SAP JCo Commit*: This action performs a commit function during a session between SAP MII and SAP ERP Central Component (SAP ECC). See Figure 7-172.

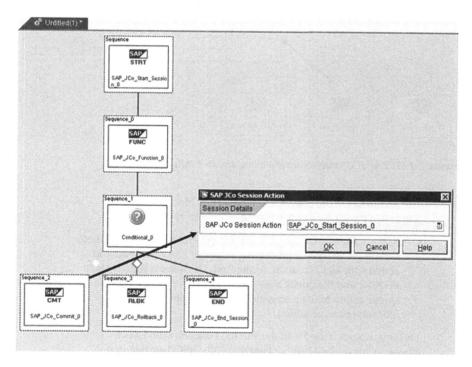

Figure 7-172. *SAP JCo commit action block and its configuration*

This action needs the JCo Start Session action block name to be referred in the JCo commit action block to commit the function.

- *SAP JCo Rollback:* This action is to roll back a function during a session between SAP MII and SAP ERP Central Component (SAP ECC). See Figure 7-173.

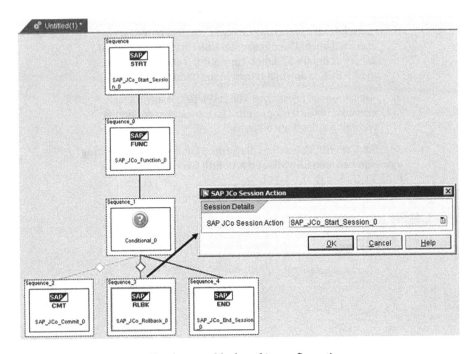

Figure 7-173. *SAP JCo Rollback action block and its configuration*

This action needs the JCo Start Session action block name to be referred in the JCo Commit action block to commit the function.

- *SAP JCo Execute Queue*: This action performs the queued Remote Function Call (qRFC) processing. Suppose a SAP JCo Function action with an RFC can be configured. The value is Exactly Once in Order and the queue name is typed. Then, SAP JCo Execute Queue action to the transaction to run the queue on the target SAP server can be added.

This action block is used with the SAP JCo Function action block whenever any queued Remote Function Calls (RFCs) are required. To achieve this, the SAP JCo Function action block needs to be configured with the RFC Type Exactly Once In Order and specified with the queue name, as shown in Figure 7-174.

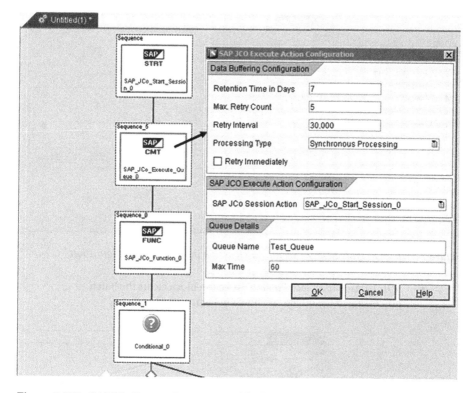

Figure 7-174. *SAP JCo Execute Queue action block and its configuration*

The system checks for an existing data buffer entry. If an entry exists, the system creates a new data buffer entry for the qRFC and adds it to the job.

New Action Blocks in SAP MII 15.X

Many new action blocks were introduced in the new versions of SAP MII. The new action blocks are described here:

- *SQL Transaction Execute Batch*: This action block is used to perform batch processing, as shown in Figure 7-175.

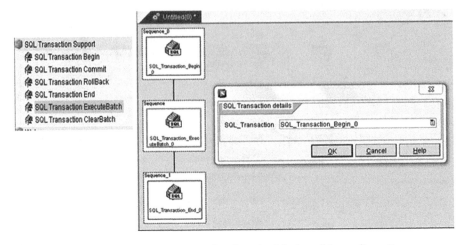

Figure 7-175. SQL Transaction Execute Batch action block and its configuration

- *SQL Transaction Clear Batch*: This action block clears the batch processing in the queue, as shown in Figure 7-176.

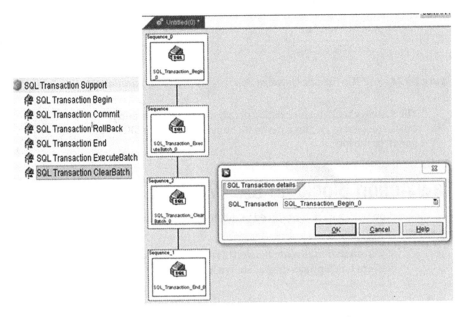

Figure 7-176. SQL Transaction Clear Batch action block and its configuration

- *JSON to XML Converter*: This XML function block converts the JSON structure into an XML structure, as shown in Figure 7-177.

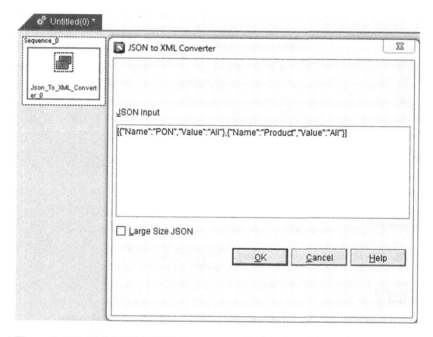

Figure 7-177. *SAP JSON to XML Converter action block and its configuration*

When an input JSON structure is provided in the JSON input and saved and executed, an XML version as an output of the action block is generated. The Large Size JSON checkbox is a Boolean flag and takes 1 or 0 when checked and unchecked, respectively. If it's selected, the large JSON Input could be provided; otherwise, it won't accept.

- *ADS Printing*: ADS printing lets you generate the file in PDF format with barcode/QR code from SAP MII. This can be directly used to print the result to a real printer, to save it in the file system, or feed it to a web browser, as shown in Figure 7-178.

Refer to http://www.sap.com/documents/2016/09/864b7d45-8a7c-0010-82c7-eda71af511fa.html.

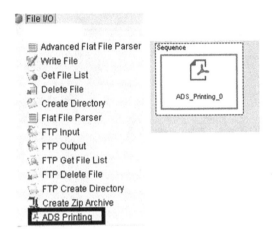

Figure 7-178. ADS Printing action block and its configuration

Summary

This chapter introduced the general concepts associated with MDO, visualization services, UI5 and SSCE, KPIs and alerts, PIC, PCo, session handling for queries and JRA, and the new action blocks introduced in SAP MII.

The next chapter discusses the best practices that should be followed for SAP MII and the frequently asked questions that will help you gain a more in-depth understanding of SAP MII.

CHAPTER 8

Best Practices and FAQs

In every programming and technical platform, there is a recommended approach by the product owner. Similarly with SAP MII, there are dos and don'ts that need to be followed. SAP MII is a platform, so there are few recommendations from SAP. The best practices explained here should be followed for best performance and effectiveness of the solution.

Best Practices

It is recommended you follow the best approaches explained in the following sections.

Project Handling

From the project creation perspective in SAP MII, it is always recommended best to use NWDI (NetWeaver Development Infrastructure) as for the proper version controlling mechanism, use the central repository feature for the entire development component, and to have zero code overwrite risk. If NWDI is used, then a shared project is created and check in and check out of the code check-in and check-out is mandatory in it. If you create a local project and store it on the local server, then anyone with access to the server can access the code. There is a good chance that the code will get overwritten, as multiple developers can edit and save the code. The latest instance of a code change will be saved.

Project Folder Structure

When creating a project, it is recommended you use a specific, easily understandable structure. For example, in the Catalog tab under Project, there should be separate folders defining different functionalities of the project, such as a report name. Under each functionality, there should be separate folders for different object types like Query Template and BLS. The exact same structure needs to be followed for the Object and Web tabs, but the Query Template and BLS is replaced with MDO, KPI objects etc., and with the web files HTML (.irpt), JavaScript, etc.

© Suman Mukherjee and Saptaparna Mukherjee (Das) 2017
S. Mukherjee and S. Mukherjee (Das), *SAP MII*, DOI 10.1007/978-1-4842-2814-2_8

Naming Conventions

Certain naming conventions should also be followed as part of your best practices. Here are a few examples:

- Scheduler: `<Project Name>_<Functionality>_<Plant (if any)>`

- Data Server: `DS_<Project Name>_<Server Name>`

- Credential Store: `<Project Name>_<Connection Name>`

- BLS: `BLS_<Functionality>`

- Query: `SQL_<Functionality>`, `[MDOQry/KPIQry/AlertQry]_<Functionality>`,`PCO_<Functionality>`, `XCT_<BLS Name>` etc.

- Display Template: `LineChrt_<Functionality>`, `iGrd_<Functionality>` etc.

- Object: `MDOObj_<Table Name>`, `KPIObj_<KPI Name>`

Note that if the customer has some pre-defined naming conventions as per company policy, those conventions should be given priority.

Development

During development, follow these recommendations to write clean code and experience better and more effective performance:

- Only the input and output properties used in the BLS should be declared as *transaction* variables. All other variables temporarily used in the BLS should be declared as *local* variables.

- Always use the `Exceptional Enabler` and `Catch` action blocks to capture any exceptions within the logic.

- Avoid using a repeater under another repeater. Avoid loops as much as possible in the logic. Instead, use XSLT to achieve good performance.

- Use XPath and XQueries to avoid looping.

- Remove all the tracers and loggers once the development is finalized (i.e., before migration), otherwise, the performance will be very poor and sometimes can lead to memory crash issues due to heavy logging.

- Avoid writing file and loader action blocks as much as possible because when they execute, they consume a considerable amount of memory.

- Avoid using a terminate action block.

- You must remove breakpoints and watchpoints once debugging is done; otherwise, the execution of BLS will stop at these breakpoints.

- If any BLS is executed in debug mode, close it with the Debug Close button. Do not close it directly by clicking the cross (X) button. Even if the BLS is closed, the cache memory will continue caching the debug log whenever the BLS executes and a Java heap space error could occur.

- Avoid storing large input in the local variable again, even if it is already coming from source, because once a value comes in a BLS, it exists until the end of the BLS execution.

- Avoid creating a local XML structure as a local variable and appending the value in it if it is possible to achieve the same effect through MII Output XML action blocks.

- Try to use asynchronous transaction calls as much as possible if they fit in the logic. Synchronous transaction calls hold the execution of primary BLS until the execution of the called BLS is complete and thus adversely affect performance.

- Use meaningful naming conventions with *Camelcasing* for all action blocks. If possible, provide action block descriptions.

- Avoid calling BLS from a scheduler where, within that BLS, a synchronous transaction call is present. It holds the execution of scheduler instance and keeps the scheduler in a running state for a long time. In such cases, try to use a wrapper BLS, which will call the primary BLS asynchronously and put the wrapper BLS in the scheduler. The scheduler instance will not be queued until the next execution since it works asynchronously.

- Do not hardcode usernames and passwords in an action block. Try to use credential aliases and refer to them in the action block. On a similar note, this is also applicable to the connection alias.

- Avoid hardcoding in the action block configuration, and try to use it dynamically as much as possible.

- Do not use select * in a SQL query if it is not required. Try to define the specific column while querying.

- Do not use hardcoded timeout in the UI. Try to handle timeouts using logic.

- Do not hardcode usernames and passwords in a URL used in the UI.

- Do not repeat any logic part in BLS and in UI. In UI try to call the function in multiple places.

- It is suggested to use sessioning during an ECC call using JCO, JRA, and similarly for query templates. It helps to commit and roll back the call.

- It is recommended to use the MVC model for UI, which helps keep code clean and easily understandable to other developers.

- Try to use separate property files for different user locales in the Web tab.

- Try to develop a utility file that will have the common functionality code for different modules so as to reuse it in other object development settings.

- Explain in the comments section the use of the code and the functions being used in the UI frontend coding. This will help other developers understand the code later.

FAQs (Frequently Asked Questions)

Here are some common queries that SAP MII professionals and practitioners have:

1. *What is SAP MII?*

   SAP MII is a platform developed in Java by Lighthammer and acquired by SAP. SAP MII can work as middleware with real-time integration and high-end intelligence capabilities. SAP MII is so advanced that lots of innovations are possible using IOT.

2. *How do I install SAP MII?*

   SAP MII can be installed on top of NetWeaver or the SAP HANA Web application server.

3. *What versions are available in SAP MII?*

   SAP MII was introduced by SAP as SAP xMII 11.5. Later on, there was SAP MII 12.0, SAP MII 12.1, SAP MII 12.2, SAP MII 14.0, and SAP MII 15.0. The latest version is SAP MII 15.1.

4. *Does SAP MII support SAP HANA?*

   Yes, from SAP MII 15.1, it is possible to expose the MII data in HANA using the OData service.

5. *What is the base component of SAP MII?*

   SAP MII is developed using Java Swing and SAP MII supports XML for all internal processing and handling.

6. *What kind of integration is possible using SAP MII?*

   SAP MII can connect with SAP ERP; any kind of databases; systems that support any kind of REST service like HTTP Post, Web service, JMS etc.; and any kind of shopfloor system that supports UDC connector.

7. *What kind of intelligence does SAP MII have?*

   SAP MII can show rich and high-end reporting using various charts and it is also possible to develop a user interactive interface using SAP MII.

8. *What kinds of applications are possible using SAP MII?*

   SAP MII based applications are always web-based applications because SAP MII runs on Web Application Server.

9. *Does SAP MII provide real-time data?*

   Yes, SAP MII is very much capable of providing near real-time data. However, as applications developed on SPA MII are web based, it is difficult to expect exact real-time data in a SAP MII-based application because the data flow is dependent on the network speed.

10. *How flexible is a SAP MII based application?*

    From an integration perspective, SAP MII can connect and fetch data bi-directionally from most of the systems. From a UI perspective, SAP MII now uses SAP UI5 for its user interface development. SAP UI5 is browser independent, which helps the application run in any kind of window or any mobile browser, regardless of the operating system.

11. *What OS servers does SAP MII support?*

    SAP MII can be executed on Windows, on Linux, and on SAP PCo, which is one of the freely distributable components with SAP MII. It's also an important integration tool with shopfloor, but it supports only Windows Server, as SAP PCo is developed using the Microsoft .NET technology.

12. *How is MDO different from a database?*

    MDO stands for Manufacturing Data Object. It is an internal database or cache for SAP MII applications. Instead of querying a database, data can be stored in MDO and queried locally to fetch data faster. There are two types of MDO—persistent and on-demand. These differ in data storing ways.

13. *How is HANA integration done with SAP MII?*

    Data from plant or manufacturing systems can be obtained in SAP HANA using SAP MII Smart Data Adapter (SDI). Using the adapter data from PCo, queries in SAP MII will be available on virtual tables in SAP HANA and the tables can be used for various analytics and calculation views in SAP HANA.

14. *What is shared memory?*

    It is a persistent memory that can be used to store limited values and can be used in transactions while developing logic as a persistent variable. Shared memory can be accessible to the users through the SAP MII menu page. To change a value in shared memory, no code change is required.

15. *What is a custom action block?*

    A custom action block is customized code developed in the Java platform to handle certain functionalities which are not available as standard functions in SAP MII. Using the standard SDK available for the custom action block, it is possible to create the .JAR file containing the Java code with the special handling functions and upload and use the file as an action block in SAP MII workbench.

16. *Is it possible to access Excel files?*

    Yes it is possible, in two ways. If the Excel filename is fixed, even if the content is refreshed periodically, it is possible to integrate the file through PCo, the file system connector and OLEDB connector in SAP MII. Another way is to develop a custom action block through Java to integrate it.

17. *Can SAP MII Transaction be called remotely?*

    Yes, it is possible to call SAP MII Transaction using runner services. A runner service is an illuminator service that can help to call MII transaction from outside using this URL format:

    ```
    http://<server>:<port>/XMII/Runner/Transaction=<fold
    er>/<TransactionName>&<InputParamName1>=<value1>&<In
    putParamNameN>=<valueN>&OutputParameter=<OutputParam
    Name>&Content-Type=<content-type>&isBinary=<true|fal
    se>&XacuteLoginName= <username>&XacuteLoginPassword=
    <password>
    ```

18. *Is it possible to expose SAP MII Transaction as a REST service?*

    Yes, it is possible in SAP MII to expose any SAP Transaction as a SOAP web service.

The MII transaction can be converted into WSDL using this URL:

```
http://<server>:<port>/XMII/WSDLGen/<projectName>/
<folderName>/<transactionname>
```

To run the SAP MII transaction as a Web Service, use the following URL:

```
http://<server>:<port>/XMII/SOAPRunner/<projectName>
/<folderName><transactionname>
```

19. *Does SAP MII support synchronous and asynchronous calls?*

Yes, it supports both synchronous and asynchronous calls. Inside a SAP MII Transaction, other transactions can be called depending on the requirements. Transactions can be called in both asynchronous and synchronous ways. In a synchronous call, parent transactions call the child transactions and wait for the child transaction to complete execution. Based on the executed result, the parent transaction completes the logic and closes the session. In an asynchronous call, the parent transaction triggers the child transactions and the parent transaction completes its full logic and closes the session. It does not wait for the completion of the child transaction being triggered and thus the child transaction is always executed independently.

20. *What is the difference between the default and active memory of a shared property?*

Shared properties in SAP MII have both a default and active memory. Default memories have default values whereas active memories have active values. Active values can be checked either from the Tools tab from workbench or from the Data Servers sections of the SAP MII Admin page. At the time of transaction execution, a value is always fetched from active memory. Initially when the default memory is created for any variable, the same value gets replicated immediately and automatically to active memory the first time.

21. *What is the difference between an iterator and a repeater?*

SAP MII Transaction gives us a wide variety of action blocks for logic assignments. To loop in, there are two main action blocks—an iterator and a repeater. An iterator is used to loop over lists, as its input source is a list. The repeater is used to loop over XML nodes.

22. *What are scheduled transactions?*

    Scheduled transactions are the ones that enable execution of
    MII Transaction as per defined schedules for required logic.
    They can be enabled or disabled any time as needed.

23. *Is there a platform from which plant hierarchy can be directly
    maintained?*

    Yes, SAP MII provides the PIC (Plant Information Catalog)
    from SAP MII version 15+. Using this, it is possible to define
    the plant hierarchy along with the tags and details from SAP
    MII.

24. *How is PCo used in SAP MII?*

    SAP Plant Connectivity (PCo) is a software component that
    enables the exchange of data between the shopfloor and
    SAP MII. In PCo, it is possible to define the shopfloor tags to
    get real-time time-series data directly from the machines; it
    can maintain the historical data too. There are two ways to
    exchange the data from PCo—one is the push methodology to
    create agents with groups of tags and define certain conditions
    based on which a notification is triggered to the specific
    defined BLS of SAP MII. The second is the Pull mechanism
    by which it is possible to directly fetch data from the tags by
    using the PCo query via PCo connector from SAP MII.

25. *Does SAP MII support any other SAP manufacturing product?*

    Yes, it supports SAP manufacturing products—SAP ME
    and SAP OEE for their integration components MEINT and
    OEEINT. As both the products are developed on top of SAP
    MII, the custom logic hooking (activity hook) and custom
    dashboard (POD for ME and operator dashboard for OEE)
    development is also possible through SAP MII and with the
    standard solutions. Hence, to summarize, SAP MII is tightly
    coupled with both manufacturing products.

26. *What is bootstrapping?*

    To begin any application in UI, it must first be loaded and
    initialized. This process of loading and initializing is called
    bootstrapping.

27. *What are the supported data models for SAP UI5 development?*

    SAP UI5 supports XML model, JSON model, OData model,
    and JS model view.

28. *What is the difference between applet-based UI coding (.irpt) and UI5 coding?*

   In Applet-based UI coding, to load any kind of display template like chart, grid etc., you need Java JRE to load initially, which consumes a significant amount of time during execution and can lead to cache issues. Sometimes JRE versions also create issues for the applet version. UI5 is a Java-independent coding for all the UI components like HTML5, as it follows MVC model. This means the processing time for UI5 is much faster compared to .irpt files and there are no cache issues in UI5.

29. *What is the difference between an i5 display template and a normal display template?*

   SAP MII introduced new display templates that are UI5 based and they have been named as i5 templates whereas the existing ones are applet-based templates.

30. *What is an IRPT page?*

   An IRPT page, also referred to as an SAP MII report, is a web page that uses the SAP MII .irpt file extension rather than the standard .html file extension. IRPT pages facilitate the dynamic generation of web pages through server-side processing. The web server sends the .irpt page to a specialized servlet, called `ReportServlet`, for processing. There are some special features used by IRPT like session variables and dynamic content insertion in web pages. This makes it different from HTML.

31. *Is there any functionality in SAP MII for tracing and logging activities?*

   Logging in SAP MII can be done with NWA logs with some configurations done in NetWeaver and this tracing can be initiated. Event Logger action blocks trace custom messages in logs from SAP MII Transaction as well.

32. *What is an illuminator service?*

   Illuminator service is the backbone of SAP MII. Using this web service, any of the SAP MII standard components can be called, modified, and updated. Apart from that, the components of SAP MII, like query template, display template, and the components of the UI, can be called directly to access them. It is the only way to work with SAP standard data stored in an internal table.

33. *How do I use illuminator services?*

Illuminator services contain two major parameters—one is the service and the other one is the mode. There are multiple services available, including admin, systemInfo, scheduler, BLS manager services, and more. Various modes are also available for each service. The way to write it is as follows:

```
http://<server>:<port>/XMII/
Illuminator?service=<service name>&mode=<mode
name>&content-type=text/xml
```

Summary

In this chapter, you learned about the best practices that should be followed in SAP MII. Along with that, the frequently asked questions are also provided. They can help you have a batter grasp of SAP MII.

Now you are ready to work in SAP MII. You have an understanding of manufacturing industries. You also know the history and types of manufacturing industries. You have gone through how SAP MII came into manufacturing industries and how it is progressed day by day along with the versioning. It will provide you with the understanding of changes and requirements for SAP MII upgrade projects. You learned why SAP MII is important and where to use it, so you can now relate the business requirements and can easily understand the probable scenarios for the business. As you got the flavor on the basics, components of SAP MII, and how to develop technical objects in the SAP MII IDE, you should be confident working in it.

Along with it, you got a detailed understanding of the various manufacturing domains and their requirements, as well as how SAP MII and other SAP manufacturing products can fulfill those requirements. Last but not least, you are also aware of various integration scenarios using SAP MII and the new features in SAP MII. So to conclude this book, you will be your perfect guide to understanding and exploring SAP MII. Further, to gain more knowledge on SAP MII, you can visit the SCN—SAP Community Network— at https://www.sap.com/community/topic/manufacturing-integration-and-intelligence.html, wherein you can read various blogs, documents, and discussions.

Index

Get the eBook for only $5!

Why limit yourself?

With most of our titles available in both PDF and ePUB format, you can access your content wherever and however you wish—on your PC, phone, tablet, or reader.

Since you've purchased this print book, we are happy to offer you the eBook for just $5.

To learn more, go to http://www.apress.com/companion or contact support@apress.com.

Apress®

Printed in the United States
By Bookmasters